Reading Jesus's Bible

Reading Jesus's Bible

How the New Testament Helps Us
Understand the Old Testament

John Goldingay

WILLIAM B. EERDMANS PUBLISHING COMPANY
GRAND RAPIDS, MICHIGAN

Wm. B. Eerdmans Publishing Co.
2140 Oak Industrial Drive NE, Grand Rapids, Michigan 49505
www.eerdmans.com

23 22 21 20 19 18 17   1 2 3 4 5 6 7

ISBN 978-0-8028-7364-4

Library of Congress Cataloging-in-Publication Data

Names: Goldingay, John, author.
Title: Reading Jesus's Bible : how the New Testament helps us understand
    the Old Testament / John Goldingay.
Description: Grand Rapids : Eerdmans Publishing Co., 2017. | Includes bibliographical
    references and index.
Identifiers: LCCN 2016054246 | ISBN 9780802873644 (pbk. : alk. paper)
Subjects: LCSH: Bible. New Testament—Relation to the Old Testament. |
    Bible. New Testament—Criticism, interpretation, etc.
Classification: LCC BS2387 .G54 2017 | DDC 220.6—dc23
    LC record available at https://lccn.loc.gov/2016054246

Contents

Acknowledgments

The seed thoughts for this book lie in an article on "The Old Testament and Christian Faith" published in *Themelios* 8.1 (1982): 4–10; 8.2 (1983): 5–12; and reprinted in revised form in my *Key Questions about Biblical Interpretation: Old Testament Answers* (Grand Rapids: Baker, 2011), 211–32.

Quotations from the New Testament are from Today's New International Version (TNIV). Translations from the Old Testament are my own and are adapted from a draft translation of *The Old Testament for Everyone*. Some biblical passages cited in this book have different chapter and/or verse numbers in English Bibles from the ones printed in Hebrew Bibles. All biblical references are to the English chapter and verse, even when citing Hebrew terms. Chapter 6 is adapted from draft material for a book on *Old Testament Ethics for Everyone*.

I am grateful to Michael Thomson and his editorial committee for pushing me to develop the book in the direction that it takes, and to Thomas A. Bennett and Kathleen Scott Goldingay for their careful reading and comments on a draft.

CHAPTER 1

Introduction

Christian faith focuses on Jesus, and we learn of him from the New Testament. But when the New Testament writers sought to understand Jesus, they assumed that the Old Testament could play a key role in helping them. My concern in this book is to look at the way they went about this task, in order then to consider a question that is the reverse of theirs: to look at the pointers they suggest for understanding the Old Testament itself. "The Gospels teach us how to read the OT, and—at the same time—the OT teaches us how to read the Gospels. Or, to put it a little differently, we learn to read the OT by reading backwards from the Gospels, and—at the same time—we learn how to read the Gospels by reading forwards from the OT."[1]

The term *Old Testament* does not occur in the New Testament, which obviously also does not refer to itself as the "New Testament." Jews call their Scriptures "the Torah, the Prophets, and the Writings"; the scholarly world today calls them "the Hebrew Bible" (slightly inaccurately, as part of them is in Aramaic). In Jesus's day, the Torah, the Prophets, and the Writings were simply "the Scriptures,"[2] and they were the fundamental basis of people's lives with God. The stories of people such as Zechariah, Elizabeth, Mary, Joseph, Simeon, and Anna (see Luke 1–2) show that people living before Jesus could gain quite an adequate understanding of those Scriptures and from them

1. Richard B. Hays, *Reading Backwards: Figural Christology and the Fourfold Gospel Witness* (Grand Rapids: Eerdmans, 2014), 4. Much of the quotation is italicized.

2. The Torah is the first five books, Genesis–Deuteronomy (hence also known as the Pentateuch, the five books); the Prophets section comprises Joshua, Judges, 1–2 Samuel, 1–2 Kings, Isaiah, Jeremiah, Ezekiel, and the Twelve (also known as the Minor Prophets); the Writings are Psalms, Job, Proverbs, Ruth, Song of Songs, Ecclesiastes, Lamentations, Esther, Daniel, Ezra, Nehemiah, and 1–2 Chronicles.

could gain quite an adequate understanding of God, of God's purpose, of God's ways with us, and of a relationship with God. But they also knew that God still needed to do something spectacular in order to sort the world out and fulfill his own purpose and sort out things for the people of God. That spectacular thing is what Jesus came to do.

In light of his coming, in due course the church developed a collection of written materials telling of what God had indeed done in him and of its implications, to set alongside those existent Scriptures. The church knew that Jesus came to inaugurate a "new covenant" and that he did so by dying for us; so this covenant was a kind of testament or will. Thus the collection came to be known as the "New Testament," and by analogy Christians came to call the existent collection of Scriptures by a new name, the "Old Testament." The expression "Old Testament" is thus anachronistic in connection with the time of Jesus or Paul. For them, these works were simply "the Scriptures." In Western cultures, at least, the phrase "Old Testament" is also something of a slight; it rather implies that this collection of writings is antique and outdated by the "New Testament." So from now on, I shall refer to that first collection as "the First Testament."

So what significance attaches to the First Testament after Jesus has come? How does the New Testament refer to these writings? What pointers does it give to our interaction with them? The New Testament books vary in how much they refer to those earlier Scriptures and in the way they use them. As it happens, however, the opening pages of the New Testament offer an instructive set of concrete illustrations of what the First Testament signifies for the New Testament. The New Testament thus begins with the First Testament. It opens its account of Jesus by relating him to the First Testament and by explaining who he is by looking at him in light of the First Testament.

Actually, most of the New Testament operates that way to one degree or another. Acts does so. Paul does so, especially in Romans. Hebrews does so. Revelation does so. But the opening chapters of Matthew happen to operate that way in a particularly systematic fashion. I do not imagine that Matthew was consciously aiming to achieve this end, but whether he was trying or not, it is what he succeeded in doing. So a convenient approach to considering our question is to start from Matthew's approach; we can then also look at insights from other parts of the New Testament alongside Matthew. Thus in this book I use Matthew's five ways of reading the First Testament to frame how we might read the First Testament for ourselves:

1. The First Testament tells the story of which Jesus is the climax. Matthew begins here (Matt 1:1–17) with a kind of summary of the First Testament story up to Jesus in the form of a list of his ancestors. The summary tells us something important about how to understand Jesus and directs us back to the First Testament story in order to expand on that understanding.

2. The First Testament declares the promise of which Jesus is the fulfillment. After the list of names, Matthew goes on to tell the story of Jesus's birth and early months (Matt 1:18–2:23). It shows how passages from the Prophets are fulfilled or filled out in what happens; it thus uses the Prophets to help us understand Jesus and directs us back to read the Prophets.

3. The First Testament provides the images, ideas, and words with which to understand Jesus. Matthew's account of Jesus's ministry begins with his baptism by John and with God's words to him from heaven, which come from the First Testament (Matt 3:1–17). So the account invites us to go back to the First Testament for an understanding of who Jesus's God is.

4. The First Testament lays out the nature of a relationship with God. Jesus models the nature of such a relationship during his temptations in the wilderness and teaches about it in the opening section of the Sermon on the Mount (Matt 4:1–11; 5:1–16). The first passage quotes extensively from the First Testament, and the second alludes extensively to its motifs, so that it invites us to discover more about the nature of a relationship with God by studying it.

5. The First Testament provides the foundation for Jesus's moral teaching. Jesus goes on to declare, "You have heard that it was said.... But I tell you . . ." (Matt 5:17–48). He is again "fulfilling" or "filling out" the First Testament, speaking like a prophet, helping people to see implications in the Scriptures that they might be avoiding, and inviting us to study what the Scriptures have to teach us about the way we should live.

The New Testament writers were concerned to help congregations understand the story of Jesus—to see more clearly who he was and what difference he should make to their lives. Their interest in the First Testament lay in helping themselves and their congregations gain this understanding. Reading between the lines of Matthew's Gospel, we may infer that he was writing for a congregation that was mostly Jewish believers, so there would be special reason to show them how the First Testament related to Jesus. The same may be true of Hebrews. Yet in writing Romans, Paul makes the same assumption about the significance of the First Testament, and he makes clear in that letter that the Roman church was not predominantly Jewish. Likewise Luke and Acts (which are two parts of the same work) concern themselves with the significance of Jesus for the world as a whole, and they also appeal frequently to the First Testament. While the First Testament is important in a particular way to Jews who believe in Jesus, it is also important to the whole church if it wants to understand Jesus, or to understand God, or to understand itself.

Paul's charge to Timothy puts it this way:

> From infancy you have known the Holy Scriptures, which are able to make you wise for salvation through faith in Christ Jesus. All Scripture is God-breathed and is useful for teaching, rebuking, correcting and training in righteousness, so that all God's people may be thoroughly equipped for every good work. (2 Tim 3:15–17)

When Paul refers here to "the Holy Scriptures," he of course means the First Testament (when Paul wrote, the documents that make up the rest of the New Testament had not yet been written). It is these writings that are "God-breathed" and useful in those different ways. Most strikingly, he says that they are able to make one wise in a way that leads to salvation *through faith in Christ Jesus*. The First Testament (Paul says) is monumentally important to anyone who wants to trust in Jesus and live for Jesus.

My approaching the First Testament by looking at what the New Testament does with it is partly pragmatic or tactical. The First Testament is intelligible in its own right, and we do not need the New Testament to tell us what it means.[3] But it is natural for Christians to assume that the New Testament ought to help us understand the First Testament. So we will consider ways in which Jesus and the first Christian writers used the First Testament and thus gave us pointers toward ways in which we might approach it. And in light of looking at and through some of those lenses that the New Testament uses, we will look at the nature of the First Testament itself.

---

3. I have argued this point in a book called *Do We Need the New Testament? Letting the Old Testament Speak for Itself* (Downers Grove, IL: InterVarsity Press, 2015).

CHAPTER 2

Story

The First Testament tells the story of which Jesus is the climax. The First Testament story thus helps us understand Jesus, and Jesus's story helps us understand the First Testament.

Neither Testament of the Christian Bible opens in the way that one might expect a religious book to begin. Each Testament opens not with direct teaching about God or with advice about prayer or with moral instruction (though they provide much of all those in due course). Each begins by telling a story, doing so at some length, and doing so more than once. They take this form because the essence of the faith in both Testaments is not direct teaching about God or advice about prayer or moral instruction but an account of what God has done, which is then the clue to formulating the teaching and the advice and the instruction. And the New Testament begins telling its story with a look back at the First Testament story and with some pointers about how to read it. Subsequent parts of the New Testament offer more pointers: we will look especially at Romans, Hebrews, and 1 Corinthians. Then we will look at the First Testament story in its own right.

2.1 Matthew 1:1–17: Jesus's Backstory

To the eyes of most modern readers, the opening verses of the New Testament form an unpromising beginning, with their unexciting list of bare names, mostly from the First Testament. But they form a telling introduction to the Gospel.

This is the genealogy of Jesus the Messiah the son of David, the son of Abraham: Abraham was the father of Isaac, Isaac the father of Jacob, Jacob the father of Judah and his brothers, Judah the father of Perez and Zerah, whose mother was Tamar, Perez the father of Hezron, Hezron the father of Ram, Ram the father of Amminadab, Amminadab the father of Nahshon, Nahshon the father of Salmon, Salmon the father of Boaz, whose mother was Rahab, Boaz the father of Obed, whose mother was Ruth, Obed the father of Jesse, and Jesse the father of King David.

David was the father of Solomon, whose mother had been Uriah's wife, Solomon the father of Rehoboam, Rehoboam the father of Abijah, Abijah the father of Asa, Asa the father of Jehoshaphat, Jehoshaphat the father of Jehoram, Jehoram the father of Uzziah, Uzziah the father of Jotham, Jotham the father of Ahaz, Ahaz the father of Hezekiah, Hezekiah the father of Manasseh, Manasseh the father of Amon, Amon the father of Josiah, and Josiah the father of Jeconiah and his brothers at the time of the exile to Babylon.

After the exile to Babylon: Jeconiah was the father of Shealtiel, Shealtiel the father of Zerubbabel, Zerubbabel the father of Abiud, Abiud the father of Eliakim, Eliakim the father of Azor, Azor the father of Zadok, Zadok the father of Akim, Akim the father of Eliud, Eliud the father of Eleazar, Eleazar the father of Matthan, Matthan the father of Jacob, and Jacob the father of Joseph, the husband of Mary, and Mary was the mother of Jesus who is called the Messiah.

Thus there were fourteen generations in all from Abraham to David, fourteen from David to the exile to Babylon, and fourteen from the exile to the Messiah. (Matt 1:1–17)

This introduction expresses an understanding of the shape of the First Testament story and its relationship to the Jesus story, and it encourages an interest both in the facts behind Israel's story and in the way the story interprets the facts.

Abraham, David, the Exile, Jesus

So the attention of modern Western readers soon moves on from this list of names to the stories in Matthew 1:18–2:23. But the Jewish reader who came to faith in Jesus through reading these verses responded to them in a way Matthew would have appreciated. This reader had seen that the genealogy embodies an assertion about Jesus—he was a Jew. Further, it is a genealogy that not only establishes that Jesus's ancestry goes back to Abraham, but also marks him as a member of the clan of Judah and of the family of David.[1] It thus gives him a formal claim to David's throne. It is a genealogy that (unusually) includes the names of several women, names that draw attention to the contribution made by some rather questionable unions to this genealogy even before and during David's own time, so that the apparently questionable circumstances of Jesus's own birth (Matt 1:19) can hardly be deemed unworthy of someone who was claimed to be David's successor. It is a genealogy arranged into three sequences of fourteen names, a patterning that itself expresses the conviction that Jesus's coming happens by the providence of God, which has been at work throughout the history of the Jewish people but now comes to its climax.

The genealogy appeals to the historical past, to real history. Matthew assumes that a person has to be a descendant of David to have a claim to David's throne, and has to be a descendant of Abraham to have a "natural" share in Abraham's promise, still more if he is to be recognized as *the* seed of Abraham. Matthew has in mind legal descent; someone who is adopted into a family comes to share that family's genealogy as fully as someone born into it. Thus Jesus's claim to David's throne comes through his adoptive, legal father, Joseph. It is in this sense that Matthew is talking about the real ancestry of Jesus, the real historical antecedents to Jesus's coming.

At the same time, Matthew schematizes the past when he appeals to it. There were not, in fact, fourteen generations from Abraham to David, fourteen from David to the exile, and another fourteen from the exile to Jesus (Matt 1:17), as one can see by comparing the genealogy with the material in the First Testament itself from which Matthew got much of his raw material. Josiah, for instance, was actually the father of Jehoiakim and thus the grandfather of Jeconiah (see 2 Kgs 23–25).

By shaping the genealogy so that it worked by fourteens, Matthew created a list that is more artistic and easier to remember than it might otherwise be, and a list that expresses explicitly that the providence of God had been at work in the ordering of Israelite history up to Jesus's time, as it was at work in his birth, life, death, and resurrection.

The shaping via the exile as well as via David implies another insight. After the exile, Jerusalem had been rebuilt and its community had been reestablished, but it did not gain its independence from imperial powers, and in Jesus's day it lived under the Romans, as in previous centuries it had lived un-

---

1. I use the word "clan" rather than "tribe," which implies that they are not ethnically related groups within the same people.

der the Assyrians, followed by the Babylonians, the Persians, and the Greeks. Jesus's coming links with a process that God set going with Abraham, with a process to which David was key, but a process that the exile put on hold.

In relating Jesus's genealogy, Matthew gives us one example of how to look at Jesus's coming in light of the story of Israel. His example encourages us to ask, with regard to other aspects of the significance of Jesus, what light is cast on Jesus's coming by its background in Abraham's leaving Ur, Israel's exodus from Egypt, David's capture of Jerusalem, Solomon's building of the temple, Ephraim's fall in 722, Jerusalem's fall in 587, the Persians' allowing the exiles to return, Alexander's unleashing of Hellenistic culture in the Middle East, and Antiochus's persecution and defeat. These events make up the story that is the background to Jesus's coming.

Act One and Act Two

So one could say that in the Bible's drama, the First Testament is Act One and the New Testament is Act Two;[2] and as in any story, we understand the final scene aright only in light of the preceding ones. The converse is also true: as well as understanding Jesus in light of the First Testament story, Matthew understands the First Testament story in light of Jesus's coming. His assumption is that the story from Abraham to David to the exile to the Second Temple period reaches its climax with Jesus's coming, and needs to be understood in light of this denouement. (He does not imply that Israel's history comes to an end with the exile to Babylon, as readers sometimes do under the influence of the story in Genesis through 2 Kings, which ends there. He follows the First Testament itself in seeing this story continuing into the Persian and Greek periods.)

It is not the only way to read Israel's history. A Jew who does not believe in Jesus will understand it differently. Whether you read Israel's story in this way depends on what you make of Jesus. If you recognize that Jesus is the Messiah, you will know that he is the climax of First Testament history. If you do not so recognize him, you will not. Conversely, however, for a Jew at least, whether you recognize that Jesus is the Messiah may depend on whether it seems plausible to read Israel's history in this way. A dialectic is involved here.

2. John Bright, *The Authority of the Old Testament* (Nashville: Abingdon; London: SCM, 1967), 202.

Once we do read Israel's history thus, it makes a difference to the way we understand the events it relates. The significance of Abraham's leaving Ur, Israel's exodus from Egypt, David's capture of Jerusalem, and so on, emerges with greater clarity when we see these events in light of one another and in light of Jesus's coming as their climax.

The interpretation of the exodus provides an example of such clarification, both because of the intrinsic importance of the exodus in the First Testament and because of interest in this event in various forms of liberation theology. On one hand, understanding Jesus's coming in light of the First Testament story supports the assertion that God is concerned for people's political and social liberation. The God and Father of our Lord Jesus Christ is one who is concerned for the release of the oppressed from bondage; Jesus's coming does not change that fact. On the other hand, understanding the First Testament story in light of Jesus's coming highlights for us the concern with the spiritual and moral liberation of the spiritually and morally oppressed that is present in the exodus story and becomes more pressing as the First Testament story unfolds. Any concern with political and social liberation that does not recognize humanity's fundamental need of spiritual and moral liberation has failed to take account of the development of the First Testament story after the exodus via the exile to Jesus's coming, his death, his resurrection, and his pouring out of the Holy Spirit.

Matthew himself later issues his own warning about misreading Israelite history, as he relates the warning John the Baptizer gave his hearers: "Do not think you can say to yourselves, 'We have Abraham as our father'" (Matt 3:9). In other words, he is saying that merely having the right history does nothing for you. It places you in a position of potential privilege, but it requires that you respond to the God who has been active in that history if you are to enjoy your privilege. The story is quite capable of turning into a tragedy if you allow it. "The ax is already at the root of the trees" (Matt 3:10). That God has been working out a purpose in history is of crucial significance for Christian faith. But it effects nothing until it leads us to personal trust and obedience in relation to God.

Events and Ordering

In his compressed summary of Act One in God's drama, Matthew implies an interest both in recording the facts and in shaping the facts. The two aspects of his appeal to the past are consistent features of the Gospels and of First

Testament narratives. The Gospels are concerned with the real, historical Jesus, but they tell his story in a schematized way, selecting and ordering material to make clear the points of central significance. Matthew 4 tells us of three temptations Jesus experienced; Luke 4 relates the same temptations but orders them differently. Matthew tells of the beginning of Jesus's ministry in Capernaum; Luke precedes this story by the account of his rejection at Nazareth, which comes later in Matthew. It is not that either Matthew or Luke has made mistakes in his presentation, but that a reordering or rewriting of a story can sometimes make the story's significance clearer than a merely chronological account does.

The First Testament narratives that were among the Gospels' models, such as Genesis and Exodus, Kings and Chronicles, were likewise concerned with relating historical events, and with selecting, ordering, and rewriting material so as to make the message of history clear for their contemporaries. Much of the opening part of Matthew's genealogy comes from Chronicles, which well illustrates this combination of a concern for real people and events with a presentation that makes explicit their significance for the writer's day so that its message will be clear for the people who listen to the story. It is the interest in communicating with their people and bringing home God's message to them that explains the substantial difference between Samuel–Kings' and Chronicles' presentation of the same story.

Matthew's example, then, directs us toward a twofold interest in the First Testament story. We are interested in the significant actual events of First Testament times that led up to Jesus. It is this instinct that made generations of students feel that their library was incomplete without a volume on the history of Israel on their shelves. If this history is the background to Jesus's coming, we had better understand the actual history of Israel. At the same time, we are also interested in the way this history has been shaped as narrative by the First Testament writers. We are not reading mere chronicles or annals but a story whose message is expressed in the way it is told. So as well as books retelling the history of Israel, more recent generations of students have felt the need of books on the interpretation of biblical narrative to help them interpret the story of Israel as the First Testament itself tells it.

In practice, it is easy to let one interest exclude the other. Readers may assume that we are concerned only with the events and may ignore the literary creativity in biblical narrative. Or we can become so aware of this creativity that we cease to recognize the fact and the importance of the fundamental historicity of Israelite history. Like the First Testament narratives themselves, Matthew implies that both matter.

Matthew assumes, then, that readers need to know something of the history behind Jesus if they are to understand Jesus himself. This assumption applies to every historical person or event. We understand others aright only if we know something of their history, experiences, and background, which have made them what they are. We understand complex political problems such as those of the Middle East only if we understand their history. We understand Jesus's coming only if we see it as the climax to a story reaching centuries back into pre-Christian times, the story of a relationship between the God and Father of our Lord Jesus Christ and the Israelite people whom God chose as his means of gaining access to the world as a whole. The First Testament story thus has an importance for Christians that (for instance) Indian or Chinese or Greek history does not have, because this story is the story of which Jesus's coming is the climax.

Story and History in the First Testament

Although both Testaments imply an interest both in the story that Israel told and in the history that actually happened, they do not concern themselves with the differences between these two. For modern readers, this omission may be puzzling. We cannot help but notice that the First Testament can tell its story in different ways. In 1 Samuel 17, David kills Goliath; in 2 Samuel 21:19, Elhanan kills Goliath. In 2 Samuel 24, God gets David to take a census; in 1 Chronicles 21, "the Adversary" (TNIV Satan) gets David to take a census. There are many such examples of what are often called contradictions in the First Testament (and in the New Testament, especially among the Gospels), and there are ways of explaining them so that they need no longer be seen as contradictions. But why do these differences bother us in a way that they apparently did not bother the scriptural writers and the communities that accepted these works into their Scriptures?

I was helped in answering this question by Hans Frei's book *The Eclipse of Biblical Narrative.*[3] In the eighteenth century, Frei argues, scholars started asking about the possible difference between the scriptural story and the actual history of Israel and of Jesus. They did so in the context of a developing interest in discovering what actually happened in history, not merely in connection with the Bible but in connection with (for instance) Greek or

---

3. Hans W. Frei, *The Eclipse of Biblical Narrative: A Study in Eighteenth and Nineteenth Century Hermeneutics* (New Haven: Yale University Press, 1974).

Roman history. Indeed, the events that lay behind Homer came to be more interesting than the story Homer told. The same dynamic applied to the scholarly study of the Scriptures.

For a couple of centuries, but especially from the last decades of the nineteenth century to the last decades of the twentieth, scholarly study of the First Testament worked hard at trying to establish the real history that lies behind the story. This venture more or less failed, in the sense that the scholarly world has not been able to reach a stable consensus on that history. Indeed, in the twenty-first century there is less of a consensus than there was in the twentieth, and there is no basis for thinking that this situation will ever change. The reason is that the First Testament narrative works are not the type of works from which we can get the kind of historical information we would like. We cannot get behind the story to the pure history. Ironically, the narratives sometimes draw attention to this fact themselves when they tell us, in effect, "If you want mere historical facts, go and look in the court records" (see, e.g., 1 Kgs 11:41; 14:19, 29). The narratives themselves have a different interest.

Realizing that this is the case is a blessing in disguise. The reason why the stories were written and why the Jewish people and the church accepted them into their Scriptures was that these stories spoke to them about God and his ways. Trying to get behind them to the actual history involves abandoning the stories that God inspired and that those communities found compelling. We are better off reading the stories and letting them speak to us, and not worrying about the boundary between fact and story.

It helps me to look at this question in light of our experience with movies. Many movies that we watch are neither pure fact nor pure fiction but stories "based on fact." They tell a historical story but they use their imagination in order to recreate what happened, to reconstruct what people might have said, to draw attention to moral issues, and so on. They do so in a way that helps bring home the story's significance for our context. If we get preoccupied by whether everything in the movie happened, we miss the point.

The analogy with movies is only partial. The Scriptures are God's inspired message to us on which we base our lives, and movies are not. However, God apparently knew that narratives based on facts but incorporating divinely inspired reflection and divinely inspired imagination were the kind of writings that could fulfill his purpose in a way that simple history would not. It is important to a movie that claims to be based on facts that it really is based on facts, and it is important to the First Testament that it is based on facts. But studying the First Testament does not mean focusing on establishing exactly what happened and finding the point where fact gives way to imagination. It means reading the story that we have.

2.2 Romans: The First Testament Story and the Gospel

Romans has no single section like Matthew 1:1–17 that suggests a way of looking at the First Testament story, but we can assemble a series of passages that refer to episodes in that story. Romans shows an interest in Adam, Abraham, Isaac and Ishmael, Jacob and Esau, Pharaoh, Moses and the giving of the Torah, and the eventual decimation of Israel, all of which help us to understand the gospel.

Romans 5: Adam

Unlike Matthew, Paul goes behind Abraham to Adam.

> Just as sin entered the world through one man, and death through sin, and in this way death came to all people, because all sinned—to be sure, sin was in the world before the law was given, but sin is not charged against anyone's account where there is no law. Nevertheless, death reigned from the time of Adam to the time of Moses, even over those who did not sin by breaking a command, as did Adam, who is a pattern of the one to come. (Rom 5:12–14)

Luke's account of Jesus's forebears also goes behind Abraham to Adam (see Luke 3:23–38), but whereas Luke traces a straight line from Adam to Jesus, Paul is more interested in a kind of compare and contrast between Adam and Jesus. He speaks in terms of a common "pattern" in their stories, but there is a sharp contrast as well as a comparison:

> But the gift is not like the trespass. For if the many died by the trespass of the one man, how much more did God's grace and the gift that came by the grace of the one man, Jesus Christ, overflow to the many! Nor can the gift of God be compared with the result of one man's sin: The judgment followed one sin and brought condemnation, but the gift followed many trespasses and brought justification. For if, by the trespass of the one man, death reigned through that one man, how much more will those who re-

ceive God's abundant provision of grace and of the gift of righteousness reign in life through the one man, Jesus Christ!

Consequently, just as one trespass resulted in condemnation for all people, so also one righteous act resulted in justification and life for all. For just as through the disobedience of the one man the many were made sinners, so also through the obedience of the one man the many will be made righteous.

The law was brought in so that the trespass might increase. But where sin increased, grace increased all the more, so that, just as sin reigned in death, so also grace might reign through righteousness to bring eternal life through Jesus Christ our Lord. (Rom 5:15–21)

The Greek word translated "pattern" is *typos*, from which we get the English word *type*. The study of the comparison and contrast in the First Testament story and the New Testament story is thus called *typology*. Like many theological words, the word *typology* is used in different ways. I usually think of it as having three features.

1. It presupposes a similarity between something God does in the First Testament and something God does in the New Testament. God redeemed Israel from slavery (to Egypt) at the exodus; God redeemed us from slavery (to sin) through Jesus. In the temple, priests offered sacrifices that enabled people to go into the holy place; Jesus offered a sacrifice that enables us to go into the holy place, into eternal life.
2. But it presupposes a heightening between the first act and the second act (hence the comparison and contrast). The redemption from sin through Jesus is like the redemption from Egypt, but better. Jesus's one-time sacrifice redeems us from death. It enables us to go into God's heavenly dwelling place in the new age, not just into the temple as God's earthly dwelling place.
3. The first time God performs the act, it is literal; the literal act then provides a metaphor for God's second act. God redeemed Israel from a literal slavery; he redeems us from a metaphorical slavery. The First Testament temple, priesthood, and sacrifices were literal; Jesus is metaphorically a priest who offers a metaphorical sacrifice that entitles him to enter a metaphorical temple. (To speak in terms of metaphor is not to imply that these things are not real; they are more real. But the language used to describe them is metaphorical.)

Typology and Romans

How does typology work out in Romans 5?

1. There is a similarity between what happened through Adam and what happened through Jesus: in each case something epoch making came about through one person who had an effect on everyone.
2. But there is a monumental heightening between what happened through Adam and what happened through Jesus. What happened through Adam was horrifically negative. What happened through Jesus was wondrously positive. Indeed, the heightening is so marked that Paul backtracks and declares that the difference is more striking than the similarity.
3. The point about literal and metaphorical does not apply in Romans 5, though a related question arises for modern readers. On the surface, Genesis speaks as if the whole of humanity is Adam's physical offspring, though it also gives hints in other directions (Where did Cain get his wife from?). The usual scientific view is that all humanity did not descend from one original couple, certainly not a few thousand years ago (though I understand that it is not impossible that we could all have descended from one couple over a much longer period). But it is worth noting that Romans does not talk about everyone physically descending from Adam, only that it was through him that everyone became sinners. Now the whole of the new humanity that comes about through Jesus are not his physical offspring. Jesus has had his effect on people through people talking to one another. Maybe the first beings to whom God spoke had their effect on others through people talking to one another. They shared sin in that way and affected us all; Jesus shared grace in that way and affected us all.

The question about our link with Adam connects to a broader one. Genesis is the beginning of a long story that continues through 1 and 2 Kings, and in its later parts certainly talks about historical events. It seems to me more likely that the opening of this long story talks in some sense about real events than that it is a purely parabolic story about how things regularly work out in human experience. That is, Genesis talks about real events in the sense that it talks about God creating, about God being systematic but also experimental, about God's creation issuing in something good, about God creating humanity to look after the world, about God providing for humanity though requiring one bit of constraint on their part, and so on. Those were real events.

On the other hand, if we do read the Adam and Eve story as a parable about how relationships regularly work between God and us and between men and women, does it undermine Paul's point? If Adam did not really sin in a way that affected all humanity and in a way that makes his story a pattern for the Jesus story, does it imperil Paul's point about Jesus? If Adam did not bring death to us, does it mean Jesus did not bring life to us?

In considering this question, we need to remember that the theology Paul is doing involves moving from Jesus to the First Testament, not the other way around. He is not saying, "Because we know that Adam brought death, we can infer that Jesus brought life." He is saying, "We know that Jesus brought life; the story of Adam bringing death can help us understand how that works." Jesus bringing life is the fact that Adam can then illuminate, and maybe he can do so whether or not he ever existed.

Some further implications of analysis in terms of typology need to be noted.

- The people who experience the first event do not know it is a pattern or a foreshadowing of what will come later. The point of the first event for them is its real importance in its own right. It was truly important that God redeemed Israel from Egypt and that Israel could meet with God in the temple.
- Thus it is only the people who experience the second event who know that the first event was a pattern or a foreshadowing. Its point for them, then, is that it helps them understand what they have themselves experienced. Like Paul, they are moving from Jesus to the First Testament to help them understand Jesus better.
- The greatness of what God does the second time does not mean that God's first-time act loses meaning. Again, it is still important that God redeemed Israel from Egypt and that Israel could meet with God in the temple.
- Thus understanding Exodus or Leviticus means focusing on their inherent meaning for the people to whom God was speaking through them—and considering their significance for us in light of what God was saying to the people of Israel. Understanding Exodus or Leviticus does not focus on looking at them in light of Jesus.

Romans 4: Abraham

The next First Testament figure who is important for Paul is Abraham—next in the order of the First Testament's story, though not in the order of Paul's argument in Romans, where he comes before Adam. Abraham is important for any Jew—hence the fact that Matthew begins with him. Israel's own story starts with Abraham. He is not as important as Moses, but he is very important.

For Jews, Moses was supremely important. And for Jews who came to believe in Jesus, too, Moses remained important—too important, Paul finds. Many Jews who believed in Jesus assumed that they were still committed to living by Moses's teaching, the Torah, and that Gentiles who came to believe in Jesus thereby became honorary Jews; therefore they too needed to live by the Torah.[4] Paul is going to have to deal with Moses, but he needs to talk about Abraham first, to subvert that inclination to attach too much ongoing importance to Moses and to the Torah.

> What then shall we say that Abraham, the forefather of us Jews, discovered in this matter? If, in fact, Abraham was justified by works, he had something to boast about—but not before God. What does Scripture say? "Abraham believed God, and it was credited to him as righteousness." Now to anyone who works, their wages are not credited to them as a gift, but as an obligation. However, to anyone who does not work but trusts God who justifies the ungodly, their faith is credited as righteousness. (Rom 4:1–5)

Now Moses knew that the foundation of God's relationship with Israel was God's love for Israel and God's delivering Israel from serfdom in Egypt. But once people had recognized that foundation, living by the teaching that God gave Israel via Moses was of vital importance. In such a statement, *vital* carries the same connotation as it does in the phrase *vital signs*. Living by that teaching is the key to life. But Paul knows that living by Moses's teaching is no longer the key to life now that Jesus has come. That assumption by Paul seems implausible to Jewish believers (and of course to Jews who do not believe in Jesus). How could Moses's teaching suddenly lose its basic importance?

---

4. The usual translation of the word *torah* is "law," but it is a misleading translation because it gives the impression that Mosaic faith was legalistic. It was not. So I shall refer to it as the Torah.

Paul needs to be able to show from the Scriptures that Moses's teaching is now less important than people think—than he himself once thought. He has to be able thus to show that his gospel fits the Scriptures. Modern Christians can have a real question about whether the First Testament fits with the gospel. For New Testament Christians, the question has to be, how does the gospel fit with the First Testament? Going back to Abraham is the way Paul answers that question. The key point is that God had a perfectly fine relationship with Abraham before there was any Mosaic teaching for him to follow.

> Under what circumstances was it credited? Was it after he was circumcised, or before? It was not after, but before! And he received circumcision as a sign, a seal of the righteousness that he had by faith while he was still uncircumcised. So then, he is the father of all who believe but have not been circumcised, in order that righteousness might be credited to them. And he is then also the father of the circumcised who not only are circumcised but who also follow in the footsteps of the faith that our father Abraham had before he was circumcised. (Rom 4:10–12)

Promise and Circumcision

If there is one nonnegotiable requirement in the Torah, it is that men should be circumcised. A man who declined to be circumcised imperiled his place in the people of God. This omission almost cost Moses himself his life (see Exod 4:24–26). It is the supreme covenant sign in the First Testament.

Now Gentiles who come to believe in Jesus thereby come to be part of that people of God. So should males among them be circumcised? It might seem quite logical. And Paul does not mind people being circumcised if they wish to be, but he is adamant that it must not be a requirement, because insisting on such a requirement compromises the basis of the relationship between God and human beings that has come about through Jesus. That relationship is based on Jesus dying for us and our simply trusting in him.

> It was not through the law that Abraham and his offspring received the promise that he would be heir of the world, but through the righteousness that comes by faith. For if those who depend on the law are heirs, faith means nothing and the promise is worthless, because the law brings wrath. And where there is no law there is no transgression. Therefore, the prom-

ise comes by faith, so that it may be by grace and may be guaranteed to all Abraham's offspring—not only to those who are of the law but also to those who have the faith of Abraham. He is the father of us all. As it is written: "I have made you a father of many nations." He is our father in the sight of God, in whom he believed—the God who gives life to the dead and calls into being things that were not. (Rom 4:13–17)

Ironically, the requirement of circumcision is one of the few rules in the Torah that antedate Moses. It goes back to Abraham. But that fact helps Paul make the point he wants to make. Not only did God's relationship with Abraham antedate the Mosaic Torah—it antedated Abraham's circumcision. God did not say, "Get circumcised and then we can be in relationship." God got into a relationship with Abraham and then some years later issued the requirement of circumcision. To put the point more theologically, the relationship between God and Abraham is based on grace, not on works.

Against all hope, Abraham in hope believed and so became the father of many nations, just as it had been said to him, "So shall your offspring be." Without weakening in his faith, he faced the fact that his body was as good as dead—since he was about a hundred years old—and that Sarah's womb was also dead. Yet he did not waver through unbelief regarding the promise of God, but was strengthened in his faith and gave glory to God, being fully persuaded that God had power to do what he had promised. This is why "it was credited to him as righteousness." The words "it was credited to him" were written not for him alone, but also for us, to whom God will credit righteousness—for us who believe in him who raised Jesus our Lord from the dead. He was delivered over to death for our sins and was raised to life for our justification. (Rom 4:18–25)

The relationship between God and Abraham was based on promises on God's part and on trust in those promises on Abraham's part. In this connection Paul quotes from Genesis 15:6, which refers to Abraham's trust in God's promise. The significance of the Abraham story is that it establishes the fundamental nature of the relationship between God and his people. That relationship does not involve the requirement of circumcision or any other rules.

Romans 9:6–9: Isaac and Ishmael

After Abraham and Sarah in Genesis come their sons, to whose story Paul has reason to appeal in another connection. Paul had needed to argue from the Scriptures that God's relationship with us is based on God's grace, not on anything that we do, such as get circumcised or work for justice. Another theological question that he needed to think about was the strange fact that in his day the Jewish people as a whole had declined to acknowledge Jesus. Paul's very stress on God's promises and God's grace adds emphasis to the question. God made a commitment to the Jewish people that it did not earn. What has happened to that commitment, if the Jewish people have not acknowledged the Messiah?

> It is not as though God's word had failed. For not all who are descended from Israel are Israel. Nor because they are his descendants are they all Abraham's children. On the contrary, "It is through Isaac that your offspring will be reckoned." In other words, it is not the natural children who are God's children, but it is the children of the promise who are regarded as Abraham's offspring. For this was how the promise was stated: "At the appointed time I will return, and Sarah will have a son." (Rom 9:6–9)

God gave his promises to Abraham with regard to his family, but the undertakings did not find fulfillment in his entire family but only in Isaac's line, not in Ishmael's. So there is nothing new in what has happened in Paul's day.

I have the sense that Paul had to wrestle with the question about the fulfillment of God's undertakings. He did not have to wrestle in this determined way with the question of grace and law, promise and circumcision. Once Jesus had knocked him off his high horse on the way to Damascus, the basics about grace and trust apparently fell into place straightaway. But reading Romans 9–11 gives the impression that he did have to wrestle with this other question, and these chapters take us through the argument he himself went though.

His discussion parallels his argument about Abraham. Both arguments concern issues that are fundamental and central to the gospel. It has often been obvious to Christians that the question of grace and works is fundamental to the gospel. It has not been so obvious that the question about the Jewish people is central. But the truth is that the Abraham story is about the promises to which God binds himself to be faithful and about the trust that Abraham places in those promises; the later story of Israel, and specifically of the Jewish people in Paul's day, puts a question mark by the idea that God is faithful to his promises.

Christians have often assumed that God abandoned the Jewish people as a result of their turning their back on Jesus, and that he replaced Israel by the church. We might then rejoice in how gracious God is to us, how blessed we are. If we do so rejoice, we have not noticed the frightening implication of God's letting go of the Jewish people. If he let go of the original chosen people, he could let go of the new chosen people that on this theory have replaced the original ones. And we can hardly claim that the church has been more consistent in its faithfulness to God than the Jewish people were, so it seems quite likely that God has let the church go. Fortunately for us, Paul's argument about the Jewish people also reassures us—if God did not let Israel go, he will not the church go.

Romans 9:10–13: Jacob and Esau

In Paul's time, most of the Jewish people have indeed not recognized Jesus. But throughout the Gospels and Acts, there are always some Jews who get it. And many of Paul's epistles presuppose that the congregations to which he writes include both Jews and Gentiles. The first stage in his argument about whether God has fulfilled his undertakings is that the existence of a solid core of Jewish people in the church is a proof that God has not let the Jewish people go. Paul himself is the most spectacular evidence of the point. His case is especially significant because his recognizing Jesus came about through a stunning act of God. Paul gives us no hint that he had any doubts about his good status with God as a Jew or about the heretical nature of belief in Jesus. He was turned upside down in his attitude to Jesus purely because God knocked him over. Paul must surely have been one of the most brilliant opponents of Christian faith in the first few decades after Jesus. So God decided that Paul was the one to turn upside down, as an indication of his own power and with the idea of using him in a different direction, but more important (in our present context) as an indication of that faithfulness.

In due course, Paul himself will make this point about the significance of God's revealing himself to him: "Did God reject his people? By no means! I am an Israelite myself, a descendant of Abraham, from the tribe of Benjamin" (Rom 11:1). But God's revelation to him is not the starting point in his argument about God's faithfulness. His starting point is once again the First Testament story of Abraham and of Abraham's family. God gave his promises to Abraham, but they did not find fulfillment in his entire family. First they found fulfillment in Isaac's line, not in Ishmael's, then not in Isaac's entire family line but only in Jacob's line, not in Esau's.

> Rebekah's children were conceived at the same time by our father Isaac. Yet, before the twins were born or had done anything good or bad—in order that God's purpose in election might stand: not by works but by him who calls—she was told, "The older will serve the younger." Just as it is written: "Jacob I loved, but Esau I hated." (Rom 9:10–13)

The reason, Paul notes, is not that Jacob was more deserving than Esau; and the same point could have been made about Isaac in relation to Ishmael. God's deciding to favor Jacob happened before he and Esau were born (as he decided to take hold of Paul before he was born; see Gal 1:15).

Paul can claim the support not only of the Genesis story but of God's scandalous declaration, "Jacob I loved, but Esau I hated" (Mal 1:2–3). There are various ways of softening that declaration. Hating and loving commonly suggest action rather than feelings, and they can suggest treating one as less important and the other as more important, as when Jesus talks about hating parents (Luke 14:26; cf. Matt 12:37). But Paul would not be very interested in making the declaration more acceptable to us, because his interest lies in its significance for an understanding of God's sovereignty and God's faithfulness to his people. What counts is the one who calls, not what the one who is called deserves.

I need to make a further comment about those references to Jacob and Esau. Paul uses the word *election*, which in Western Christian parlance suggests that God chooses some people and not others to have eternal life. But when the Scriptures talk about election, they are referring to God's deciding whom to use in his service in one way or another. That Esau is not chosen, even that he is "hated," does not say anything in itself about his eternal destiny.

We might think that Paul's comments about Isaac and Ishmael and about Jacob and Esau still raise the question whether God is fair. God's choice of one brother rather than the other is based on his freedom, not on what the brothers deserve. Is that fair? The modern instinct is to seek to establish God's fairness. Paul's instinct is to plead guilty as charged. No, God is not fair. He is God. Deal with it.

Romans 9:14–26: Pharaoh

In Romans 9, Paul moves on from the Genesis story to the Exodus story and notes that the same principle applies to God's dealings with Pharaoh, the king who likes having the Israelites as conscript labor and does not want to let them leave the country.

> What then shall we say? Is God unjust? Not at all! For he says to Moses,
>
>> "I will have mercy on whom I have mercy,
>>   and I will have compassion on whom I have compassion."
>
> It does not, therefore, depend on human desire or effort, but on God's mercy. For Scripture says to Pharaoh: "I raised you up for this very purpose, that I might display my power in you and that my name might be proclaimed in all the earth." Therefore God has mercy on whom he wants to have mercy, and he hardens whom he wants to harden.
>
> One of you will say to me: "Then why does God still blame us? For who is able to resist his will?" But who are you, a mere human being, to talk back to God? "Shall what is formed say to the one who formed it, 'Why did you make me like this?'" Does not the potter have the right to make out of the same lump of clay some pottery for noble purposes and some for disposal of refuse? (Rom 9:14–21)

The story of the exodus constitutes a brilliant portrait of the interweaving of (1) things that we can empirically see, (2) human decisions that we cannot see, and (3) God's sovereignty, which we also cannot see. God declares the intention to have Pharaoh be tough; Pharaoh simply is tough; Pharaoh decides to be tough. We have to allow for all three and not water down any one of them.

> What if God, although choosing to show his wrath and make his power known, bore with great patience the objects of his wrath—prepared for destruction? What if he did this to make the riches of his glory known to the objects of his mercy, whom he prepared in advance for glory—even us, whom he also called, not only from the Jews but also from the Gentiles? As he says in Hosea:
>
>> "I will call them 'my people' who are not my people;
>>   and I will call her 'my loved one' who is not my loved one,"

and,

> "In the very place where it was said to them,
>   'You are not my people,'
>   they will be called 'children of the living God.'" (Rom 9:22–26)

The issue that interests modern people is Pharaoh's free will. The one that interests Paul is God's free will. The exodus story is the account of a battle between God and Pharaoh. There was no need for God to engage in this long-running battle; he could have airlifted the Israelites straight out of Egypt. Indeed, he later speaks as if he did so: "I carried you on eagles' wings" (Exod 19:4). But God does not usually do things quickly (we have been waiting for Jesus for two thousand years), partly because he likes to give people maximum chance to acknowledge him (as 2 Pet 3:9 comments in that connection).

One significance of the exodus story is that God is giving Pharaoh plenty of chances, though the way Exodus tells the story, Pharaoh is pretty well doomed from the beginning. God himself is going to strengthen Pharaoh's resistance (Exod 4:21). Pharaoh can still give in if he chooses; he is not being manipulated. But it will suit God if Pharaoh carries on resisting, because his resistance is going to make it necessary for God to display his power and thus provide the nations of Israel's world (not to say Israel itself and not to say our world) with evidence that he is God. After all, it is tempting for world powers to think that they are God, and for people within their empires and the vassals and subalterns of those imperial powers to make the same assumption. Yahweh is going to demonstrate that things are otherwise.

Taking up the exodus story, Paul fastens on the fact that God can be nice to anyone he wishes, and can also be nasty to anyone he wishes, as the Jacob-Esau story has already shown. It is not that Pharaoh was a nice guy who got a raw deal. Pharaoh was a nasty guy. The unfairness to which God pleads guilty is that he can choose to show mercy and compassion even when people do not deserve it.

You are probably someone who acknowledges Yahweh, otherwise you would not be reading this book. You do not deserve to be among the people who acknowledge Yahweh, as I do not. God just had mercy on us and enabled us to open our eyes to the truth. If we are looking to justify God for this favoritism, the only way to do so is to remember that God opened our eyes so that through us he might open some other people's eyes. God chose Abraham and chose Israel not in order to exclude other nations but in order to include them. But that is not Paul's argument. Paul's argument is simply that God is God, so be quiet. (You do not have to do as Paul says: Abraham does not, and Moses does not, and Job does not, and Habakkuk does not, and sometimes they get away with it. Just be ready for that response.)

Romans 10 and 7: Sinai

We move on from Moses and the conflict with Pharaoh to Moses and the giving of the Torah at Sinai. Paul makes a teasing comment on this subject in the course of Romans 9–11 (actually he makes a few teasing comments on various subjects). The King James Version and the original New International Version have Paul declaring that "Christ is the end of the law" (Rom 10:4). If you are among those people who think that you can be right with God only if you do what the Torah says as well as believing in Jesus, then Paul's comment challenges you. The Torah was significant before Jesus's coming. It loses significance when Jesus has come.

But the TNIV puts it another way: "Christ is the culmination of the law." Both "end" and "culmination" are possible translations of the Greek word that Paul uses (*telos*), and both fit Paul's thinking. But "culmination" fits nicely with his argument a little bit earlier in Romans, where he declares that the proper expectations of the Torah are fulfilled in people who believe in Jesus and "do not live according to the sinful nature but according to the Spirit"[5] (Rom 8:4); in other words, through Jesus we fulfill the aim of the Torah, whether or not we fulfill its concrete commands. And it fits with Jesus's declaration that he came to fulfill the Torah (Matt 5:17).

The puzzling question is, why did God give Moses the Torah at Sinai, if it was going to come to an end or if it was not going to reach its aim for another thousand years, when Jesus came and the Holy Spirit was given? Paul's explanation in Romans starts from another puzzling fact about the First Testament story, one that he hints he can see replicated in his own life. Back at the beginning, he implies, Adam and Eve were fine until God said, "Do not take the fruit of that tree." The effect of the prohibition was to make them want the fruit. So there was a sense in which the very prohibition generated the coveting.

---

5. It is hard to know when to say "spirit" and when to say "Spirit." When quoting from the TNIV, I have followed its practice. Otherwise, I use "spirit" except when it is preceded by the word "holy"; then I use "Holy Spirit."

I would not have known what sin was had it not been for the law. For I would not have known what coveting really was if the law had not said, "You shall not covet." But sin, seizing the opportunity afforded by the commandment, produced in me every kind of coveting. For apart from the law, sin was dead. Once I was alive apart from the law; but when the commandment came, sin sprang to life and I died. I found that the very commandment that was intended to bring life actually brought death. For sin, seizing the opportunity afforded by the commandment, deceived me, and through the commandment put me to death. (Rom 7:7–11)

Again, not surprisingly, Paul's argument fits with something Jesus says. A young man plausibly claims that he has not committed murder, adultery, false witness, and so on, but he makes no claim about the tenth commandment, not to covet. Jesus bids him sell all he has and give to the poor (Matt 19:16–30; Luke 18:18–30). That challenge raises the question about coveting.

What Paul implies about the Eden story and what Jesus implies about the Ten Commandments apply to the Torah as a whole. Some believers in Jesus think that obeying the Torah can be life-giving. Paul has already indicated that he does not see that it can be. It is death-dealing: "The law was brought in so that the trespass might increase, . . . so that . . . sin reigned in death" (Rom 5:20–21). While the last of the Ten Commandments helps to establish the point, the opening of the Ten Commandments also does so. Before Sinai, the First Testament never said that there was anything wrong with making images of God. It is one of a number of things that seem to have been okay in Abraham's day but are no longer okay. As soon as God begins his revelation at Sinai, he says that making images of God is forbidden.

He gives no reasons there, but he later implies that the trouble with images is that they can only misrepresent God, even though they are supposed to represent God. The God of Israel, the only real God, is a singing and dancing God, a speaking and acting God. An image can only give the impression that God is static (see Deut 4). So it is unexplained but explicable that the Ten Commandments ban images of Yahweh.

But as soon as Yahweh bans them, Israel makes one (see Exod 32:1–8). It is almost as if the prohibition provokes the disobedience. Some people say that if you put negative possibilities into someone's imagination, you always risk making them do the thing you draw attention to. It could almost look as if God is doing so. And if we assume that God can guess how things will work out but still speaks in this way, we could say that God accepts responsibility for this dynamic.

The aim of giving Israel the Torah was to lead them in a way of holiness, but the effect of giving Israel the Torah was to make Israel do things that made them guilty. In yet another sense, then, Jesus is the aim of the Torah. Precisely because the existence of the Torah (accidentally, one could say) leads to people sinning more, it drives people to Jesus because it is through him that they find forgiveness and the gift of the Holy Spirit, who can enable them to fulfill the expectations that the Torah can lay down but not help them fulfill.

Romans 9 Again: Israel's Decimation

Romans 9 takes up one further aspect of the First Testament story. At Sinai, Israel ignored that command about images, and many Israelites died as a result. On the way to the promised land, Israel rebelled against Yahweh, and many people died as a result. The pattern repeated itself when Israel was living in Canaan. In the aftermath of Solomon's reign, most of Israel turned their back on Yahweh's temple in Jerusalem and on Yahweh's commitment to David, and Judah became just a rump state. And (Paul notes) the situation gets still worse.

Isaiah cries out concerning Israel:

"Though the number of the Israelites be like the sand by the sea,
only the remnant will be saved.
For the Lord will carry out
his sentence on earth with speed and finality."

It is just as Isaiah said previously:

"Unless the Lord Almighty
had left us descendants,
we would have become like Sodom,
we would have been like Gomorrah." (Rom 9:27–29)

The people of God have already been decimated before Isaiah's time by being cut down to Judah alone, and Isaiah declares that this rump state is itself going to be decimated (so Paul's first quotation, from Isa 10:22–23). And it happened in Isaiah's day (so Paul's second quotation, from Isa 1:9). In his quotations, Paul reverses their order from the order in Isaiah, but he thereby makes them clearer (the book of Isaiah is not always arranged chronologically). God had declared that he would cut Judah down until all that is left is some sad remains. And Paul's second quote looks back on the fact that God has done so.

Paul picks up from Isaiah the key word *remnant* or *remains*. That expression has different meanings in different contexts. Originally it indicated that God's judgment would be such that almost nothing would be left—only enough to make clear that there once was something. But then it can be turned on its head to suggest that at least some remains would still exist to open up the possibility that there could be a future. Finally, it can become a challenge: being the remnant carries no necessary implication that you have survived because you deserved to, but if you do survive undeservedly, you can become the faithful remnant. You are not the remnant because you are faithful. You are faithful because you are the remnant.

Paul's quotations from Isaiah relate to that logic. In Isaiah's day, Judah was invaded by the Assyrians and devastated. Only Jerusalem itself survived siege. If things had been worse, it would have been as disastrous a destruction as the one that overcame Sodom and Gomorrah. But it was not, because God does not let total annihilation happen.

The pattern of Israel's history is the one Paul has seen repeated in his own day. Once again God has let most of his people fall by the wayside. There were not many people like Paul himself whose eyes God miraculously opened—but there were some. In a sense there was nothing odd about the way most of the Jewish people failed to recognize Jesus. It was of a piece with the way the story has always been. The First Testament helps Paul understand what has happened, though the gospel also helps Paul understand an issue that the First Testament hardly recognized was an issue.

2.3 First Corinthians 10 and Hebrews: The Story as Warning

In Romans 9–11, Paul makes the point that the community of people who believe in Jesus cannot afford to start feeling superior to the Jewish people because such arrogance could mean that we get cut out of the tree into which we have been grafted, in the same way as many Jewish branches had been: "If God did not spare the natural branches, he will not spare you either" (Rom 11:21). He expands on that theme in 1 Corinthians, and Hebrews expounds it more systematically.

First Corinthians 10: The Exodus Generation as a Warning

So Gentile believers are not to think that they are "safe" because they have been grafted into the place vacated by the current generation of Israel. Paul's exhortation in 1 Corinthians makes the story of Israel's beginnings a warning example in this connection.

> Our ancestors were all under the cloud and . . . they all passed through the sea. They were all baptized into Moses in the cloud and in the sea. They all ate the same spiritual food and drank the same spiritual drink; for they drank from the spiritual rock that accompanied them, and that rock was Christ. Nevertheless, God was not pleased with most of them; their bodies were scattered in the wilderness. (1 Cor 10:1–5)

Paul retells Israel's story but translates it into Christian imagery. The Israelites went through the Red Sea; in effect, they were being baptized. God gave them food and drink in the wilderness; in effect, Jesus was nourishing them. They had the full Christian experience. But then God let that generation die.

In Romans, Paul talks about these realities in order to make a point about theology, about the relationship between God's discipline and God's faithfulness. In 1 Corinthians, he talks about them to make a point about behavior.

> Now these things occurred as examples to keep us from setting our hearts on evil things as they did. Do not be idolaters, as some of them were; as it is written: "The people sat down to eat and drink and got up to indulge in revelry." We should not commit sexual immorality, as some of them did—and in one day twenty-three thousand of them died. We should not test Christ, as some of them did—and were killed by snakes. And do not grumble, as some of them did—and were killed by the destroying angel.
>
> These things happened to them as examples and were written down as warnings for us, on whom the culmination of the ages has come. So, if you think you are standing firm, be careful that you don't fall! No temptation has overtaken you except what is common to us all. And God is faithful; he will not let you be tempted beyond what you can bear. But when you are tempted, he will also provide a way out so that you can endure it. (1 Cor 10:6–11)

The Corinthians must learn the lesson from the story. The Israelites are a warning example. Christian congregations need to see that they should not take the Israelites of the wilderness period as a role model.

Christians sometimes operate with a supersessionist model of the church's relationship with Israel, according to which the church superseded Israel as God's people. Paul does not think that way. To revert to the image from Romans 11, he does not think in terms of God cutting down one tree (Israel) and planting another (the church). But neither for that matter does he think of God planting a second tree beside the first tree. There is only one tree, the Israel tree into which Gentiles are grafted.

So when the church reads stories about Israel's idolatry or immorality or testing or grumbling, its appropriate reaction is not to congratulate itself for not being people like that, but to make sure that it learns from the negative example of these other members of the family.

Hebrews 3:7–11: The Exodus Generation Hardened and Rebellious

Hebrews 3–4 makes the same point by means of an exposition of the last part of Psalm 95. Most of the psalm is an act of praise to God, but a strange thing happens in the last section: the psalm does a complete turnaround and becomes a statement from God to us rather than from us to God. Perhaps God recognizes that the praise that dominates the psalm can be words without substance. Hebrews quotes this last part of the psalm, which says:

> Today, if you listen to his voice,
>> don't toughen your mind as you did at Meribah [Argument],
> As on the day at Massah [Testing] in the wilderness,
>> when your ancestors tested me.
> They tried me, though they'd seen my action;
>> for forty years I loathed the generation.
> I said, 'They're a people who go astray in mind,
>> and they—they have not acknowledged my ways,
> Of whom I swore in my anger,
>> "If they come to my place to settle down. . . ."' (Ps 95:7–11)

Congregations often use just the praise part of the psalm and stop before the last part, perhaps in the conviction that the divine anger expressed in the psalm may have been a feature of the First Testament God but is hardly a feature of the God we know in Jesus. Ironically, it is the last part, the part about God's anger and judgment, that the New Testament quotes in order to bring its own message home to congregations. Hebrews describes the psalm as a message that the Holy Spirit is bringing now ("the Holy Spirit says"). No doubt Hebrews assumes that the Holy Spirit was speaking those words back then to Israel, but they are not just words that the Holy Spirit spoke centuries ago. The Holy Spirit is speaking them now.

According to the psalm, a congregation needs to note several features of Israel's story. First, Israel's time in the wilderness on the way from Egypt to the promised land is a time of Israel's hardening its heart. Oddly enough, the exodus story does not refer to Israel hardening its heart, though the phrase would be a fair description of what Israel was doing. Exodus refers only to Pharaoh hardening his heart. So it is ironic and telling that the expression is here applied to Israel itself. Israel was behaving like Pharaoh, a mistake that even the Philistines knew to avoid (1 Sam 6:6).

Second, it is a time of rebellion. Again, the term *rebellion* does not occur in Exodus, but the Psalms and the Prophets often use it in this connection. When God wanted Israel to take courage and enter the promised land, Israel rebelled. When God then said, "Okay then, wander about the wilderness for a generation," they rebelled again, tried to enter the land, and failed.

Hebrews 3:12–19: The Exodus Generation Testing God

A third feature of Israel's story is that it is a time of testing. Like Exodus and like 1 Corinthians, the psalm and Hebrews do not talk about God testing his people (though other parts of the Scriptures do). The psalm and Hebrews rather speak about the people testing God, referring directly to Exodus 17:

> The entire Israelite community moved on from the Sin Wilderness by stages at Yahweh's bidding. They camped at Rephidim, but there was no water for the people to drink, and the people got into an argument with Moses. They said, "Give us water so we can drink!" Moses said to them, "Why argue with me? Why test Yahweh?" But the people were thirsty there for water. So the people protested against Moses: "Why was it that you brought us up from Egypt to have me and my children and my livestock die of thirst?" Moses cried out to Yahweh, "What shall I do about this people? A little while and they will stone me!" Yahweh said to Moses, "Pass before the people, take some of Israel's elders with you and take in your hand your staff with which you struck the Nile, and go. There, I will be standing before you there on the crag at Horeb. You are to strike the crag, and water will come out of it, and the people will drink." Moses did so before the eyes of Israel's elders. He

named the place Testing and Argument, because of the Israelites' arguing and because of their testing Yahweh by saying, "Is Yahweh among us or is he not?" (Exod 17:1–7)

Testing God can have at least two implications. It can imply that we are not sure that God can live up to what he is supposed to be or is supposed to be able to do. It can imply that we are unconsciously seeing how far we can push God. Both dynamics are there in this story.

Having introduced its quotation from the psalm, Hebrews goes on:

See to it, brothers and sisters, that none of you has a sinful, unbelieving heart that turns away from the living God. But encourage one another daily, as long as it is called "Today," so that none of you may be hardened by sin's deceitfulness. We have come to share in Christ, if indeed we hold firmly till the end our original conviction. As has just been said:

> "Today, if you hear his voice,
> do not harden your hearts
> as you did in the rebellion."

Who were they who heard and rebelled? Were they not all those Moses led out of Egypt? And with whom was he angry for forty years? Was it not with those who sinned, whose bodies perished in the wilderness? And to whom did God swear that they would never enter his rest if not to those who disobeyed? So we see that they were not able to enter, because of their unbelief. (Heb 3:12–19)

Israel had a sinful, unbelieving heart and turned away from the living God. In Hebrews, the point is that it is not guaranteed that a congregation would be different from Israel because people believe in Jesus. It is easy for a congregation to be the same as Israel. People need to learn from Israel's story. Like 1 Corinthians, Hebrews notes that a whole generation of Israel experienced the exodus, but in the end it did them little good. They got out of Egypt but they did not get into the promised land. The congregation(s) that Hebrews addresses could go the same way.

Hebrews 4: The Exodus Generation Failing to Enter

The argument continues in Hebrews 4 (as we would expect, since Hebrews as originally written did not have chapter breaks).

> Therefore, since the promise of entering his rest still stands, let us be careful that none of you be found to have fallen short of it. For we also have had the good news proclaimed to us, just as they did; but the message they heard was of no value to them, because they did not share the faith of those who obeyed. Now we who have believed enter that rest, just as God has said,
>
> > "So I declared on oath in my anger,
> > 'They shall never enter my rest.'"
>
> And yet his work has been finished since the creation of the world. For somewhere he has spoken about the seventh day in these words: "On the seventh day God rested from all his work." And again in the passage above he says, "They shall never enter my rest." (Heb 4:1–5)

I tell budding preachers not to confuse people by cross-referring to other texts in their sermons (though it might be a good way to get people to dip into the First Testament), but Hebrews does not play by my rules. In a neat collocation it puts Genesis alongside Psalm 95. God rested after completing creation, and it was evidently that divine rest that Israel was to enter in the promised land. Hebrews goes on to make an explicit link with Joshua's leading people into the land, the place of rest where people were to enjoy God's rest.

> Therefore since it still remains for some to enter that rest, and since those who formerly had the good news proclaimed to them did not go in because of their disobedience, God again set a certain day, calling it "Today." This he did when a long time later he spoke through David, as in the passage already quoted:
>
> > "Today, if you hear his voice,
> > do not harden your hearts."
>
> For if Joshua had given them rest, God would not have spoken later about another day. There remains, then, a Sabbath-rest for the people of God; for

those who enter God's rest also rest from their own work, just as God did from his. (Heb 4:6–10)

Now the psalm is speaking to people who are in the promised land, but it is warning them about the possibility of not getting there. Apparently you can be physically in the land of rest, but not really be there, or you can lose your place there, or you can fail to see that there is more to enter into.

Israel's failure to enter God's rest, then, leaves it open to people who believe in Jesus, and "we who have believed enter that rest" (Heb 4:3). The comment again looks supersessionist, that is, the church supersedes Israel as God's people. But Hebrews steps back from that implication by noting (as Rom 9–11 does) that the church could go the same way as Israel and not enter God's rest. The point in Hebrews is not that Israel failed to enter but we do enter. It is that Israel failed to enter so we need to make sure we do not fail.

In the final line of its exposition of Psalm 95:7-11, Hebrews makes explicit its interpretive approach to the First Testament story.

Let us, therefore, make every effort to enter that rest, so that no one will perish by following their example of disobedience. (Heb 4:11)

Israel is an example that we must make sure we do not follow.

Hebrews 11:1–22: Heroes of Faith

In its exposition of the story of Israel, then, Hebrews takes Israel as a warning example. It later takes the stories of a whole sequence of individuals in the First Testament as positive examples. For instance,

By faith Abel brought God a better offering than Cain did. By faith he was commended as righteous, when God spoke well of his offerings. And by faith Abel still speaks, even though he is dead.

By faith Enoch was taken from this life, so that he did not experience death: "He could not be found, because God had taken him away." For before he was taken, he was commended as one who pleased God. . . .

By faith Noah, when warned about things not yet seen, in holy fear built an ark to save his family. By his faith he condemned the world and became heir of the righteousness that is in keeping with faith. (Heb 11:4–7)

A student recently told me that two of his great role models were Joseph in Genesis and David. "What?" I replied. "You mean the Joseph who made all the Egyptians into Pharaoh's slaves? And you mean the David who raped a married woman, then had her husband killed, then failed to bring up his sons with anything much by way of a moral code, then did nothing when one his sons raped his half-sister (like father, like son)? And that is not all that could be said about David." The student knew about David's failures, but somehow he could ignore them and focus on David's strengths. He had never noticed that other aspect of Joseph's story (it is in Gen 47). Hebrews, too, does not draw attention to it, or to similar ambiguities about a hero such as Noah.

Looking to the First Testament for examples of faithfulness or warnings of unfaithfulness is a standard strategy for us, but Hebrews 11 is a rare example of this approach within the Scriptures themselves. A striking feature of the stories in the First Testament (the New Testament, too) is that they commonly portray their heroes with the ambiguity that regularly attaches to human beings—even heroes of faith. Using the stories to provide good or bad examples involves using them selectively, in a negative way or in a positive way as that student did and as Hebrews does. So Hebrews 11 continues with Abraham:

> By faith Abraham, when called to go to a place he would later receive as his inheritance, obeyed and went, even though he did not know where he was going. By faith he made his home in the promised land like a stranger in a foreign country; he lived in tents, as did Isaac and Jacob, who were heirs with him of the same promise. For he was looking forward to the city with foundations, whose architect and builder is God. And by faith even Sarah, who was past childbearing age, was enabled to bear children because she considered him faithful who had made the promise. . . .
>
> By faith Abraham, when God tested him, offered Isaac as a sacrifice. He who had embraced the promises was about to sacrifice his one and only son, even though God had said to him, "It is through Isaac that your offspring will be reckoned." Abraham reasoned that God could even raise the dead, and so in a manner of speaking he did receive Isaac back from death.
>
> By faith Isaac blessed Jacob and Esau in regard to their future.
>
> By faith Jacob, when he was dying, blessed each of Joseph's sons, and worshiped as he leaned on the top of his staff.
>
> By faith Joseph, when his end was near, spoke about the exodus of the Israelites from Egypt and gave instructions concerning the burial of his bones. (Heb 11:8–22)

Hebrews 11:23–31: Ambiguity and Grayness

There are several other interesting features about this chapter in Hebrews that takes up these First Testament stories. In some cases, it builds on positive affirmations expressed in them—for instance, Genesis commends Enoch as someone who walked with God, and Abraham as a person who had faith in God's promise. In other cases, Hebrews draws inferences from the stories that fit with the way the stories are told—for instance, the inference that Noah, Jacob, and Joseph were operating by faith. In other cases, Hebrews draws inferences about First Testament stories that issue from its own reflection (or from reflection expressed in Jewish tradition)—for instance, Genesis leaves unexplained God's acceptance of Abel's sacrifice and not Cain's, and it says nothing about Abraham looking for a city.

In yet other cases, Hebrews appeals selectively to aspects of the lives of people who were more complex than it indicates. The story of Cain and Abel is ambiguous: from Genesis, one could infer that Cain is doing just what God said in Genesis 2 in serving the ground and bringing some of its fruit to God, and that he is operating on the basis of faith; while Abel has gone in for a vocation that God did not commission, and in making his offering he is just following his brother's example but trying to do better than him—though Cain does then let himself be tripped up by Abel and by God's positive response to Abel. Noah is a more ambiguous figure than is implied by an appeal to his boat-building (see Gen 9:20–27). Abraham, too, is a more ambiguous figure than Hebrews indicates (see, e.g., Gen 12:10–20). And did Sarah really operate on the basis of faith? Genesis gives the opposite impression. Hebrews goes on:

> By faith Moses' parents hid him for three months after he was born, because they saw he was no ordinary child, and they were not afraid of the king's edict.
>
> By faith Moses, when he had grown up, refused to be known as the son of Pharaoh's daughter. He chose to be mistreated along with the people of God rather than to enjoy the fleeting pleasures of sin. He regarded disgrace for the sake of Christ as of greater value than the treasures of Egypt, because he was looking ahead to his reward. By faith he left Egypt, not fearing the king's anger; he persevered because he saw him who is invisible. By faith he kept the Passover and the application of blood, so that the destroyer of the firstborn would not touch the firstborn of Israel.
>
> By faith the people passed through the Red Sea as on dry land; but when the Egyptians tried to do so, they were drowned.

> By faith the walls of Jericho fell, after the army had marched around them for seven days.
>
> By faith the prostitute Rahab, because she welcomed the spies, was not killed with those who were disobedient. (Heb 11:23–31)

Moses, too, is more ambiguous than Hebrews implies. There is no mention here of panicking about Pharaoh and running for his life on account of being wanted for murder, or causing God to try to kill him because he has not circumcised his son, or losing his place in the promised land for an act of disobedience. And certainly ambiguity attaches to Gideon, Barak, Samson, Jephthah, and David, about whom Hebrews wisely refrains from going into detail.

Hebrews, then, works with the First Testament story on the basis of an agenda and of convictions that it brings to the text, and it uses that agenda and those convictions as the basis for the way it selects from the text and the way it interprets the text. It is not offering a definitive exegesis of the text that provides a lens for our reading the text in its own right to discover what the Holy Spirit was saying to the people for whom those stories were originally told. The Holy Spirit inspires or at least permits what Hebrews is doing, and I cannot critique my student for following its example. At the same time, by appealing to the First Testament, in effect Hebrews invites readers to go and look at the text itself, and as we do so we will find more (or less) there than Hebrews notes.

So the lesson Hebrews 11 draws from the stories involves some inference, not least because the First Testament itself does not give us a moral interpretation of them. The First Testament is being used to make a point that comes from the agenda in Hebrews itself. The point that the Holy Spirit inspires Hebrews to make is a good First Testament point, but it is not the point that most of the passages make. When modern preachers and Sunday school teachers make moral points on the basis of First Testament stories, they may be First Testament points (in which case the only problem is that they are ignoring the stories' own point). But they may be points that do not come from the Scriptures at all.

Examples and Characters

While the popular way to read First Testament stories is as moral examples, then, this can hardly be an appropriate default approach to them. They were not designed for reading that way. They do not usually divide people into good guys and bad guys. Generally their characters have both strong points and weaknesses. They sometimes act faithfully and sometimes fail. While many readers do like to have heroes whose faith and bravery they can aspire to, the First Testament's approach portrays people who are more like us, more like real people—complicated people whose stories are worth thinking about precisely because they are not plaster saints.

Further, the stories' common omission of moral evaluation of their characters also suggests something about their own aim. Sometimes the evaluation is indeed obvious, and sometimes the stories are explicit about an evaluation. While 2 Samuel 11:27 tells us that David's date rape and murder did not please God (in case we would not have realized), it does not tell us what to think about much of the last ten chapters of David's story, and the answer is not obvious at every point. The story works by drawing us in and making us think about what goes on, which may help us more than simply telling us the answer. The same consideration applies to the ambiguity in the story of Cain and Abel.

Maybe the stories were designed to have that effect, though I think their omission has another significance. It links with Paul's dominant way of reading them. Paul is interested in the First Testament stories primarily because they tell us about how God was at work in Israel's story. The astounding message on which the stories focus concerns the way God worked at his purpose of blessing for the world and then for Israel. God used people like Abraham, Sarah, Joseph, Moses, Miriam, and David, but it was not because they were great people. They were just the people God could get hold of. God worked by means of them, sometimes through their trust and obedience, sometimes despite their self-centeredness and stupidity.

Whereas we are often interested in the stories because of things they tell us about these people's characters and lives that we can put alongside our own, the Scriptures would like us to be more interested in God than in the people God used. A scene from David's story (2 Sam 7) illustrates the point. Having built himself a nice house in Jerusalem, David has a guilty conscience and thinks he had better build one for Yahweh. David's prophet knows it is his job to encourage his boss's ideas if they are not obviously immoral, but then Yahweh taps him on the shoulder with a message for David. Part of the message is that David has the relationship between David and God back to front. David wants to build God a house. God is more interested in building David a house, in the sense of a household, a royal line.

Now we have seen that the New Testament does use the First Testament as a source of good and bad examples, and its practice corresponds to an element within the First Testament that is instanced by Psalm 95 and by the Philistines' urging themselves not to follow the Egyptians' example in being stubborn. It is not illegitimate to use stories that way, but it is a subordinate feature of the New Testament's use of the First Testament and a subordinate element in the nature of the story that the First Testament tells. We need to wean ourselves from it.

2.4 The Story and the Stories (Part 1)

So a consideration of the First Testament story as examples of people and actions to emulate or avoid will not do as a default understanding of the First Testament. What happens when we look at the First Testament in its own right or when we look at it from the perspective of its main character, Yahweh?

The New Testament presupposes that the First Testament story is one story. Matthew explicitly treats it that way; Paul also implies that he sees it thus. What the First Testament itself presents us with, however, is a series of separate stories. By far the biggest is the huge narrative that runs from Genesis through 2 Kings, telling the story from creation to the fall of Jerusalem and the exile of many Judahites in 587.

I have suggested a comparison between the First Testament story and movies that are based on fact yet incorporate a lot of creative imagination. There is also a point of connection between the First Testament story and dramatic series on television. It is quite common for a television series to go on for a year and achieve semiclosure, then to come back for another year and another year. . . . Something similar happens in the First Testament. Genesis, Exodus, Leviticus, and so on, through 2 Kings, are self-contained books, though only to some extent. Genesis ends with a cliff-hanger—Israel's ancestors are stuck in Egypt, which is not where they are supposed to end up. Exodus ends with one part of God's commission to Moses fulfilled (he has organized the building of a sanctuary) but the other part unfulfilled (he has not yet ordained its ministers). So the story goes on through twelve "seasons." Even 2 Kings does not end very well, because it concludes with Jerusalem destroyed and with many of its people taken off to Babylon. But we know it is the end of that entire work, because when we turn over the page this time, there is no continuation of the story.

Genesis through 2 Kings: A Narrative Arc and a Context

As is the case with some long-running television series, a narrative arc runs through Genesis–2 Kings as a whole. It is like a range of hills with two high points. The first high point is the time of Moses, which is significant for the Israelites' deliverance from Egypt and also for their being given copious instructions through Moses. The second is the time of David and Solomon, which is significant for the establishment of Jerusalem as Israel's capital, for God's making a promise to David about his line, and for the building of the temple in Jerusalem.

Before the first high point, the story has downs as well as ups as it builds; creation leads to trouble, but God's involvement with Abraham and his family promises to bring God's purpose of blessing to fulfillment. In between the two high points are more downs and ups: Israel's faithlessness on the way to Canaan, its partial occupation of Canaan, and its faithlessness there. After the second high point, there are more downs than ups as the nation divides into two, there is more faithlessness, and the reforms of some kings do not reverse the inexorable drift toward disaster.

The books do not give us any information on who wrote them, nor do they give us explicit information on when or why they were written. One certainty is that the complete work (the eleven seasons) must have been finished after the last events it relates, events associated with the collapse of the Judahite nation in 587. Outside of that certainty are many uncertainties.

The story does not look as if it was written by one person all in one go. It reads more like a compilation of materials, much of which had accumulated over the centuries. Again the analogy with a television series works: it is common for many different writers to contribute to the scripts over the years. But in the case of Genesis through 2 Kings, there are no credits to identify the writers. Over the past two centuries, as part of the focus on history that we have noted, scholars have worked with monumental ingenuity at trying to uncover the process, but no progress has been made, and it seems to me best to assume that we are never going to know.

Yet it is illuminating to see the story in its eventual form as written for Judahites in those decades after 587, and one can see that it fulfills various functions and brings various messages for them. Was it read out for people in installments in some prayer services? We do not know how it would become known, or even whether only a few literary people could read it.

The period after 587 is commonly referred to as "the exile," though the disadvantage of that term is that it makes one think simply of Judahites whom the Babylonians have taken geographically into exile. But the figures that the First Testament gives for the number of people taken to Babylon at various points are quite small: over four thousand on this occasion, over ten thousand on that occasion. It seems that the Babylonians naturally focused on removing the important people, the leaders, the troublemakers—people such as the royal family, the members of the court, the priests, and the prophets. Most Judahites escaped exile and may have been quite glad to see the back of many of the people who did go. So not so many people went into exile, and instead of using the term *exile* to refer to the period when Genesis through Kings came into the form that we know, I shall use expressions such as "the time when Babylon ruled." Babylon's control of the Middle East was a dominant factor in the life of the people in Judah as well as the people who were exiled.

In the Beginning (Genesis—Seasons 1 and 2)

When your nation has collapsed, your capital has been destroyed, your leaders have been taken off into exile, and you are the shattered underlings of a great imperial power, what would you notice when you read this gargantuan work that tells your story up to this point?

Its beginning would strike you, especially if you were in Babylon, because it would remind you of the Babylonians' own creation story—both by comparison and by contrast. There are individual points in the Genesis story that ring bells with the Babylonians' story, such as the reference to the Deep and the fact that human beings are made to serve God; but the contrasts are also striking. The Babylonian story involves lots of gods, and they are inclined to fight with one another. Genesis speaks of only one God. It emphasizes how good the original creation was; strife and violence came only later. Not unreasonably, the Babylonians would claim that their god Marduk had defeated the Judahites' God, Yahweh. Genesis boldly declares that the God of Israel is the God who created the world. The Babylonians would be puzzled by the Judahites' discipline of avoiding work for one day in seven, and the Judahites might wonder if this was just their private peculiarity. Genesis implies that this practice reflects the way God went about the process of creation. It portrays the God of Israel as the God of the whole world and the one through whom all the nations came into being. In the Babylonian version, the story of creation ends up in Babylon. It is interesting that the Genesis story of creation also ends up there, but with a snide touch: Babylon is the place where humanity reaches a peak in its resistance to God's purpose. The story of the tower in Babylon would remind people of the ziggurats, and Babel becomes the place the language of the nations is turned into babble (Gen 11).

That story is the end of season 1 in this drama, though Genesis 1–11 occupies only one-fifth of Genesis. This is another parallel with television series: some seasons are shorter than others.

Season 2 comprises Genesis 12–50, the story of Israel's own ancestors: the families of Abraham and Sarah, of Isaac and Rebekah, and of Jacob and his sons. It transpires that Israel's own story has a double preamble. The earlier preamble sets Israel in the context of the world's story. The second preamble tells of those ancestors. It would not be surprising if the ancestors' story was written as the prequel or backstory to Israel's story; and it would not be surprising if the world's story was written as the prequel or backstory to that prequel.

If Judahites in Babylon might have wondered about their relationship with the world as a whole and about their God's relationship with the world as a whole, they would be even more likely to wonder about their own future and about their relationship with their own country now that they have been exiled from it. Season 2 reminds them that their great ancestors, Abraham and Sarah, came from—Babylonia. The prequel to Israel's story is the story of God making and (partially) fulfilling a number of promises.

- Yahweh promises that they will have their own country, specifically the country of Canaan. While I assume that this promise indeed goes back to the time of Israel's ancestors, it is not hard to see how it would speak to Judahites who had been moved away from that country back to where their ancestors came from.
- Yahweh promises to make them into a big nation. When Babylon ruled, Israel had been decimated in numbers and in importance compared with what it had once been. This element in the promise would again speak to the present situation of the people.
- These two promises constitute great blessing. Yahweh promises that the blessing will be so great that other peoples will pray to be blessed as Abraham and Sarah's descendants are blessed and/or that these descendants will actually be the means of these other peoples' blessing.

Covenants

These promises indicate how season 2 picks up from season 1, because the very first episode of season 1, the story of creation in Genesis 1, had spoken of land and increase and blessing. The rest of season 1 makes us wonder whether the original plan is going to find fulfillment. The promises to Abraham and Sarah reaffirm that it will. The way season 2 picks up from season 1 also clarifies something that is a bit ambiguous in some formulations of the promises to Abraham and Sarah. Is the blessing mainly for them or is it for all the nations? The answer is that it is for both. It really is for them; it really is for the world. God had that intention from the beginning.

The divine promises are undergirded by Yahweh's making them the subject of a covenant. The essential nature of a covenant is that it involves an especially solemn and binding commitment. When you make a covenant, you signify that it is a commitment you cannot get out of without being unfaithful to yourself as well as to the other person. In the Scriptures, covenants are sometimes two-sided, sometimes one-sided. Two individuals or two peoples may make a covenant with one another; God and his people may make a covenant with each other. In addition, one person may make a covenant to another person, one person or a group may make a covenant to God, God may make a covenant to people.

The first covenant in the Scriptures is the one God makes to Noah, that he will never again destroy the earth. The second is the one he makes to Abraham, the covenant that undergirds those promises. Both these covenants are one-sided. They are not conditional on a commitment the other party makes. The covenant with Abraham looks for a response, but it does not say, "This covenant will require a response before it will become effective." It says, "This covenant will be effective, so you should make a response." That characteristic of God's dealings with Abraham and Sarah is the one Paul picks up in Romans. The covenant involves a promise on God's part and a response of trust on Abraham's part. What God does through Jesus follows the pattern of what God did with Abraham and Sarah.

One can see how significant would be the nature of that covenant for people living in the time when Babylon was king. Well before their time, God had supplemented the one-sided covenant with a two-sided one, as we shall see in considering season 3. The problem is, Israel had failed to keep their side of the two-sided covenant; it was why they had ended up with nationhood terminated, capital and temple destroyed, and many people exiled. The question is, has Yahweh simply terminated his relationship with them because of their failure? On what basis can one imagine that Yahweh has not done so? The basis is as Paul argues. Behind the two-sided covenant was the one-sided one. People's response was not integral to the original covenant. So their failure to respond does not imperil it.

Paul notes that the addition of the covenant sign of circumcision (Gen 17) came after the original establishment of the covenant (Gen 15). It became integral to the relationship, but it was not integral at the beginning. It thus does not compromise the principle that the covenant was based simply on God's promise and Abraham's trust.

For Judahites in Babylon, the addition of circumcision would be significant in a second way. While other peoples around Israel did practice circumcision, the Babylonians did not. So this Judahite practice would raise the same question as the distinctive Judahite practice of a weekly Sabbath. Is this just their cultural oddity? The Abraham story would affirm to them that this "cultural oddity" was really important. It was an example of God's taking a practice that some other people knew and reworking it so that it became integral to God's relationship with them.

From the Service of Pharaoh to the Service of Yahweh (Exodus, Leviticus, Numbers 1:1–10:10—Seasons 3 and 4)

As season 2 followed on from season 1, season 3 (Exod 1–18) follows on from season 2. The cliff-hanger at the end of season 2 left Israel's ancestors in the wrong country, though doing rather well there. At the beginning of season 3, things get much worse as the Egyptians turn the people of Israel (as we may now call them) into state serfs. They become conscript labor on building projects. But they cry out to Yahweh, and Yahweh is mindful of that covenant he made to Abraham. It is time to set about fulfilling the next stage of his promises. He eventually acts spectacularly in order to get them out of their serfdom and brings about a number of disasters in Egypt on the way to the final one. The calamities are designed to persuade the Egyptian king to acknowledge him and to get the king to let the Israelites go of his own free will. Paradoxically the story also speaks in terms of God's desire that he should not do so, because each new disaster makes clearer that Yahweh is God and Pharaoh is not. It is the dynamic Paul refers to in Romans 9.

So Israel leaves Egypt in order to realize its destiny to serve Yahweh rather than Pharaoh. The implications are worked out at great length in season 4 (Exod 19:1–Num 10:10), the whole of which is spent at Mount Sinai. The people are outside Egypt, but they are still nearer where they have come from than where they are going. At Sinai, God spells out what it means to serve Yahweh. Read in its own context, season 4 lays out what Yahweh expects Israel to fulfill.

The significance of season 4 is more complicated when we look back on it from the time when Babylon is king. That time is one when Yahweh has now committed Israel to serving someone other than him. Israel is to serve Babylon, though Babylon is Yahweh's servant. The reason is that Israel has been refusing to serve Yahweh over the centuries. He has now validated their refusal. To see the nature of that refusal, they do not have to look beyond the very beginning of the expectations detailed in season 4 (the Ten Commandments). The first four commandments are to acknowledge no gods other than Yahweh, not to make images of Yahweh, not to misuse Yahweh's name, and to keep the Sabbath. People living in the time when Babylon ruled would know that they failed miserably in connection with these basic expectations. The significance of season 4 in this context is like the significance that Paul attributes to it, and that Martin Luther especially emphasized. When we read the expectations expressed in season 4, we do not think, "Oh, good, I know now what God expects, I can go and do it." We think, "Oh, no, that is just the kind of thing that we have not been doing, and the more guidance God has given us, the more guilty it makes us."

At Sinai, Yahweh declares to Moses that the people are to keep his statutes and rulings, "by doing which a person will live" (Lev 18:5). Paul picks up that declaration and contrasts it with what the right relationship with God that is based on faith says, about Christ being accessible and the word being "near you, in your mouth and in your heart" (Rom 10:5–8). Ironically, Paul is paraphrasing Moses himself (in Deut 30:12–14). Yes, Moses proclaims that grace and faith are basic to our relationship with God; Moses also declares that people who belong to God need to live in the appropriate way. If we take the declaration in Leviticus out of its context (as Paul's opponents were perhaps doing), we pervert the Scriptures. But if we take no notice of the challenge to obedience, we also pervert the Scriptures.

Sometimes Christians think that the complexity and detail of the Torah make it a burden and make it impossible to fulfill, or that it makes people hopelessly guilty if they fail to obey one tiny rule. Neither season 4 nor later seasons give that impression. The basic requirements of the Torah (such as the opening four of the Ten Commandments, noted just now) are not all that complicated. But Israel will not resist the temptation to ignore them. Indeed, season 4 recounts how they already disobey them at Sinai (see Exod 32).

From Sinai to Moab (Numbers 10:11–25:18; Numbers 26–Deuteronomy—Seasons 5 and 6)

Season 5 (Num 10:11–25:18) takes Israel from Sinai to the area of Moab down in the Jordan Valley that stands on the edge of the promised land. The caravan would have needed only a few weeks to make this trek from Sinai (Num 33 gives a list of the way stations), yet the series covers enough time for the whole exodus generation to die out so that the next generation will be the one that actually enters the land. The reason is the problem advertised by that failure at Sinai. A failure of trust and commitment continues to characterize the people, and Yahweh finally gives up on them, except for two faithful men, Joshua and Caleb.

Paul does not appeal to season 5 in Romans, though he might have done. It illustrates the way God acts in drastic chastisement, cutting down his people to virtually nothing, though not actually to nothing. Paul does appeal to season 5 in 1 Corinthians 10, for its warning value. It illustrates the devastation that can fall on the people of God for failures that the Corinthian congregation is imitating only too well.

On the edge of the promised land, season 6 (Num 26–Deuteronomy) stands still, like season 4. Deuteronomy is Moses's monumental farewell address or sermon or lesson, which recapitulates much of season 4. Why does it do so? There are two or three sorts of reasons. In terms of the story, this whole new generation needs to face up to Yahweh's expectations and commit themselves to fulfilling these expectations. In a literal sense they are a wholly new people who did not experience the exodus, though Deuteronomy emphasizes that in another sense they need to see themselves as the same people. Yahweh did not make the covenant just with their parents' generation. He made it with them.

Later generations of Israelites are implicitly invited to look at themselves in light of the same dynamic. They are not the exodus people; but in another sense they are. They need to identify themselves as such. The dynamic is one that continues into Christian faith; we were crucified with Christ. We were there when they crucified our Lord.

On the eve of Babylon's becoming king, the Judahite king Josiah led Judah in a renewal of its covenant commitment to Yahweh that constituted its identifying itself as the exodus people. There is enough overlap between the reforms of Josiah and the contents of Deuteronomy for us to infer that Josiah knew what he was doing here. Indeed, the overlap points to another reason why season 6 recapitulates season 4. It does more than repeat or summarize what came before. It brings it up to date for a later generation. A neat concrete example is Deuteronomy's comments on the need to distinguish between real prophets and false prophets. It was not a need in Moses's day or for centuries afterward, but it was a need in Josiah's day, as we discover from Jeremiah.

Josiah knew that he had to take action that would forestall the warnings at the end of Deuteronomy about what would follow from failing to keep the covenant. But the reform did not last, and the warnings were fulfilled. Yet Deuteronomy also holds up the possibility that the catastrophe it envisages need not be the end. It would be possible for Israel to turn back after the catastrophe, if it failed to turn back before. Deuteronomy offers hope as well as explanation to people living in the time when Babylon ruled.

From Victory to Loss (Joshua, Judges—Seasons 7 and 8)

Seasons 7 and 8 comprise the story told in Joshua and Judges. The Joshua narrative covers a decade or three; the Judges narrative covers a century or three.

The first half of Joshua relates the exciting story of how Yahweh gives the country of Canaan to the Israelites under Joshua; the second half relates how Joshua allocates the country to the different Israelite clans. The first half raises sharply the question about the relationship of history and story. Whereas the book of Joshua emphasizes the Israelites' capture and destruction of Jericho and Ai, archaeological discoveries suggest that neither Jericho nor Ai was occupied by anybody at the time when the Israelites took them (which would obviously make the job easier). On the other hand, Joshua also emphasizes the capture and destruction of Hazor in the north. Hazor was inhabited at the time, and it was destroyed by someone. Archaeological discoveries also indicate a vast increase in the number of smaller settlements spread over the Canaanite hill country in the period that now begins. The implication is that the nature of Joshua is not so different from that of Genesis and Exodus. It is a story that combines fact and imagination in telling how God gave Israel its land.

Yahweh does not throw the Canaanites out of their land just because he wishes to give the country to Israel (though if he had seemed to do so and you told Paul it was not right, he would again put you in your place by declaring that God can do as he likes, so be quiet). The Torah and Joshua justify God's throwing the Canaanites out by appealing to the Canaanites' waywardness, not least their practice of human sacrifice. This rationale might be food for thought for people living when Babylon is king. Israel has behaved the same way as the Canaanites, including offering human sacrifice, and Israel has proved that Yahweh is not so unfair. Israel too has lost control of the land, and the people who led Israel in its waywardness have been taken far away.

The allocation of the land among the clans in the second half of Joshua would carry some poignancy. On one hand, it would underline the sadness of what had happened to the land by the time when Babylon ruled. It would also underline what had gone wrong in the way many kin groups and families had lost their land through their bad luck or laziness and through being taken advantage of or swindled by people who were luckier or cleverer. Control of much of the land had become concentrated in the hands of a small number of landowners, and many families had been reduced to working what had been their own land as tenants of those landowners. Yet the story would also raise the question whether the allocation might still stand. The book indicates that there are still records of how the land was distributed among the clans. Maybe there could be a fresh start. Significantly, the book closes with another challenge to covenant making, which will be a necessity if there is to be such a fresh start.

The book of Joshua declares that all Yahweh's promises have now been fulfilled. So season 7 could be the end. After all, seven is the number that suggests completeness. Yet the book of Joshua also declares in a series of notes between the lines of its story that of course Israel's occupation of the country is not really complete. The Canaanites stay in control of vast areas. So as a good TV series will continue if the company commissions another season, the book of Joshua leaves openings for the story to continue.

Season 8 takes up the book of Judges, and an audience-pulling season it is, with a sequence of rip-roaring, funny, violent, scatological, salacious, and finally deeply disturbing and distressing stories.

When we get to the end of a story or a season, sometimes it throws light on all that has preceded, and so it is with Judges. The book's conclusion notes that it is a tale about people doing what was right in their own eyes when there was no king in Israel. That comment announces how this season leads into season 9. When Babylon is king, however, the comment carries an irony, because having kings has commonly meant Israel has done what was right in the eyes of Israel's kings, not in Yahweh's eyes. It is hardly surprising that Yahweh later terminated the rule of kings in Israel. So the question that arises for the readers is where we go from here.

King, Capital, and Promise (1 and 2 Samuel—Seasons 9 and 10)

Seasons 9 and 10 themselves articulate that ambiguity about kingship. Actually, Judges has already implied it—the best thing Gideon ever does is decline to become the first in a line of hereditary rulers. He will not do so because Yahweh is Israel's ruler. But the natural development of Israel's life as a nation pushes it toward having a central government, and the external pressure of the Philistines does the same. When Israel asks for a king, Yahweh takes the view that Gideon is right—they are thereby rejecting Yahweh as king. Samuel also warns them of the inevitable cost that central government will bring. But Yahweh gives in and chooses first Saul, then David (and in due course Solomon). In different ways they embody the ambiguity of central government. They both start well, and they are the means of God's solving some of Israel's problems and of taking Israel to the most complete experience yet of the keeping of those promises whose fulfillment Joshua exaggerated. But they then fall for the temptations of power.

The story of each king is thus a tragedy in the classic sense: it takes them to a height of achievement but then relates how they throw almost everything away and watch their life unravel. We feel sorry for Saul, who takes actions that are understandable in the pressure of circumstances but with whom God operates in tough fashion. It is almost as if he pays the price for being the first person to occupy the position that God did not really want occupied. David acts in ways whose morality is more obviously reprehensible, yet God is more merciful with him. It is almost as if he gets away with things because God has made his point with Saul and can now afford to be merciful.

Arguably the high point in his story comes in 2 Samuel 7, some of whose significance we have already noted. It points up another facet of his ambiguity. He has won his great victories, captured Jerusalem, and built himself a palace, and he feels a bit sheepish about the fact that Yahweh has no palace (Hebrew uses the same word for palace and temple). His prophet Nathan encourages his idea of building one for Yahweh, until Yahweh intervenes and wonders if he might be allowed an opinion on the matter. He likes being on the move, not being fixed in one place. Further, David is reversing the relationship between himself and God in taking this initiative, and God intends to build him a house (i.e., a household). The impression the promise gives is that there will be a line of Davidic kings ruling in Jerusalem forever. They did rule for four hundred years, but the generation living in the time when Babylon is king is the generation that has experienced the termination of the Davidic monarchy. This promise to David is vital to that generation's hope that the Davidic monarchy cannot really have come to an end, and to the development of what comes to be called the messianic hope.

Paul could have used the way God deals with Saul and David in expounding the theme that God deals with people as he wishes, so be quiet, and the theme that it is God's grace, not human merit, that decides things.

We have noted that David is a great hero and spiritual model for Jews and Christians. Reading his story in 2 Samuel may make this fact puzzling. The popular veneration of David is a product more of the references to David in the Psalms than to a reading of his story in 2 Samuel. The wickedness of his action in relation to Bathsheba and Uriah is taken to be a one-time aberration. But the veneration is encouraged by seasons 11 and 12, where David becomes the gold standard by which many later kings are evaluated. The question there is, do the kings walk rightly with Yahweh in the way that David did? That affirmation of David does correspond to an element in his picture. He was always loyal to Yahweh rather than serving other gods, and he nearly always relied on Yahweh rather than trusting other resources. One might say that the story implies a contradiction at the heart of his life, a split between his relationship with God and his relationship with people. The latter failures mean that his life and his rule fall apart; they will reach their nadir in the account of his last days in the opening episode of season 11.

Temple, Division, and Downfall (1 and 2 Kings—Seasons 11 and 12)

So season 11 begins with the humiliating account of David's last days and of his wife and senior priest's involvement in manipulation and jockeying to ensure that Solomon succeeds. The trajectory of Solomon's story then follows that of Saul's and David's, and unlike David he cannot claim to have stayed loyal to Yahweh all his life. As a penalty, the realm he inherited from his father in fulfillment of God's promise falls apart after his death through the stupidity of Solomon's own son.

For two centuries there are then two Israels whose stories interweave in seasons 11 and 12. The big Israel to the north inherits the name Israel as its usual political designation, but it does not behave much like an Israel that serves Yahweh. For the little Israel to the south, the political designation is Judah, but over these two centuries it is a bit more faithful to Yahweh. More fundamental to the sense that it is the real Israel is that it has the Davidic line and the temple in Jerusalem. The Israel of the north appoints its own kings, and they often get assassinated rather than dying in their beds. And it sets up its own worship centers and its own forms of worship, which look uncomfortably like those of the Canaanites.

In the middle of season 12, the Assyrian Empire to the east starts taking an interest in the land of the Bible, but especially in the northern Israel, which is on the trade routes. Failing to win its submission to the empire's authority, Assyria eventually puts it out of business, removes most of its population to other parts of its empire, and brings people to the geographical area of Israel from those other parts in exchange. There are thus political reasons for Israel's downfall after two centuries, though 2 Kings is more interested in the religious and theological reasons. To put it another way, there is a political level of explanation for the fall of the northern kingdom, but it is the religious and theological explanation that interests the season 12 scriptwriters.

The latter decades of the northern kingdom see the emergence of prophets who confront its kings, especially Elijah, Elisha, and Micaiah. The scriptwriters are especially interested in the northern kingdom's cavalier attitude to these figures, who represent Yahweh's insistence on breaking into Israel's life.

The plot line of the second half of season 12 is less complicated because it needs to tell only the story of Judah. Its two heroes are the reforming kings Hezekiah and Josiah; between them is the antihero king Manasseh. Again there is likely a political angle to his compromise on real commitment to Yahweh and to Josiah's subsequent reforms; Judah, too, is coming under pressure from Assyria, but Josiah lives in the context of Assyria's increasing weakness. Once again, however, the scriptwriters are more interested in the religious and theological explanation of events. Manasseh is faithless; Josiah sets about reforming the worship of the temple, knows how to respond when a Torah scroll is discovered there, and knows how to relate to prophets.

Josiah's reforms are not enough to undo Judah's ingrained rebelliousness, which asserts itself after his death in a way that brings the nation's downfall to Babylon, the next superpower. The series almost closes with a pained detailing of the horrific destruction of city and temple. But after the credits have rolled and while some people are making tea, it actually closes with an event from twenty-five years later. The Babylonians had deposed and exiled the next-to-last king of Judah, but he is still alive in Babylon, and the Babylonians now release him from prison and give him something like honored foreign resident status in Babylon.

Now from time to time season 12 has referred to God's promise to David and to the necessity for God not to allow Davidic rule in Jerusalem finally to disappear. Jehoiakin's Judahite contemporaries in Judah and in Babylon cannot but see his release as a little sign that God has not forgotten his promise. This coda to season 12 thus leaves open the possibility that another series will follow. Strangely, viewers look at the schedules next fall and find no season 13. Something else appears in the schedules.

2.5 The Story and the Stories (Part 2)

After Genesis–Kings, the next longest series of stories is Chronicles–Ezra–Nehemiah, an alternative version of the story from Genesis–Kings that also goes on to narrate some episodes from the century after the exiled Judahites were allowed to return. Beyond Chronicles–Ezra–Nehemiah, the First Testament incorporates three independent short stories: Ruth, Esther, and Jonah. Further, the book of Daniel includes a number of stories and also an overview of the great empires that dominate the second half of Israel's history, Babylon, Media, Persia, and Greece.

Chronicles–Ezra–Nehemiah

When we turn over the page at the end of 2 Kings, we get a surprise, though it is a different surprise according to whether we are reading the Hebrew Bible or an English translation. In the Hebrew Bible, 2 Kings leads into Isaiah. In English Bibles, it leads into Chronicles, where the first person we meet is . . . Adam. That name alerts us to the fact that we are beginning to read an alternative version of the story in Genesis–Kings.

English Bibles present what follows as a four-part work comprising 1 and 2 Chronicles, Ezra, and Nehemiah. The first two are a revisionist version of Genesis–Kings. The second two continue the story beyond where Kings and Chronicles both stop. The first lines of Ezra repeat the last few lines of Chronicles, as an episode or series of a television drama may provide a recap of the preceding stage in the story. So Ezra–Nehemiah seems to belong with Chronicles, the remake of that first long series in Genesis–Kings.

Hebrew Bibles locate Chronicles–Ezra–Nehemiah at the end of the Scriptures. Oddly, they appear there not in chronological order, but with Ezra–Nehemiah preceding Chronicles. As there is no suggestion that Genesis–Kings was written in one go by one scriptwriter, so there is no suggestion that the whole of Chronicles–Ezra–Nehemiah was written in one go by one scriptwriter, and the variation between the Hebrew and the English order also suggests that there is no need to assume that the books were written in the order of the story they tell. Maybe Ezra–Nehemiah was written first. In fact, I have wondered whether the opening of Ezra was a draft for the missing season 13 that one might have expected to follow Kings. Either way, Chronicles was then written as a revisionist prequel for Ezra–Nehemiah. (Actually, the same might be true about Genesis-Kings: maybe Joshua–Kings was written first, and Genesis–Deuteronomy is the prequel.)

Why would someone produce another version of the story from Genesis-Kings? One aspect of the answer is that good stories just do commonly get retold; for example, the New Testament incorporates four versions of the Jesus story. Another aspect is that new insight emerges from the events the story relates. There are also new ways in which the story speaks to people in a different situation from the one the previous version addressed.

Second Kings ends with the release of a Judahite ex-king, a quarter of a century after the fall of Jerusalem, and it makes no explicit reference to any subsequent events. Second Chronicles ends with something that happened another quarter of a century later, when Cyrus the Persian took over the Babylonian Empire and thus became the Judahites' king. It is that event which makes possible the freeing of Judahites in Babylon to go home and rebuild Jerusalem.

The freeing and the rebuilding are the subject of Ezra–Nehemiah. Further, the period whose story Ezra–Nehemiah tell is also the background against which Chronicles tells its story. That is, Chronicles was written during Ezra and Nehemiah's time (or maybe a bit later). There is therefore something to be said for reading Ezra–Nehemiah before Chronicles, as the Hebrew Bible's order encourages, because it helps us understand why Chronicles tells the story the way it does.

The plot structure of the story in Chronicles–Ezra–Nehemiah corresponds to the one in Matthew's opening chapter—or rather, vice versa. Act One extends from Adam to David. Act Two extends from David to the exile. Act Three covers the time after the exile. The difference is that Matthew is starting from Jesus and working backward, and therefore we know where Act Three is going. For Chronicles–Ezra–Nehemiah, the times that Ezra–Nehemiah records are simply the present in which the community lives.

From Adam to the Fall of Jerusalem Again (1 and 2 Chronicles)

Chronicles retells the story of the entire period covered by Genesis–Kings in about one-seventh of the pages (in the Hebrew Bible). One way it achieves this is the device with which we are familiar from the opening of Matthew; in other words, Matthew took from Chronicles his idea about how to introduce his story. The period from Adam to David (from Genesis through 1 Samuel) is summarized by lists of names. The summary has the effect of the lightning recap of previous episodes in a television story with which a new episode or new season may begin. Such a summary is little use to a new viewer, but it may be enough to jog the memory of a returning viewer.

So Chronicles implies the assumption that its audience is familiar with the story from Genesis through 1 Samuel, and it begins by affirming that it takes up that story. But its real interest lies in David, and then in the temple that he conceived. It recognizes that Solomon built the temple, but it emphasizes that David made all the plans and the provisions for it. In its account of the story that follows the temple building, what subsequently happens to the temple is central.

When northern Israel set up its own state after Solomon's death, 1 and 2 Kings have noted that it thereby cut itself off from David and from the temple. Its own line of kings and its places of worship were devised by the nation itself, not by God, and they had no promise of God attaching to them. Chronicles expresses that point in more radical fashion than Kings. It simply does not tell the story of northern Israel. "Judah" (the political entity) is itself "Israel" (the people of God). The so-called Israel, the political Israel, could be ignored.

Someone who does read Ezra–Nehemiah before reading Chronicles discovers that one aspect of the community's life in that later time is the tension in which Judah lived with people in the other nearby provinces of the Persian Empire, one of which is Samaria. Samaria is roughly equivalent to the old territory of northern Israel. Its inhabitants seem to have combined people with two sorts of background. Many were descendants of people whom the Assyrians had settled there two centuries previously, when they moved people from northern Israel to other parts of their empire. Others were people who escaped removal. The leadership of Samaria presents its people as a whole as worshipers of Yahweh who therefore want to join in building the temple. The Judahites are suspicious of their motivation and their commitment. When Chronicles leaves northern Israel's story out of its narrative, it is making a theological judgment that has significance for its readers in this connection.

Chronicles' great emphasis on David and the temple thus has several sorts of importance for its audience. If people are inclined to be depressed by the discouraging side to life in the Second Temple community, Chronicles encourages them to realize the fantastic privilege of being a people that worships Yahweh in accordance with the way David laid out. If the power of their neighbors impresses them, it tries to encourage them by their past story and by the position they have. And if they read this story in light of the way prophets such as Jeremiah speak of a coming David, it gives content to that hope.

The Scriptures frequently affirm that God blesses people who honor him and brings judgment on people who do not, but they also recognize that this principle does not always work out. Second Kings provides a spectacular example of its not working out when it acknowledges that King Manasseh reigned a long time and King Josiah was cut short in his prime. Chronicles does not want people to give up on that principle about honor and judgment; it wants to motivate people to honor God. So it provides some rationale for why Manasseh lived a long time and why Josiah did not.

Rebuilding: Temple, Community, City (Ezra and Nehemiah)

The end of the story in Genesis–Kings and in Chronicles leaves the people of Judah in a mess. Its temple in Jerusalem and the city itself have been destroyed, and the underlying reason is the community's unfaithfulness to Yahweh. Ezra–Nehemiah tells the story of how steps were taken to put things right.

The time when Babylon was king came to an end when the Persians put down the Babylonian Empire in 539 BC, as the Babylonians had put down the Assyrians less than a century previously. In one sense, for Judah this change simply meant moving from one overlordship to another, but the end of Chronicles and the beginning of Ezra are prepared to view the change more positively, because the Persians were the means whereby a number of things got put right.

1. Cyrus the Persian commissioned people to return to Judah if they wanted to do so, to rebuild the temple. The first half of the book of Ezra relates how they did.
2. One of Cyrus's successors agreed to give a commission to Ezra (Ezra had nothing to do with the original return of people from exile and the

rebuilding of the temple—in fact, he was not born yet). He was to take a Torah scroll to Judah so as to get the people to shape their lives by it in a way they had not done before.

3. This same Persian king agreed to give a commission to Nehemiah to go and rebuild the walls of Jerusalem.

The disaster that had overcome Judah had another aspect that never got put right. No Davidic king now ruled the people of God, and the restoration of Judah did not include the restoration of the monarchy. Indeed, the story incorporates a feature that contrasts with this idea. A remarkable feature of it is the involvement of the Persian administration in approving and even facilitating the work. Alongside that feature of the story is a kind of mirror image of it. Throughout the story, relations are fraught between Judah and its neighbors such as Ammon, Moab, Samaria, and Edom, which in previous centuries had been independent peoples that were often in conflict with Judah. Now all these peoples are Persian provinces or colonies, and the Judahites' account of things implies (plausibly) that these other peoples were not keen on Judah gaining a status like theirs. They tried to get the Persians to put Judah in its place. But they failed.

The omission of any reference to reinstating the Davidic monarchy is an aspect of the way the rebuilding of Judah after the disaster of 587 was wonderful yet partial. The completion of the temple made people who remembered the First Temple cry. Ezra and Nehemiah have to battle hard to get Judah to take the Torah seriously and not risk assimilation to those other peoples surrounding them. Nehemiah is scandalized at the way Judahites are taking advantage of the situation when their fellow Judahites are having a hard time.

Yes, it is a miraculous restoration—but an incomplete one, and it will stay that way. Persia will give way to Greece, and Greece to Rome, and people will still be longing for restoration. In the Gospels, the point is more explicit in the opening of Luke than in the opening of Matthew. Mary rejoices in the way God is now putting down the mighty (read: the latest imperial power) and acting to help Israel. John the Baptizer's father rejoices that God is saving Israel from its enemies so as to enable Israel to serve God without fear. Yes, the time when Babylon is king, or Persia is king, or Greece is king, or Rome is king, will not be the end.

Three Heroes (?) (Ruth, Jonah, Esther)

The First Testament includes three stand-alone dramas outside the frame of Genesis–Kings and Chronicles–Ezra–Nehemiah.

While Ruth is set in the context of Judges and 1 Samuel in English Bibles, it stands alone in Hebrew Bibles, We have noted that Ruth appears in Matthew in the company of three other women whose presence in the Messiah's genealogy might raise eyebrows: Tamar in Genesis, Rahab in Joshua, and Uriah's wife in 2 Samuel. Let no one suggest there was anything odd about Jesus being the son of an unmarried woman, then. Matthew's appeal to Ruth provides an appropriate way into her story, which keeps emphasizing that she is a Moabite. Moabites or Canaanites who held onto their commitment to Kemosh or Baal could hardly be members of Israel, but the principle for determining inclusion or exclusion was faith commitment, not ethnicity. Israel was never ethnically exclusive.

The declaration that Israel is open to people such as Moabites is not the only point about the Ruth story. It is a story about a woman who loses everything as a result of a famine and the need to move to a foreign country to find food. It is a story about a man who accepts his responsibilities as a family guardian and restorer. It is a story about David. It is a story about a number of other people with cameo roles. So Matthew presupposes just one of its key themes.

Esther does not appear in the New Testament, but Paul's argument in Romans 9–11 meshes with Esther's place in the Bible as a whole. Esther is the story of an attempted final solution to the Jewish problem of the kind that Adolf Hitler sought, an attempt to eliminate the Jewish people. The attempt fails. The book never refers explicitly to God or to other aspects of Jewish faith, but its delicacy in almost referring to them but never quite doing so has the effect of drawing attention to them yet indicating that on this occasion God delivered his people through coincidences and through human beings accepting responsibility for the Jewish people's destiny, rather than through the kind of divine intervention that the exodus story involves. One way or another, God will not let his people be eliminated, though (the story emphasizes) this certainly is not reason for us to do nothing.

Jonah appears in the New Testament in Jesus's appeal to an analogy between himself and Jonah. In Luke 11:29–30, the analogy lies in Jonah's preaching to the Ninevites, with an implication that again opens up an appropriate reading of Jonah's story. For Israel, one possible implication of the story is, Nineveh knew how to repent—do you? God canceled its judgment—he could cancel yours. As is the case with Esther and Ruth, there are other aspects to the richness of the Jonah story, including its challenge about God's desire to forgive the foreign, pagan nation, and the ease with which a true prophet becomes a resistant prophet (hence the question mark after the word "heroes" in my subheading above).

The allusion to Jonah in Matthew 12:40 works the analogy in a different way, by noting the parallel between Jonah's time in the fish and Jesus's coming time in the tomb. While I assume that Jonah is a fictional story, it has a historical background; Jonah was a real prophet (he is mentioned in 2 Kgs 14:25). While much of the First Testament is (divinely inspired) fictionalized history, the book of Jonah is (divinely inspired) historical fiction. I do not think that historically Jonah spent three days in a fish, though of course God could have made that possible. But that fact about Jonah does not mean Jesus will not or did not spend (part of) three days in the tomb. It is the Jonah of the fictional story that provides Jesus with his illustration. I sometimes use Lady Macbeth's awareness that her hands are stained with King Duncan's blood as an illustration of the stain that wrongdoing imposes on us, from which Jesus cleansed us. Lady Macbeth existed, but the fact that her awareness of her stain is fictional, as far as I know, does not mean that Jesus cleansing me is fictional.

Daniel

The first half of the book of Daniel focuses on incidents in the life of Daniel and three other young Judahites taken off to Babylon after Nebuchadnezzar conquered Judah. The New Testament does not refer to the stories, but one can see how New Testament believers might have found them encouraging and illuminating. They are stories about living in exile, and the New Testament sometimes sees believers as people living in exile insofar as their real citizenship lies somewhere else (see, e.g., 1 Pet 1:2). The image would be especially telling for people living outside Judea and closer to the center of the Roman Empire.

One question they would have to handle would be, who is Lord? Is it Jesus or Caesar? Believers in Jesus were taking some risk in declaring that Jesus is Lord and Caesar is not. Would they lose their lives? If they were not risking their lives, were they risking their livelihood? Were they condemning themselves to a marginal position within the empire? The stories in Daniel would speak directly to such questions. The stories concern people who live and work in the service of the empire and who are challenged to change their diet and to worship an idol. They model what faithfulness means when under such pressure, and they prove that God is faithful. God makes it possible for them to show that they are better, more useful, more recognized citizens of the empire. The stories portray God's involvement with them, rescuing them and making it possible for them to succeed.

The second half of the book (to oversimplify slightly) speaks to a different question, and one to which the New Testament does refer. The visions relate to the persecution of Judahites by the Seleucid emperor Antiochus IV in the 160s BC. He banned worship in accordance with the Torah and instituted in the Jerusalem temple a form of worship involving "a desolating abomination," which was apparently some form of idolatrous object. Jesus and the New Testament writers can refer to it as providing them with a way of describing the abomination that Rome was expected to introduce into the temple in their time.

Like the stories, the visions in Daniel encourage believers with a promise that God will put the empire down. The visions actually speak of four empires beginning in Daniel's own day: Babylon, Media, Persia, and Greece (which includes Seleucids such as Antiochus). They promise that God will crush the final empire, and in the 160s God does so in an extraordinary way.

The New Testament can see the pattern being repeated in its day. Like other Jews reading Daniel, those in New Testament times can now identify the fourth empire as Rome and can look forward to God putting it down as he put Antiochus down.[6]

In connection with Chronicles–Ezra–Nehemiah, we have spoken of Act One extending from Adam to David, Act Two extending from David to the exile, and Act Three covering the time after the exile. Whereas Chronicles–Ezra–Nehemiah makes no overt promises about Act Three coming to an end, the visions of Daniel focus on Act Three and describe it as covering the empires from Babylon to the time when God brings an end to their meaningless but self-deifying story and introduces his own reign.

Questions for Discussion

1. What does the summary of the First Testament story that opens Matthew's Gospel suggest to you about Jesus?

---

6. See further the discussion of Rev 13 on pp. 154–55 below.

2. How do you think Adam and Eve, Abraham and Sarah, Isaac and Ishmael, Jacob and his sons, Pharaoh and Moses are significant for you?
3. Do the stories about Israel in the wilderness have any specific significance for your congregation?
4. Which version of Israel's story (Genesis to Kings or Chronicles–Ezra–Nehemiah) speaks more powerfully to the church as you know it?
5. Of Ruth, Jonah, Esther, and Daniel and his friends, which resonates most with your life?

CHAPTER 3

Promises

The First Testament makes the promises that Jesus fulfills. The New Testament shows how passages from the prophets are fulfilled or filled out in what Jesus does and in what happens to him; it thus uses the prophets to help us understand Jesus, and it directs us back to read the prophets.

When Christians think about the relationship of the First Testament to Jesus, their default model comes from the fact that the First Testament incorporates prophecies or promises of which Jesus is the fulfillment. Matthew does not begin here (though Mark does), which signals to us that this Christian approach is narrower than the New Testament's own. But it is one important way in which the New Testament sees the link between the Testaments.

3.1 Matthew 1:18–2:23: Jesus Filling Out Promises

For most readers, Matthew really begins with the five scenes from the story of Jesus's birth in Matthew 1:18–2:23. How do these scenes relate to the First Testament? The passages from prophecy that Matthew quotes help him in various ways to understand Jesus. But a number of them do so as a result of his not focusing on the way the Holy Spirit was speaking to the people to whom the prophecies were given. They illumine Jesus through the Holy Spirit giving new significance to them as Matthew asks his question about who Jesus is.

Scenes from the Beginning

Each scene gives a key place to a prophecy that is "fulfilled" in the event related.

1. Joseph is reassured that his fiancée's pregnancy results not from her promiscuity but from the Holy Spirit's activity that will bring about the birth of one who will save his people. The point is clinched by a reference to what the Lord had said by means of Isaiah concerning a virgin who would have a child called "God with us" or Immanuel (Matt 1:18–25; cf. Isa 7:14).
2. The place where "the king of the Jews" is to be born is discovered to be Bethlehem through a consideration of the prophecy in Micah about the birth there of a ruler over Israel (Matt 2:1–12; cf. Mic 5:2).
3. The account of Joseph, Mary, and Jesus's sojourn in Egypt is brought to a climax by relating this event to what the Lord had spoken by means of Hosea about his son having been called out of Egypt (Matt 2:13–15; cf. Hos 11:1).
4. The story of Herod's massacre of baby boys is brought to a climax by linking it to Jeremiah's words describing Rachel mourning for her children (Matt 2:16–18; cf. Jer 31:15).
5. The account of the family's move back to Nazareth is concluded by describing it as a fulfillment of the statement in the prophets that the Messiah was to be called a Nazarene (Matt 2:19–23).

The reference of this last passage is unclear, there being no prophecy that says, "he will be called a Nazarene." Three texts might perhaps have been in Matthew's mind.

First, Isaiah 11:1 and other texts describe a coming ruler as a "branch" growing from the "tree" of Jesse, which was "felled" by the exile, and these texts use the Hebrew word *netser* for "branch." So describing Jesus as a Nazarene, a *notsri*, could be taken as an unwitting description of him as "Branch Man."

Second, the description of the servant in Isaiah 52:13–53:12 as despised and rejected could link with Nazareth's being a city in the despised and alien far north, Galilee of the Gentiles, the land of darkness (Matt 4:14–16, quoting Isa 9:1–2); it was a city proverbially unlikely to produce anything good (John 1:46). So it would not be surprising if a Nazarene were despised and rejected, as the prophecy described Yahweh's servant.

Third, the angel's appearance to Samson's mother describes Samson's calling to be a Nazirite to God from birth (Judg 13:5). A Nazirite was someone especially dedicated to God, of which the signs were that he didn't drink, he avoided contact with anything dead, and he kept his hair long. There isn't a link of substance between being a Nazirite and being a Nazarene, but the words are similar. The events surrounding the birth of Jesus's forerunner also recollect that angelic visitation to Samson's mother (see Luke 1:15; also Luke 1:31).

In each of these vignettes from the beginning of Jesus's life, then, a key place is taken by a reference to a First Testament prophecy, as if to say, "You will understand Jesus aright only if you see him as the fulfillment of a purpose of God contemplated and announced by God centuries before." In particular, if you find it surprising that he should be conceived out of wedlock, born in a little town like Bethlehem rather than in Jerusalem, hurried off to Egypt at an early age, indirectly the cause of the death of scores of baby boys, and eventually brought up in unfashionable Nazareth, then consider these facts in light of what the prophets say.

How are we to understand the use of prophecy by Matthew and other New Testament writers? Is it a way of proving that Jesus is the Messiah? And if so, is such "proof from prophecy" designed to remove the scandal from the story of Jesus and to win cheap debating points over against non-Christian Jews?[1]

Actually, Matthew's use of prophecy is of a piece with his interest in other aspects of the First Testament. He is concerned with understanding Jesus and with understanding the First Testament; he is not out to prove something to unwilling hearers or to explain away something to disciples of shallow faith. He is writing to people who believe in Jesus. He is not trying to convince them that Jesus is the Messiah. They are aware that Jesus is the Messiah. Matthew knows that Jesus is to be understood in light of the promise of which he is the fulfillment, and he therefore seeks to interpret his significance in that light.

This understanding of Matthew's attitude is supported by the next episode he relates, the ministry of John the Baptizer (3:1–12). Here too a passage from prophecy has a key place: John is the voice preaching in the wilderness of which Isaiah 40:3 speaks. The idea that Matthew is utilizing apologetic

---

1. See, e.g., Friedrich Baumgärtel, "The Hermeneutical Problem of the Old Testament," in *Essays on Old Testament Interpretation,* ed. Claus Westermann (London: SCM, 1963) = *Essays on Old Testament Hermeneutics* (Richmond: John Knox, 1963), 134–59, especially 143.

"proofs from prophecy" is even less plausible here. He is seeking to help himself and his readers to understand what Jesus's messiahship means.

Understanding Jesus

Putting it this way raises a further question about the passages from Matthew 1–2. The modern instinct is to interpret prophecy, like other biblical material, by concentrating on the meaning the prophecy had for its author and hearers. A passage such as Micah 5 with its reference to a birth in Bethlehem is future-oriented in its original context, and in this sense Matthew's quotation of it fits its inherent meaning. One cannot prove exegetically that Jesus is the ruler of whom Micah speaks; Matthew's use of his text goes beyond its statements, in light of his faith in Jesus. But his use of this text is not alien to it.

At another extreme, his appeal to Hosea 11 takes the text in a quite different way from what Hosea meant. Hosea 11 is a report of God's wrestling over whether to act toward Israel with love or with wrath. It opens by recalling the blessings God had given to the people, beginning by calling them out of Egypt at the time of the exodus. Hosea 11:1 is not prophecy in the sense of a statement about the future that could be capable of being "fulfilled" at all. It is history.

Between these two extreme examples are passages that are future-oriented but that relate to the future within the prophet's day (Mic 5, too, may have had such a shorter-term future reference to an imminent king). Rachel's weeping (Jer 31:15) is the lament she will utter as Judahites trudge past her tomb on their way to exile after the fall of Jerusalem in 587 BC. The voice in the wilderness (Isa 40:3) to which Matthew 3:2 goes on to refer is a voice commissioning Yahweh's supernatural servants to prepare the road for Yahweh's return to Jerusalem when the exile is over, fifty years later.

The child of Isaiah 7:14 is a more controversial figure. To begin with, it is debated whether "virgin" is the right translation of the Hebrew word *almah*. That word may denote a virgin, or it may simply denote a young girl. But let us assume it refers to a virgin. This reference still hardly means that the girl in question will be a virgin when she conceives and gives birth. At the time of writing, I can say that the Prince of Wales will one day rule Great Britain; but it does not mean he will rule as a prince but that he will become king and will then rule. In Isaiah 7, the prophet would be promising that by the time a girl who is not yet married, and who may therefore be designated a virgin, has married and had her first child (say, within a year), the crisis Ahaz fears will be over. She will be able to call her child Immanuel, "God with us," in her rejoicing at what God has done for the people. (If the word just means "young girl," Isaiah may be talking about a girl who is already pregnant, in which case the time frame is even shorter.)

Finally, if "he will be called a Nazarene" refers to Judges 13, this reference, too, takes up a statement about a specific imminent event involving a specific individual. If it is an allusion to Isaiah 11, it more resembles the appeal to Micah 5. If it alludes to Isaiah 52:13–53:12, it more resembles the appeal to Hosea 11. Isaiah 52:13–53:12 presents itself not as a prophecy about the future but as a vision or picture of someone whose humiliation is past and whose exaltation is future. It is not directly a portrait of either crucifixion or resurrection. As Jews who believe in Jesus can find Jesus in the chapter, Jews who do not believe in Jesus can point out ways in which it does not literally apply to him. Indeed, part of what happens when we study this passage is that knowing Jesus is the Messiah helps Christians make sense of this otherwise enigmatic picture. At the same time, Jewish people reading the passage make sense of its enigmatic picture in light of their own suffering as God's people.

Fulfillment, Meaning, and Significance

I once received a phone call from a Jewish lawyer in Los Angeles named Asher Norman, who had written a book entitled *Twenty-Six Reasons Why Jews Don't Believe in Jesus.*[2] He wanted me to check out what he had said about Christian faith to make sure he had not misrepresented it. In the book he argued, among other things:

- Isaiah 7:14 is not a prophecy of the virgin birth of the Messiah.
- Isaiah 9:6 does not prophesy that the Messiah will be named Mighty God.
- Isaiah 52:13–53:12 is describing someone who has already suffered but who will be restored, not someone who will suffer in the future.
- Isaiah 59:20 (quoted in Rom 11:26) does not refer to the Messiah.
- Psalm 22:16 is not a prophecy that the Messiah's hands and feet would be pierced.

2. Asher Norman, *Twenty-Six Reasons Why Jews Don't Believe in Jesus* (Nanuet, NY: Feldheim, 2007).

Although I dispute numerous points in Mr. Norman's book, I cannot dispute that he is right in his comments about these and other biblical texts. In most if not all the passages in Matthew 1–3, Matthew sees significance in prophecies that they would not have had for their authors.

Speaking of their prophecies as being "fulfilled," then, may mean more (or less) than we conventionally mean by "fulfilled." The Greek word usually translated "fulfilled" here is *plēroō*; it is the regular verb meaning "fill." The other New Testament verbs sometimes translated "fulfill" are *teleō* and *teleioō*, which mean "complete" or "accomplish." None of these verbs is a technical term like the English word *fulfill* for the idea that prophecies that were statements about the future now come true. Applied to a prophecy, *plēroō* could suggest "filled" or "filled up" or "filled out" as well as "fulfilled" in the sense of "(caused to) come true." To put it another way, it is useful to distinguish between the meaning of a passage and its significance for us. Its *meaning* is what the Holy Spirit was saying to the people whom the human author was addressing, and the people who received that message and ensured it found a place in the Scriptures. Its *significance* is the way the message was filled out in a context when people saw new implications in it for their situation.

If we understand "fulfilled" as meaning something like being filled out or brought to its goal, then Matthew's quotations are easier to handle. In this sense, Isaiah 52:13–53:12 is indeed fulfilled by Jesus's crucifixion and resurrection. And it is in this sense that one might think in terms of the New Testament's revelation of the "fuller meaning" of a prophecy. That expression is misleading if it implies that the New Testament is unveiling the prophecy's own inherent meaning. It is rather revealing a fuller meaning that the prophecy has for later readers—what I prefer to call its further significance. In this sense the prophets were a resource for the New Testament church, and continue to be a resource for us, in understanding who Jesus is; and Jesus was a resource for their understanding of the prophets, and continues to be so for our understanding.

A story in John 11 suggests the way of thinking that may lie behind Matthew's interpretation. Caiaphas declares, "It is better for you that one man die for the people than that the whole nation perish." Jesus must be killed lest he continue to arouse messianic expectations and ultimately cause a revolt that the Romans would have to crush violently. But John can see a hidden significance in Caiaphas's words: "He did not say this of his own accord, but being high priest that year he prophesied that Jesus should die for the nation" (11:50–51). Now Caiaphas did of course speak of his own accord, and he knew what he meant. But in light of later events (that Jesus did die for the nation, in a different sense), John intuits that Caiaphas spoke the way he did by a divine prompting that gave his words a further significance. Jesus will die to avert from his people not merely Rome's wrath but God's wrath.

John's words, then, point to a way of understanding Matthew's assumptions about the prophets. Whatever meaning prophecy may have had historically, Matthew finds within it particular sentences that were in a special sense not spoken by the prophets "of their own accord" but by a divine prompting that gave them a significance that was not part of the meaning for the prophets and for their original hearers but that is apparent in light of the event they refer to. All the words of a prophet had a God-given historical meaning; some also had a God-given messianic significance, a way in which they illumine the significance of Jesus. It is this latter significance to which 2 Peter 1:21 refers when it declares that "prophecy never had its origin in the human will, but prophets, though human, spoke from God as they were carried along by the Holy Spirit."

When New Testament writers looked back to the words of the prophets in light of Jesus, sometimes they found statements so appropriate to Jesus's coming that this reference must have been present in them from the beginning by God's will, if not in the awareness of their human authors. Like John, they moved from some aspect of the later event back to a passage that turned out to illumine it. No one would have thought that a passage such as Hosea 11:1 was a prophecy awaiting fulfillment until someone thought about it in light of what happened to Jesus.[3]

Inspired Interpretation

Can we continue to interpret prophecy in Matthew's way? There is a possible instance in Psalm 22. This protest of someone abandoned by God and attacked by enemies is several times quoted in the New Testament as "fulfilled" in Jesus. In the psalm (v. 16) the supplicant says, "they pierce my hands and my feet" (TNIV); text and translation are problematic, but for the sake of argument we will assume a version that is most open to a prophetic inter-

---

3. This, incidentally, reduces the plausibility of the theory that stories in the Gospels were developed to provide fulfillments of prophecies. The hermeneutical movement is *from* the puzzle of Jesus's flight *to* a reinterpretation of Hosea 11, not from the natural meaning of Hosea 11 to a story that assures people that it has been fulfilled.

pretation. The New Testament does not quote this line, but many Christians have found a prophecy of the crucifixion here. There is no hint that the psalm's author saw this prayer as a prophecy, or that other Israelites would have understood it so. The suggestion that it refers to Jesus works back from Jesus's coming to the text and intuits that the facts of the crucifixion must have been in the back of God's mind when God welcomed into the Psalter this prayer by an afflicted Israelite.

This suggestion seems feasible. Such possibly inspired interpretation of the Scriptures is similar to other forms of inspired utterance: difficult to test, possible sometimes to disprove, but hard to prove. I accept Matthew's intuitions about the First Testament because I believe he was inspired; I could not ask you to accept mine on the same basis. Yet I do rejoice that God sometimes speaks to me and through me by means of interpretations of the Scriptures that do not correspond to their original meaning and that I believe come from the Holy Spirit.

Similar considerations apply to the study of the precise form of the biblical text. In Psalm 22:16, the Masoretic Text actually reads not "they pierce my hands and my feet" but "like a lion [at] my hands and my feet" (cf. TNIV margin) or "my hands and feet have shriveled" (New Revised Standard Version). The familiar translation follows the Greek, Syriac, and Latin versions of the psalm. Thus the Christian textual tradition preserves a reading amenable to a Christian interpretation, while the main Jewish textual tradition (the Masoretic) preserves one that is not. Either could be working back from what they believe: Jesus is the crucified Messiah, and the text can be expected to hint at that fact; or he is not, and the text cannot be expected to hint at it. The text's preservation can be influenced by the same factors as its interpretation; the movement is from contemporary beliefs to the text, as well as vice versa.

This post–New Testament phenomenon instanced by Psalm 22 is paralleled within the passages from Matthew that appeal to prophecy. The quotation from Micah (Matt 2:6) provides an example, since Micah's "insignificant Bethlehem" has become Matthew's "by no means insignificant," which was the result of Micah's prophecy being fulfilled or filled out. It is characteristic of textual work in New Testament times (within the New Testament and, for instance, at Qumran) to pay close attention to the text itself in the awareness that one is handling Holy Scripture; and the conviction that one now sees God acting in fulfillment of promises enables one to specify more precisely in the Scriptures themselves the nature of the filling out. As with his way of interpreting prophecy, Matthew's way of handling the text of prophecy is one that we sometimes follow when we choose the translation that best makes the point we want to bring home to people. It will be important to be self-conscious about what we are doing and to complement it with a concern to work with a text of the Scriptures as near as we can to the one that issued by God's providence from its human authors.

Thus Matthew's ignoring the First Testament's inherent meaning at some points does not undermine our conventional emphasis on texts' historical meaning. The parallel with John 11 does not suggest that every human statement, or even every statement by a high priest, or even every statement about the future by a high priest, or even every statement about the future by this particular high priest in this particular year, has a second significance. Rather, on occasion the words of a particular person may be so striking in another connection that they raise the question of a second significance. The way Matthew or John can identify this second significance is by considering what they already know about Jesus as the Messiah. But generally it is appropriate to understand the prophets or to understand a high priest such as Caiaphas in light of what they themselves meant. It is generally how we will discover what the Holy Spirit meant in inspiring the prophets.

This approach to interpretation makes it possible to argue about the meaning of a text. Theologically, it reflects the awareness that God indeed spoke and acted in the life of Israel in a way that can also be instructive for us. Some passages of the Scriptures may have an inspired second significance, an extra level of significance in the back of God's mind that we may need a special revelation to identify. All the Scriptures have an inspired first meaning, their meaning as a communication between God and people in a particular context in their lives, to which we can have access by the usual methods for understanding written texts.

Learning from Prophecy

If our study of First Testament prophecy is to attend to its meaning for its authors and their hearers, our interpretation of passages such as the ones Matthew quotes will not be limited to noting the significance he finds in them when he interprets them in light of the circumstances of Jesus's coming.

Isaiah 7, for instance, belongs in a context of dire peril for preexilic Judah, and it relates how its king was challenged to a radical trust in God despite the reality of this threat. Such a trust would issue in doing the right thing before God and before human beings, despite the temptation to yield to Syria and Ephraim's attempts to lean on him to join their rebellion against Assyria, or to seek help against Syria and Ephraim from Assyria itself. The power of Syria and Ephraim threatens to destroy Judah; but within a year (says Isaiah) it will all be over, and Judah will know that "God is with us." That promise is reserved in the Scriptures for the impossible situations that most need it (see, e.g., Gen 28:15; Exod 3:12; Jer 1:8; Matt 28:20). In those contexts it lifts people back on their feet by promising that they do not face the future alone and that God will deal with whatever crisis threatens. So it does in Isaiah 7:14 (see also 8:8, 10), and in the situation of crisis in Matthew 1:18–25.

Jesus's beginning his work in Galilee provides another puzzle like the ones raised by the stories in Matthew 1:18–2:23. Why Galilee rather than Jerusalem? Matthew answers with another passage from the prophets that is thereby filled or filled out or filled up. Isaiah 9:1–2 speaks of light dawning in Galilee; Yahweh has not finished with the Ephraimites, who were the first victims of Assyria in the eighth century. One could say that the pattern is repeated in Jesus's preaching when he begins in Galilee,

to fulfill what was said through the prophet Isaiah:

"Land of Zebulun and land of Naphtali,
the Way of the Sea, beyond the Jordan,
Galilee of the Gentiles—
the people living in darkness
have seen a great light;
on those living in the land of the shadow of death
a light has dawned." (Matt 4:14–16, quoting Isa 9:1–2)

Isaiah 9 thus gains new significance in light of Jesus's action. In its own context it speaks of the darkness, anguish, gloom, and distress of war (Isa 8:21–22). But it speaks of more than that darkness, for these are the darkness, anguish, gloom, and distress of the day of Yahweh (cf. Amos 5:18–20), embodied in historical events for Ephraim, which is the despised "Gentile Galilee." But then the prophecy portrays darkness dispelled, anguish and distress comforted (Isa 9:1–3). It goes on to speak of a son of David ruling the world by the faithful exercise of authority (9:4–7). It is not a vision we see fulfilled yet, but it is one that will be fulfilled.

What of the branch, the *netser*, in Isaiah 11:1? If a branch can grow from the trunk of a tree that has been felled, then no one and nothing is ever finished. If God says there will be new growth, there will be. For five centuries it must have seemed as if that promise was as dead as the trunk it referred to, but then there *was* new growth, in the person of the Nazarene.

As well as understanding Jesus in light of prophecy, we understand prophecy in light of Jesus, as the one who fulfills it. The notion of "God with us" is capable of suggesting a presence of a much fuller kind than we would have guessed from the words in their First Testament context. The darkness into which God brings light is not merely the darkness of this-worldly suffering but that of God's absence. In the person of the Branch Man, the growth from the felled tree is more extraordinary even than Isaiah pictured it.

Matthew and the Qumran Community

Whereas Matthew 1:18–2:23 and 4:12–16 use passages from the Scriptures to help people make sense of events that might raise questions, this dynamic is not so obvious in the quotation that comes in between:

> In those days John the Baptist came, preaching in the wilderness of Judea and saying, "Repent, for the kingdom of heaven has come near." This is he who was spoken of through the prophet Isaiah:
>
> > "A voice of one calling in the wilderness,
> > 'Prepare the way for the Lord,
> >   make straight paths for him.'" (Matt 3:1–3, quoting Isa 40:3)

Matthew has now reached the point where Mark actually begins the story of Jesus, incorporating the same quotation as Mark (Mark 1:1–4). So Matthew is not unique in incorporating such quotations, though he has more of them and he uses them in distinctive ways. Luke also includes this quotation, and we will shortly look at further examples from Luke and Acts. At the same time, in including many quotations early on, Matthew is flagging the way his Gospel will continue; there are similar quotations in Matthew 8, 11, 12, 13, and so on.

As is the case with Matthew's earlier quotations, in Isaiah 40 the prophet is not talking about a figure who will come in some centuries' time but about a proclamation that is being made in the context of the sixth century BC when Yahweh had abandoned Jerusalem but is now intending to come back, bringing Judahite exiles with him. The prophecy thus reports the commissioning of some supernatural engineers to construct a suitable highway for this return. It is not clear whose voice the prophecy is reporting. The prophet simply hears a voice, without seeing anyone. The point is the commission of the work, not the one commissioning it. Matthew thus once again makes use of a prophecy to help people understand what Jesus is about (more strictly, what John the Baptizer is about) and to set him in the light of the Scriptures. In Isaiah, Yahweh is coming (back) to Jerusalem. In Matthew, Jesus is (eventually) coming to Jerusalem.

In Isaiah 40:3, "the Lord" is Yahweh. In the Gospels' quotation, "the Lord" is Jesus. During Jesus's lifetime and in light of his death and resurrection, his disciples come to realize that while he was a human being, he was also an embodiment of what it means to be God—in character (e.g., his faithfulness, mercy, toughness) and in power (e.g., his creating, stilling, healing). When people met him and saw him operating, they might well realize that they had met and seen someone who embodied God as well as embodying humanity. The instinctive application to Jesus, the Lord, of passages about Yahweh, the Lord, helped to articulate the point.

In another connection, Matthew takes the prophecy in a different direction from its original meaning. Five miles from where John was baptizing, the Qumran community had their monastery. The Qumran Community Rule (col. 8, lines 13–16) declares that when people become members of the community,

> they are to be separated from within the dwelling of evil men to walk in the desert to prepare there his path. As it is written, "In the desert prepare the way of Yhwh, straighten in the steppe a causeway for our God." This is the study of the Torah that he commanded by means of Moses, to act in accordance with all that has been revealed from age to age, and in accordance with what the prophets have revealed through his holy spirit.[4]

While Matthew and the Qumran community would have differing views over who was preparing the way for the Lord, and thus would have differed over who was fulfilling the prophecy in Isaiah 40, they were agreed that the preparing involved the people of God putting their lives right in accordance with the Lord's expectations. Typically, this expectation does fit with the

---

4. See, e.g., Florentino García Martínez and Eibert J. C. Tigchelaar, eds., *The Dead Sea Scrolls Study Edition*, 2 vols. (Leiden: Brill; Grand Rapids: Eerdmans, 2000), 1:88–91.

general expectations of the book of Isaiah, though it does not relate to this particular prophecy in Isaiah 40.

God's Yes

There is another link between the text's inherent meaning and the text as interpreted by John, by the New Testament, and by the Qumran community. In Jesus's day, the Jewish people were living under the overlordship of the Roman superpower, and they were thus in a situation not so different from the one presupposed by Isaiah 40. The Persians did put down the Babylonians and did encourage Judahites in Babylon to return to Judah, where they did rebuild the temple. The exile came to an end. Judahites who stayed where their families had gone into exile did so voluntarily, so that exile became dispersion. Yet life under Persia and under Greece and in due course under Rome hardly counted as Yahweh reigning in his people's life, and people in Judea thus looked for God to come to his people to restore them. In this sense, there is more than a verbal link between Isaiah 40 and Matthew 3 (and the Qumran Community Rule). Yahweh had fulfilled the promise to return to Jerusalem at the end of the sixth century BC. But the fulfillment was incomplete, as is commonly the case with the fulfillment of prophecies. In Jesus, God brings about a fuller fulfillment, though still not a final or complete one.

In connection with each of the prophecies that Matthew quotes, then, we will see more of their implications for the significance of Jesus's coming if we go back to the prophecies themselves. Matthew's appeal to particular aspects of particular prophecies becomes an encouragement to undertake a broader study of God's promises in the First Testament so that we can learn more about Jesus from them. Matthew's use of a number of specific passages (and the references elsewhere in the New Testament to other passages) does not indicate the total range of First Testament prophecies that are to illumine Jesus's coming for us. They only instance the process of understanding Jesus in light of prophecy, and they invite us to look at the total range of these prophecies in order more fully to understand the Jesus in whom all God's promises find their "Yes" (2 Cor 1:20). These promises extend right back even beyond God's promise of blessing to Abraham to the words of God about blessing in the opening chapters of Genesis.

In Genesis through 2 Kings, God's original promises keep receiving fulfillments, yet no fulfillment is complete or final, and each experience of fulfillment or of loss stimulates renewed hope in God's overarching promise. This hope becomes more overt in the prophetic books themselves. What the prophets offer is an updated version of God's ancient promises.

It is this overarching and ever-reformulated promise that is fulfilled and filled out in Jesus. He is to be understood in light of the ongoing promise, and we are encouraged to look at those promises in order to understand what he came to achieve. As much interest, then, attaches to aspects of those promises that did not obviously find their fulfillment in Jesus's coming as to aspects that did. Insofar as all God's promises are reaffirmed in Jesus, all reveal aspects of his significance and calling. Further, given that the promises of a new world in which authority is exercised in faithfulness have not been fulfilled through Jesus's first coming, we are to look forward to their being fulfilled through his second coming. They must be, because (if one may put it this way) if Jesus is truly God's Messiah, he has no choice but to be the means of fulfilling all God's promises.

So we interpret the prophets in light of their meaning in their context, and we interpret them in light of the way Jesus confirms them and fills out their significance. But neither the prophets themselves nor Matthew provides a warrant for interpreting them in light of the newspaper, which is the approach to prophecy taken by books abounding in Christian bookstores and sites abounding on the Internet that refer prophecies to events in the Middle East in our own day. They ignore the texts' meaning for the prophets whom God inspired and for the readers God addressed through them. Matthew does that too; the question is, can such interpretation be acknowledged as inspired like Matthew's? It fails one test: Matthew begins from Jesus's coming and he interprets prophecy in light of it. His interpretation has part of its justification in its faithfulness to God's revelation in Jesus. The newspaper is not as inspired a starting point.[5]

3.2 Luke: Jesus Interpreting the Scriptures

Luke's Gospel does not include the sequence of prophecies relating to Jesus's birth and his beginning his work in Galilee, though it does include the quotation of Isaiah 40:3–5 relating to John the Baptizer that Matthew and Luke

---

5. I have written further on this matter in "Can We Read Prophecy in Light of the Newspaper?" in *Key Questions about Biblical Interpretation: Old Testament Answers* (Grand Rapids: Baker, 2011), 297–310.

have in common with Mark. It also incorporates a significant quotation from Isaiah early on in Jesus's story, and a significant comment about prophecy near the end.

Luke 4: The Spirit of the Lord Is on Me

One could see Luke's account of Jesus's preaching at Nazareth on a text from the prophets as his equivalent to Matthew's sequence of references to the prophets. We do not know whether Jesus chose a passage from Isaiah 61 or whether it was one of the set readings for the day. Either way, he came to the synagogue there and read out:

> The Lord Yahweh's breath is on me,
> because Yahweh has anointed me.
> He's sent me to bring news to the humble,
> to bind up the people broken in mind,
> To call for release for captives,
> the opening of eyes for prisoners,
> To call for a year of Yahweh's acceptance.

. . . He then told the congregation, "Today this scripture is fulfilled in your hearing." (Luke 4:18–19, 21)

The book called Isaiah incorporates prophecies from later prophets as well as prophecies from Isaiah himself. They were all inspired by the Holy Spirit, and one can see how many of them were in another sense inspired by Isaiah himself: one can see ways in which they take up his prophecies. The way the New Testament takes up prophecies from the First Testament is thus continuing a process one can perceive within the First Testament. In Isaiah 61, then, one of these later prophets gives his testimony to Yahweh's call. The context suggests that he worked two centuries after Isaiah himself, beyond the time when Babylon was king and into the time when Persia was king. We have noted that the Persians' arrival was itself a fulfillment of Yahweh's prophetic promises, and in a good way. Yet in another sense one imperial overlord was simply replaced by another.

The prophet who speaks in Isaiah 61 is inspired to declare that things will not continue in this way forever. The people as a whole are poor, oppressed, controlled by the imperial power, and metaphorically speaking they are in the dark of a prison cell. The prophet has been commissioned to tell them some good news about freedom and a metaphorical recovery of sight because they will now be released from that cell. It is thus the year of Yahweh's favor. According to the Torah, every fifty years there was to be a year heralded by horn blowing—*yobel* in Hebrew, from which we get the English word *Jubilee*. When this year came, families that had lost their land through debt or had been compelled by debt to become bondservants were to be freed and enabled to go back to their land. Life could start again for them.

We do not know if the horn-blowing year ever happened or whether it was simply a nice idea like universal health care, but either way it provides this prophet with an image for what God intends to do for his people. They will be released from their serfdom in a parallel fashion.

In Jesus's day things had not changed a lot. Once again only the superpower is different—it is now Rome. The situation of God's people is still one of serfdom, poverty, darkness, and oppression. Rome is now the agent of these afflictions. Jesus takes up the testimony of the Isaianic prophet and declares that it is "fulfilled," filled out, in the congregation's ears.

The prophet goes on to speak of a day of redress. The year of favor and the day of redress are different ways of describing the same event, from two angles. Putting the superpower down and setting Israel free are two sides of a coin. Jesus reworks the parallelism between the two expressions. In his sermon, he stops before the words about redress, but he takes up the theme later in his ministry, when he speaks of the "fulfillment of all that has been written" (see Luke 21:22). His ministry is the day of God's favor, but favor will be succeeded by redress. The redress is not on the imperial power (as in Isa 61) but on the Jewish people itself. The prophecy is thus filled out in a chilling way.

Luke 24: Concerning Himself

Starting from Jesus's first reference to fulfillment helps to illumine his last reference to fulfillment, on resurrection day.

> Two of them were going to a village called Emmaus, about seven miles from Jerusalem. They were talking with each other about everything that had happened. As they talked and discussed these things with each other, Jesus himself came up and walked along with them; but they were kept from

recognizing him. He asked them, "What are you discussing together as you walk along?" They stood still, their faces downcast. . . .

He said to them, "How foolish you are, and how slow to believe all that the prophets have spoken! Did not the Messiah have to suffer these things and then enter his glory?" And beginning with Moses and all the Prophets, he explained to them what was said in all the Scriptures concerning himself. . . .

He said to them, "This is what I told you while I was still with you: Everything must be fulfilled that is written about me in the Law of Moses, the Prophets and the Psalms." Then he opened their minds so they could understand the Scriptures. He told them, "This is what is written: The Messiah will suffer and rise from the dead on the third day, and repentance for the forgiveness of sins will be preached in his name to all nations, beginning at Jerusalem." (Luke 24:13–17, 25–27, 44–47)

In what sense are the Torah, the Prophets, and the Psalms about Jesus? They do not actually say that the Messiah will suffer and rise from the dead on the third day, and that repentance for the forgiveness of sins will be preached in his name to all nations, beginning at Jerusalem. We cannot be literalistic about what Jesus says. In what sense do the Scriptures say these things?

Jesus's earlier quotation from Isaiah 61 indicated one way they relate to him: we can understand his ministry with the help of that prophecy. His relationship to it is like his relationship to the passages quoted in Matthew 1:18–2:23. Luke 24 makes the point more explicitly. How are Jesus's disciples to make sense of the extraordinary events they have been through? Methodologically, Jesus's answer is, Look at them in light of the Scriptures. No one could have worked forward from the prophets that the Messiah would suffer and then rise again on the third day, as no one could have worked out that he would be born of a girl who was a virgin or would be taken to Egypt or would go and live in Nazareth. But when these things happen, and we look back in the Scriptures, we find passages that help us understand them.

Does this understanding make the relationship of Jesus to the Scriptures seem phony? It might do so, if there were not another level to the coherence between the Scriptures and Jesus's story. While the Scriptures do not talk about the Messiah suffering, they do talk about God suffering. All through Israel's story, God was living with the world's rejection and with his people's rejection. All through that story God was bouncing back from the experience of his people crucifying him. All through, the horizon of his vision was the nations coming to recognize him. All through (or nearly all through), that revelation began from Jerusalem. Jesus is the incarnation of the God whose story the First Testament tells. What happens to Jesus as the Messiah is what has been happening to God. I have noted the striking way Matthew links Jesus with a prophecy in Isaiah 40:3 that refers to "the Lord" in the sense of Yahweh. In the Gospel of Luke, Jesus is called "Lord" more often than in any other Gospel, matching also the usage in Acts and in Paul. Luke sees Jesus as doing things that the First Testament attributes to Yahweh.[6] Jesus also experiences the things that Yahweh experiences.

When we read Yahweh's story as Jesus's story, we are then not reading into it something that is not there. We are able to see something that was always there but was easy to miss. The process of interpretation is similar to the one in Romans, whereby Paul can draw attention to a real plot feature of Genesis that he had not seen before but that becomes clear in light of Jesus. Israelites had not read their story as an account of God's paying the price for their wrongdoing. But looking back at the First Testament story in light of Jesus, one sees that this is the implication of the story.

3.3 Acts: The Holy Spirit Said . . .

Acts further illustrates the nature of this process of interpretation. It uses passages from the First Testament to elucidate who Jesus is, what it means to be an apostle, how most of the Jewish community declines to recognize Jesus, why Judas needs to be replaced, what was happening at Pentecost, and what was the general drift of Israel's story.

Acts 8: The Ethiopian Official

It is illuminating to begin from the story of Philip and the Ethiopian official.

> An angel of the Lord said to Philip, "Go south to the road—the desert road—that goes down from Jerusalem to Gaza." So he started out, and on his way he met an Ethiopian eunuch, an important official in charge of all the treasury of the Kandake (which means "queen of the Ethiopians"). This man had gone to Jerusalem to worship, and on his way home was sitting in

6. Cf. Richard B. Hays, *Reading Backwards: Figural Christology and the Fourfold Gospel Witness* (Grand Rapids: Eerdmans, 2014), 55–74.

his chariot reading the Book of Isaiah the prophet. The Spirit told Philip, "Go to that chariot and stay near it."

Then Philip ran up to the chariot and heard the man reading Isaiah the prophet. "Do you understand what you are reading?" Philip asked.

"How can I," he said, "unless someone explains it to me?" So he invited Philip to come up and sit with him.

This is the passage of Scripture the eunuch was reading:

"He was led like a sheep to the slaughter,
     and as a lamb before its shearer is silent,
     so he did not open his mouth.
In his humiliation he was deprived of justice.
     Who can speak of his descendants?
     For his life was taken from the earth."

The eunuch asked Philip, "Tell me, please, who is the prophet talking about, himself or someone else?" Then Philip began with that very passage of Scripture and told him the good news about Jesus. (Acts 8:26–35)

The form of the official's question and the form of Philip's response are suggestive. The official's question is whether Isaiah 53 refers to the prophet himself or to someone else. Exegetically, it is a fine question that has not gone out of date. In my view, his first option is the correct one—the prophet is talking about his own suffering and potential martyrdom. But exegetes over the past couple of centuries have suggested many others to whom he could have been referring, such as Moses or David or Jeremiah or King Jehoiakin. The context of the passage in Isaiah might also make one think of the people of Israel itself, since it was identified as God's servant in Isaiah 41. Not much in the context suggests a reference to a not-yet-born Messiah.

Yet beginning with this passage, it is easy for Philip to talk about Jesus. Ever since New Testament times, Christians have found it hard not to see Jesus in Isaiah 53. Once again, the interpretive process works backward, from Jesus to the text that then illumines him, rather than forward from the text to Jesus. The text was not about him; it was about the prophet himself (on my interpretation). But we could say that the prophet (or whoever one thinks the passage directly refers to) was a type of Christ—that is, Jesus was like the suffering servant, only more so. The servant's ministry helps us understand Jesus's ministry. So Isaiah 53 becomes key to the New Testament's understanding of Jesus. It helps us understand him. He does not help us understand the meaning of Isaiah 53, though he does help us understand its significance or its afterlife.

Acts 13: A Light to the Gentiles

Paul's appeal to one of the passages about Yahweh's servant provides a neat riff on this study. In a sermon in Turkey, he argues:

"The people of Jerusalem and their rulers did not recognize Jesus, yet in condemning him they fulfilled the words of the prophets that are read every Sabbath. Though they found no proper ground for a death sentence, they asked Pilate to have him executed. When they had carried out all that was written about him, they took him down from the cross and laid him in a tomb. But God raised him from the dead, and for many days he was seen by those who had traveled with him from Galilee to Jerusalem. They are now his witnesses to our people.

"We tell you the good news: What God promised our ancestors he has fulfilled for us, their children, by raising up Jesus. As it is written in the second Psalm:

'You are my son;
today I have become your father.'

God raised him from the dead so that he will never be subject to decay. As God has said,

'I will give you the holy and sure blessings promised to David.'

So it is also stated elsewhere:

'You will not let your holy one see decay.'

"Now when David had served God's purpose in his own generation, he fell asleep; he was buried with his ancestors and his body decayed. But the one whom God raised q1from the dead did not see decay. Therefore, my brothers and sisters, I want you to know that through Jesus the forgiveness of sins is proclaimed to you. Through him everyone who believes is set free from every sin, a justification you were not able to obtain under the law of Moses. Take care that what the prophets have said does not happen to you:

'Look, you scoffers,
    wonder and perish,
for I am going to do something in your days
    that you would never believe,
    even if someone told you.'"

As Paul and Barnabas were leaving the synagogue, the people invited them to speak further about these things on the next Sabbath. When the congregation was dismissed, many of the Jews and devout converts to Judaism followed Paul and Barnabas, who talked with them and urged them to continue in the grace of God.

On the next Sabbath almost the whole city gathered to hear the word of the Lord. When the Jews saw the crowds, they were filled with jealousy. They began to contradict what Paul was saying and heaped abuse on him. Then Paul and Barnabas answered them boldly: "We had to speak the word of God to you first. Since you reject it and do not consider yourselves worthy of eternal life, we now turn to the Gentiles. For this is what the Lord has commanded us:

'I have made you a light for the Gentiles,
    that you may bring salvation to the ends of the earth.'"
(Acts 13:27–47)

We will come back to the characteristic New Testament appeal to Psalm 2. At present, our interest lies in Paul's closing allusion to Isaiah 49:6. I can argue a bit less controversially that the "I" who is giving his testimony in Isaiah 49:1–6 as a whole is the prophet who is speaking throughout Isaiah 40–55. After all, a prophet who says "I" is regularly speaking either as God's mouthpiece (so the "I" is God) or speaking as himself (so he is the "I"), unless he gives some indication to the contrary.[7] So Isaiah 49:1–6 is the prophet's testimony to how God commissioned him to be his servant, "But I have been tempted to think that my work is pointless, and I told God so"

---

7. I like the idea that the prophet who speaks in Isa 40–55 might have been a "she," which fits with the manifold awarenesses of a woman's experience that surface in these chapters; but the prophet seems to have a beard (Isa 50:6).

he now tells us. God's response (now in v. 6 God is the "I" whose words the prophet is reporting) is to give him a bigger commission: he is to be the means of God's message reaching the Gentile world.

As Philip finds the account of the servant's significance in Isaiah 53 illuminating for an understanding of Jesus, Paul finds the account of the servant's significance in Isaiah 49 illuminating for an understanding of his own ministry. He too has sought to preach to Israel and has failed. He too is not released by God as a failure but is given a bigger task. He can understand himself and urge his listeners to understand him in light of that prophet's testimony.

It is not explicit whether Paul's reference to Isaiah 49 implies that he takes the prophecy to refer directly to him rather than to the prophet himself. Maybe he did not think about the question. But one of his other quotations from Isaiah, in Acts 28, suggests that he might well have assumed that some words that *originally* applied to the prophet *also* applied to him.

Acts 28: The Jewish Community in Rome

On his arrival in Rome, Paul arranges to meet with some leaders of the Jewish community.

> He witnessed to them from morning till evening, explaining about the kingdom of God, and from the Law of Moses and from the Prophets he tried to persuade them about Jesus. Some were convinced by what he said, but others would not believe. They disagreed among themselves and began to leave after Paul had made this final statement: "The Holy Spirit spoke the truth to your ancestors when he said through Isaiah the prophet:
>
> > 'Go to this people and say,
> > "You will be ever hearing but never understanding;
> >   you will be ever seeing but never perceiving."
> > For this people's heart has become calloused;
> >   they hardly hear with their ears,
> >   and they have closed their eyes.
> > Otherwise they might see with their eyes,
> >   hear with their ears,
> >   understand with their hearts
> > and turn, and I would heal them.'

Therefore I want you to know that God's salvation has been sent to the Gentiles, and they will listen!" (Acts 28:23–28)

The dynamic is the same as the one in Acts 13, but the quotation from Isaiah comes from yet another testimony by a prophet concerning his commission, this time from Isaiah 6, the original commission of Isaiah ben Amoz himself. He is told to go and tell people that they will never understand God's message. Such a commission may seem strange, but a prophet's job was often to encourage people to prove him wrong, to shake them out of their dullness, and I understand this to be an example of that prophetic function.

Now Acts 28 is not the only passage where these verses from Isaiah feature. Jesus quotes them in his response to a puzzled question from his disciples about the rationale for his speaking in parables.

This is why I speak to them in parables:

> "Though seeing, they do not see;
>   though hearing, they do not hear or understand."

In them is fulfilled the prophecy of Isaiah:

> "You will be ever hearing but never understanding;
>   you will be ever seeing but never perceiving.
> For this people's heart has become calloused;
>   they hardly hear with their ears,
>   and they have closed their eyes.
> Otherwise they might see with their eyes,
>   hear with their ears,
>   understand with their hearts
> and turn, and I would heal them." (Matt 13:13–15)

So was Isaiah talking about Jesus and his audience, or about Paul and his audience? Maybe the right answer is no, in several senses. When the Holy Spirit inspired Isaiah to speak in those terms, his immediate audience was Judah in Isaiah's day. They were the people who had been shutting their eyes to what Yahweh said to them through Isaiah and through other prophets; they were the people whom God was threatening to harden; and they were the people who were implicitly challenged to repent. But Jesus sees the same dynamic at work in the Jewish people in his day and in his ministry to them.

So Isaiah's words are filled up or filled out once more (this time Matthew uses a less common verb—not *plēroō*, "fill," but *anaplēroō*, which does more literally mean "fill up"). Prophecies can be filled out more than once.

It is not the case that the fulfillment in Isaiah's day is less important than the fulfillment in the New Testament, though many Christians think the latter is the one that really counts. God was doing something that really counted in Isaiah's day, and it is this fact that makes it possible for Jesus and Paul to see the prophecy at work in their day. Further, this example shows that the process is not one that involves simply two fulfillments, one in the prophet's day and one in Jesus's day. Prophecies can be fulfilled (filled out) many times. Maybe Jesus and Paul saw it that way, though if they had not had reason to think about the question, my suggestion is that it is the way the Holy Spirit might have thought of it.

Acts 4: The Holy Spirit by the Mouth of David

We do have some information on how the New Testament saw the Holy Spirit at work in this connection. Peter and John had been arrested for preaching about Jesus, but they then got released.

> On their release, Peter and John went back to their own people and reported all that the chief priests and the elders had said to them. When they heard this, they raised their voices together in prayer to God. "Sovereign Lord," they said, "you made the heaven and the earth and the sea, and everything in them. You spoke by the Holy Spirit through the mouth of your servant, our father David:
>
> > 'Why do the nations rage
> >   and the peoples plot in vain?
> > The kings of the earth rise up
> >   and the rulers band together
> > against the Lord
> >   and against his anointed one.'
>
> Indeed Herod and Pontius Pilate met together with the Gentiles and the people of Israel in this city to conspire against your holy servant Jesus, whom you anointed. They did what your power and will had decided beforehand should happen." (Acts 4:23–28)

What interests us here is the incidental reference to God's speaking in Psalm 2 *by the Holy Spirit* through the mouth of David. Why make that point? As often happens, believers in Jesus have been bowled over by a link between the First Testament and what is happening to them and by the way the First Testament helps to interpret what is happening. It is uncanny how the First Testament does so, and we wonder how it does so. How can it? The answer is that the Holy Spirit was involved in the formulation of Psalm 2.

Christian theology often speaks in terms of "the inspiration of the Scriptures by the Holy Spirit," but in the study of theology that idea of scriptural inspiration gained a life of its own; notably, it came to be a basis for claiming that the Scriptures were wholly accurate, on the basis of the assumption that the Holy Spirit would hardly inspire something inaccurate. Now the New Testament does show some concern with accuracy, not least in the opening to Luke's Gospel (see Luke 1:1–4); but it links this concern with the careful work of the human writers (which we can assume God honored), not with the work of the Holy Spirit. The recent theological concern with accuracy lost touch with the significance of the New Testament linking of the Scriptures and the Holy Spirit. There the significance of the Holy Spirit's involvement with the Scriptures is that this involvement explains the Scriptures' extraordinary capacity to speak to a quite different context than the one they originally addressed.[8]

Paul makes the general point when he comes nearer than anyone in the Scriptures to using the actual word *inspired* (2 Tim 3:15–17): the First Testament Scriptures are "God-breathed," which explains their extraordinary capacity to teach people about salvation through faith in Christ Jesus and to be instructive in connection with taking believers in Jesus to maturity. What on earth explains their capacity to do so for people who live after Jesus came, centuries after they were written, and in quite different circumstances? The fact that they were God-breathed explains it.

It is the Holy Spirit's involvement that lies behind the author of Psalm 2 speaking to the circumstances of believers in Jerusalem after Pentecost. I have noted Paul's appeal in Acts 13 to different lines from Psalm 2. That allusion also matches a reference to the psalm by Jesus:

> While Jesus was teaching in the temple courts, he asked, "Why do the teachers of the law say that the Messiah is the son of David? David himself, speaking by the Holy Spirit, declared:

8. See further my *Models for Scripture* (Grand Rapids: Eerdmans; Carlisle: Paternoster, 1994), 209–21.

'The Lord said to my Lord:
    "Sit at my right hand
until I put your enemies
    under your feet."'

David himself calls him 'Lord.' How then can he be his son?"
The large crowd listened to him with delight. (Mark 12:35–37)

I bet they did! Jesus too is explaining the way Psalm 2 speaks not just about things in David's day but about something that has significance in the context of Jesus's ministry and in the context of the idea that he might be the Messiah. It is the Holy Spirit's involvement in inspiring the psalm that makes it possible to entertain the idea that it has this significance.

Acts 1: Judas

Another intriguing reference to the Holy Spirit's involvement with the First Testament comes right at the beginning of Acts.

In those days Peter stood up among the believers (a group numbering about a hundred and twenty) and said, "Brothers and sisters, the Scripture had to be fulfilled in which the Holy Spirit spoke long ago through David concerning Judas, who served as guide for those who arrested Jesus. He was one of our number and shared in our ministry." . . .
"For," said Peter, "it is written in the Book of Psalms:

'May his place be deserted;
    let there be no one to dwell in it,'

and,

'May another take his place of leadership.'

Therefore it is necessary to choose one of the men who have been with us the whole time the Lord Jesus went in and out among us." (Acts 1:15–21)

Peter refers to Psalms 69 and 109, and he gets the prize for the New Testament's most startling appeal to the First Testament. Each psalm is a despairing plea to Yahweh for deliverance from desperate peril and to this end for Yahweh to put down the people who are imperiling the life of the person who prays the psalm. The prayer includes words that Peter sees as especially appropriate to God's judgment on Judas and to the need to appoint someone to replace him in the Twelve. How on earth could they be thus relevant? It is because the Holy Spirit spoke these words.

Again, it is hard to know whether Peter thought that the application of these words to Judas is the only significance they ever had. Maybe he would not have demurred if someone had pointed out to him that Jews had been using these psalms for centuries as their own prayers, and that this use corresponded to the way these psalms would have come into existence as humanly devised expressions of prayer. If so, however, he would not have been very interested. What interested him was their uncanny significance in connection with a question that concerned the group who believed in Jesus: What are we to do about Judas's place in the Twelve? It is the activity of the Holy Spirit that explains the psalms' significance in this connection. They managed to express something that God wanted to say in this connection as well as something that some Israelites needed to say to God.

The two psalms are an embarrassment to Western Christians for another reason. It is amusing that Western Christians think that people who believe in Jesus should not pray the way these psalms do. So when the Holy Spirit inspired Peter to appeal to these psalms at this point and inspired the author of Acts to include his appeal, I wonder whether there was a twinkle in the Holy Spirit's eye and a satisfaction at countering that Western Christian embarrassment. My wondering is increased by the fact that Paul also quotes positively from nasty lines in Psalm 69 (Rom 11:9–10).

In Acts, Peter declares that the Holy Spirit *spoke* in these psalms, whereas we have noted that Hebrews speaks in terms of what the Holy Spirit *says*, when it comes at the First Testament with the same hermeneutic (Heb 3:7; cf. 9:8; 10:15–16). The two formulations complement each other. The Holy Spirit *was* involved in the formulation of the biblical text in a way that would speak with extraordinary relevance in wholly other contexts. The Holy Spirit *is* also involved in enabling people living in those other contexts to see the significance of those texts.

Acts 2: Joel

Following on the appointment of Matthias, the Pentecost event itself cries out for interpretation, and it receives it through the Scriptures.

> Peter stood up with the Eleven, raised his voice and addressed the crowd: "Fellow Jews and all of you who live in Jerusalem, let me explain this to you; listen carefully to what I say. These people are not drunk, as you suppose. It is only nine in the morning! No, this is what was spoken by the prophet Joel:

> 'In the last days, God says,
>   I will pour out my Spirit on all people.
> Your sons and daughters will prophesy,
>   your young men will see visions,
>   your old men will dream dreams.
> Even on my servants, both men and women,
>   I will pour out my Spirit in those days,
>   and they will prophesy.
> I will show wonders in the heaven above
>   and signs on the earth below,
>   blood and fire and billows of smoke.
> The sun will be turned to darkness
>   and the moon to blood
>   before the coming of the great and glorious day of the Lord.
> And everyone who calls
>   on the name of the Lord will be saved.'" (Acts 2:14–21)

More literally, in his introduction to the quotation, Peter says, "This is that." He equates what people can see ("this") with what Joel once said ("that"). And it is evident that what Peter says overlaps with what Joel says, though typically the New Testament interpretations are not identical with the meaning of the First Testament. At Pentecost, sons and daughters are not prophesying, young and old are not seeing visions and dreaming dreams, there are no signs in the heavens and on the earth, no blood or billows of smoke, no transforming of sun and moon. Conversely, Joel says nothing about speaking in foreign tongues. The relationship between prophecy and fulfillment is not one that suggests a prophet's receiving a preview of the event that resembles a movie preview.

Usually the prophetic books give us the names of kings in whose time the prophet worked; like Malachi, Joel does not. If there were no kings to date by, then both Joel and Malachi lived in the Second Temple period, when Judah had only half-recovered from the fall of Jerusalem and the exile (though if that is wrong, it will not make a significant difference to the point Joel makes). Judah needed material and physical renewal; it also needed renewal in its relationship with God. Joel promises that both will come, and his declaration that God will pour out his spirit is the heart of the second aspect of this promise.

God's spirit is God's powerful, dynamic, active presence, which brings life and makes extraordinary things happen. Israel had known that spirit involved in its life in the past and in the present. Through Haggai, God assures his people, "My spirit is staying among you" (Hag 2:5). They will therefore succeed in rebuilding the temple; and they did succeed. The implication of Joel's prophecy is not that God's spirit had not been involved with Israel all through its story or that God's spirit was not involved with his people now. Rather, their position was like the position the church has often been in—not least when we look back on how things were in New Testament times. Joel promises a spectacular new outpouring of God's spirit.

Acts 2 and Hebrews: Fulfillment and Fulfillments

Whatever fulfillments of God's promise people experienced in the centuries after Joel's day, Peter can invite people in Jerusalem in his time to recognize the link between what was happening now and what had been promised then. Joel's promise had related to "Yahweh's day," the time when his purpose for his people would be fulfilled. Peter knows that the execution and resurrection of Jesus were the events that brought in that fulfillment of God's purpose, and the outpouring of God's spirit is another aspect of that fulfillment. There could be fulfillments before Pentecost and there could be fulfillments after Pentecost.

The dynamics of the talk about the pouring out of the Holy Spirit overlap with those of the talk about a new covenant. Taking up Jeremiah 31:31–34, Hebrews declares,

> If there had been nothing wrong with that first covenant, no place would have been sought for another. But God found fault with the people and said:
>
> > "The days are coming, declares the Lord,
> >   when I will make a new covenant

with the house of Israel
   and with the house of Judah.
It will not be like the covenant
   I made with their ancestors
when I took them by the hand
   to lead them out of Egypt,
because they did not remain faithful to my covenant,
   and I turned away from them,
     declares the Lord.
This is the covenant I will establish with the house of Israel
   after that time, declares the Lord.
I will put my laws in their minds
   and write them on their hearts.
I will be their God,
   and they will be my people.
No longer will they teach their neighbors,
   or say to one another, 'Know the Lord,'
because they will all know me,
   from the least of them to the greatest.
For I will forgive their wickedness
   and will remember their sins no more." (Heb 8:7–12)

Hebrews later reaffirms the point:

The Holy Spirit . . . says:

"This is the covenant I will make with them
   after that time, says the Lord.
I will put my laws in their hearts,
   and I will write them on their minds."

Then he adds:

"Their sins and lawless acts
   I will remember no more."

And where these have been forgiven, sacrifice for sin is no longer necessary.
(Heb 10:15–18)

So Jeremiah promises a new covenant that involves the writing of the Torah into people's minds, and Hebrews declares that Jesus fulfills that promise. The dynamics of this declaration compare with the dynamics of Peter's declaration about Joel's promise concerning the outpouring of the Holy Spirit, when what happened at Pentecost was not the first outpouring of the Holy Spirit, and neither would it be the last.

Hebrews and Romans: The New Covenant

There are at least four difficulties about the idea that Jesus simply fulfills Jeremiah's promise.

1. In Romans 11, Paul also quotes it:

    Israel has experienced a hardening in part until the full number of the Gentiles has come in, and in this way all Israel will be saved. As it is written:

    > "The deliverer will come from Zion;
    >   he will turn godlessness away from Jacob.
    > And this is my covenant with them
    >   when I take away their sins." (Rom 11:25–27)

    Paul begins with a quotation from Isaiah 59:20–21 but then goes on to quote Jer 31:33. For our present purposes, what matters is that he associates the fulfillment of Jeremiah's prophecy with events still to come when God's purpose is finally fulfilled, not with what Jesus has already achieved.
2. This difference from Hebrews fits in with a point readers may have noticed. It is not the case that the Torah has been written into the minds of people who believe in Jesus in such a way that we now do what it says. Indeed, it is not obvious that, on the whole, people who believe in Jesus have God's expectations written into their thinking any more than Jews who do not believe in Jesus. Certainly, teaching people to know the Lord does not seem to have become unnecessary.
3. Jeremiah and his hearers would surely have been bemused by the idea that this promise given by Jeremiah to his contemporaries was not due to be fulfilled for them or for anyone for six hundred years.
4. God actually did fulfill his promise to Judah in the nearer future af-

ter Jeremiah. The background to his prophecy is Judah's inclination to practices such as serving other gods, making images, and Sabbath breaking—failures over fundamental aspects of the Torah expressed in the Ten Commandments. These were the failures that had led to the exile. In the Second Temple period, Judahites gave up serving other gods and making images, and committed themselves to keeping the Sabbath (to such an extent that the problem Jesus sees in their attitude to the Sabbath is the opposite to the one Jeremiah identified). Within the First Testament, Psalm 119 expresses a comprehensive, enthusiastic commitment to keeping the Torah (see also Pss 1 and 19), and I would not be surprised if that commitment is a fruit of God keeping the Jeremiah promise to people in Judah.

We can make sense of these data if we look at them the same way as we look at how the two Testaments talk about the Holy Spirit. Jeremiah promises a new covenant whose implementing belongs to the end that we still await, when God's expectations will really be written into our minds (so Paul). But in the meantime, people not long after Jeremiah's day experienced some fulfillment of that promise. God did renew his covenant with his people. The promise's most spectacular fulfillment came about through Jesus, through whom the covenant was renewed (so Hebrews). And from time to time the church experiences renewal that constitutes a further interim fulfillment of the promise.

Acts 2: David

In Acts 2, Peter goes on:

> People of Israel, listen to this: Jesus of Nazareth was a man accredited by God to you by miracles, wonders and signs, which God did among you through him, as you yourselves know. This man was handed over to you by God's deliberate plan and foreknowledge; and you, with the help of wicked men, put him to death by nailing him to the cross. But God raised him from the dead, freeing him from the agony of death, because it was impossible for death to keep its hold on him. David said about him:
>
>> "I saw the Lord always before me.
>> Because he is at my right hand,
>> I will not be shaken.

Therefore my heart is glad and my tongue rejoices;
  my body also will rest in hope,
because you will not abandon me to the realm of the dead,
  you will not let your holy one see decay.
You have made known to me the paths of life;
  you will fill me with joy in your presence." (Acts 2:22–28)

Peter quotes from Psalm 16, which is an appeal to God for protection and a declaration of confidence that God will protect. It contains nothing that is strictly a word from God. Yet when Peter looks back at the words of the psalm, he cannot but see them as prophetic. His way of describing them differs from his earlier description of words from Psalms 69 and 109, but the implication is the same. In connection with those psalms, he refers to the Holy Spirit speaking; in connection with Psalm 16, he refers to David prophesying. He could have used the "prophesying" language in connection with Psalms 69 and 109 or used the Holy Spirit language in connection with Psalm 2. There is no indication in Psalm 16 that the author (whether it was David personally or some anonymous Israelite songwriter) thought of himself as prophesying. But in light of what has happened to Jesus in dying, resting temporarily in the grave, then rising to new life, Peter cannot believe it is a coincidence that the psalm speaks that way. So the psalm is useful as a prayer; it is also useful as a prophecy.

Peter goes on,

Brothers and sisters, we all know that the patriarch David died and was buried, and his tomb is here to this day. But he was a prophet and knew that God had promised him on oath that he would place one of his descendants on his throne. Seeing what was to come, he spoke of the resurrection of the Messiah, that he was not abandoned to the realm of the dead, nor did his body see decay. God has raised this Jesus to life, and we are all witnesses of the fact. Exalted to the right hand of God, he has received from the Father the promised Holy Spirit and has poured out what you now see and hear. For David did not ascend to heaven, and yet he said,

"The Lord said to my Lord:
  'Sit at my right hand
until I make your enemies
  a footstool for your feet.'"

Therefore let all Israel be assured of this: God has made this Jesus, whom you crucified, both Lord and Messiah. (Acts 2:29–36)

Peter thus again refers to Psalm 2. This appeal may not seem as surprising as the appeal to Psalm 16, because although it is a psalm, by its nature it is also a prophecy in the sense that it reports a promise from God to the king. Generally, by their nature, psalms speak from people to God; God was then happy enough with what people said to let them come into his book. But a few psalms speak from God to us, like prophecies. Psalm 2 is an example.

Acts 7: Stephen

On the eve of his martyrdom, and doing nothing to discourage it, Stephen treated his fellow Jews to a revisionist account of their people's history. I might have considered it in chapter 2, but I would rather look at it here in light of the references to prophecy that it incorporates.

Our ancestors . . . told Aaron, "Make us gods who will go before us. As for this fellow Moses who led us out of Egypt—we don't know what has happened to him!" That was the time they made an idol in the form of a calf. They brought sacrifices to it and reveled in what their own hands had made. But God turned away from them and gave them over to the worship of the sun, moon and stars. This agrees with what is written in the book of the prophets:

"Did you bring me sacrifices and offerings
    forty years in the wilderness, house of Israel?
You have taken up the tabernacle of Molek
    and the star of your god Rephan,
the idols you made to worship.
    Therefore I will send you into exile beyond Babylon."

Our ancestors had the tabernacle of the covenant law with them in the wilderness. It had been made as God directed Moses, according to the pattern he had seen. Having received the tabernacle, our ancestors under Joshua brought it with them when they took the land from the nations God drove out before them. It remained in the land until the time of Da-

vid, who enjoyed God's favor and asked that he might provide a dwelling place for the God of Jacob. But it was Solomon who built a house for him.
(Acts 7:39–47)

Stephen's argument and his quotation radically undermine belief in the significance of the temple; in a moment he will take the point further. That kind of speaking had been a key factor in taking Jesus to his death, and it is a key factor in taking Stephen the same way. The Jewish people rightly attached great significance to the temple. Stephen alludes to God's agreement to its building, as a place where he could live. It meant Jews could go to the temple and know they could meet God there. Yet God also pointed out to David that he was not so enthusiastic about being tied to one place (see 2 Sam 7). Here Stephen quotes from Amos 5. At first sight the answer to its opening question is, "Of course we did." But the temple was not built then, so sacrifices were not offered in the way they were later. Further, in the way the Torah tells the story, Yahweh's first instructions did not concern sacrifices and offerings; they do not feature in the Ten Commandments.

Solomon, who actually built the temple, also recognized the illogic about the idea that the God of the heavens and the earth could be located in an earthly building, while also rejoicing in God's grace in doing so (see 1 Kgs 8). Stephen goes on to a second quotation, from Isaiah 66, which makes Solomon's own point.

However, the Most High does not live in houses made by human hands. As the prophet says:

"Heaven is my throne,
and the earth is my footstool.
What kind of house will you build for me? says the Lord.
Or where will my resting place be?
Has not my hand made all these things?" (Acts 7:48–50)

This later prophet, too, underscores the illogic and the downside to temples. Isaiah 56–66 both recognizes the significance of the temple and draws attention to its insignificance. Indeed, the prophets in general recognize the ambiguity about the temple and its offerings. It is hard to hold onto that ambiguity. Either people focus too much on the temple, as many people did in Jesus's day; or people discount that kind of offering, as we are more inclined to do today.

3.4 The Prophets in Themselves

What happens when we look at the prophets in their own right? Christian tradition saw the prophets as foretellers of what God intended to do, not least in sending the Messiah. Nineteenth-century scholarly study reacted against that idea by declaring that the prophets were forthtellers, not foretellers: they were people who told forth God's expectations of us, not people who focused on predicting what God intended to do. Actually, they were a bit of both. Matthew 1–2 indeed focuses on their significance for an understanding of Jesus as the Messiah. But Jesus also notes the way Hosea emphasizes mercy, not sacrifice (Matt 9:13; cf. Hos 6:6).

Isaiah 1–39

When we start reading Isaiah (or one of the other prophets), we may well find it confusing. It is not organized the way we would expect a book to be organized. While there is more structure than we might at first see, the organization is a bit subtle. One thing to grasp is that the contents of Isaiah were not originally designed to be part of a book. The book is more like a collection of sermon notes.

It is worth trying to recreate how we might imagine a prophet such as Isaiah ben Amoz working. It is not so different from the way we might imagine Jesus working. Isaiah would go up to the temple courtyards when he knew people would be there (for instance, when sacrifices were going to be offered) and declare something that God gave him—maybe he knew ahead of time what he was going to say, or maybe God gave it to him there and then. In due course, he subsequently had his various messages written down; Isaiah 8:16 refers to his doing so. That initiative would have been the beginning of the process whereby the book of Isaiah came into existence. Isaiah 1:1 is, then, an editorial introduction to the book, and 1:2–9 is a prophecy Isaiah delivered in the temple courtyards on one occasion, 1:10–20 is another, 1:21–31 is another, 2:1–5 is another, and so on. Sometimes we can see why one prophecy has been placed next to another (see 1:9 and 1:10), but we can get a fair idea of Isaiah's message by reading each prophecy on its own, and we do not need to focus too much on the logical links between them.

In Isaiah 1–12, two kinds of message dominate the chapters. First, there are the *foretelling* messages that we would expect to find on the basis of the New Testament: promises of a new David and of Yahweh leading the whole world into ways of peace. Second, there are the *forthtelling* messages that declare how Yahweh has looked for mercy, not sacrifice, and not found it—which means he is going to discipline this resistant people. Broadly, the warning kind of message is more prominent at the beginning, the promise kind of message more prominent later.

In Isaiah 13–27, the focus changes. Isaiah 13–23 comprises a series of declarations about what Yahweh intends to do about the other nations in Judah's world. Here it is easier to see where one section begins and another ends. Although the messages are about these other peoples, we can again imagine Isaiah delivering them in the temple courtyards, because they are designed for Judah to hear. They are designed to shape Judah's foreign policy—to make Judah trust in Yahweh, rather than being afraid of these other peoples as threats or trusting in them as allies. Isaiah 24–27 then broadens the horizon even more, to embrace the world as a whole. It speaks of the chastisement and the blessing that Yahweh intends for all the nations.

When we get to Isaiah 28–39, we have another series of messages directly addressed to Judah, but they come from twenty or thirty years later than the ones in the opening chapters. Earlier, the people threatening Judah were Syria and Ephraim, and the potential ally was Assyria. Now Assyria has already invaded Syria and Ephraim (as Isaiah said it would), Assyria itself has become the threat (as Isaiah said it would), and Egypt has become the potential ally. So the challenges in terms of Judah's relationship with Yahweh are similar, but the political situation has changed.

Once again there are promises that the New Testament takes up. When John the Baptizer is puzzled about why Jesus's ministry takes the form it does, Jesus points out the kinds of things he is doing, and they are things that Isaiah 34 said God intended to do. But Isaiah 1–39 closes with solemn warnings about the descendants of the Judahite king ending up exiled to Babylon.

Isaiah 40–66

When we turn over the page into Isaiah 40 (as I literally do in a Bible I often use), the good news is that we may find the arrangement of the chapters less jumbled, but we may get a double sense of disorientation. Isaiah ben Amoz had talked about exile to Babylon, which would happen a century later. In Isaiah 40, this exile is not in the future but in the past. The prophet is not now preparing people for a future exile but promising them that this exile is coming to an end. We have noted that the Gospels see John the Baptizer as an embodiment of the voice shouting in the wilderness in Isaiah 40:3. Originally, this passage described God's commission for the building of a highway by which Yahweh would go back to the Jerusalem he had abandoned, taking the exiles in his train.

This change indicates that the prophecies in Isaiah 40–66 do not come from the Isaiah who features in the first part of the book (who would have to be two hundred years old to be looking back on the exile) but from a later prophet or prophets whose names we do not know. At the same time, there are lots of links between these prophecies and the work of Isaiah. Isaiah was the inspiration for their work; these prophets are continuing his ministry. They are thus often appropriately called Second Isaiah (Isa 40–55) and Third Isaiah (Isa 56–66).

The second disorienting feature is that the emphasis in Isaiah 1–39 lies on warning Judah that trouble is coming. The emphasis in Isaiah 40–55 lies on bringing good news to the people. There is good news in chapters 1–39 and there is rebuke in chapters 40–55, but the balance is different.

The difference finds expression in the way the prophecy describes God. Isaiah ben Amoz was given his commission as a prophet during a vision of Yahweh as the Holy One (see Isa 6), and he thus emphasizes that Yahweh is "the Holy One of Israel." He spells out that fact about God solemnly as the basis for warning Judah that trouble is coming to it. Isaiah 40–55 turns this argument on its head. That Yahweh is the Holy One of Israel is now an encouragement. He is the Holy One committed to Israel. Therefore he is going to restore his people, not because they deserve it (they do not), but because he is committed to them. One way he affirms that he is still committed to them involves reassuring them that they are still his servant. It is both their security and their challenge. Actually, they need someone to fulfill a servant ministry to them, but it does not mean they have lost their place or their role.

When we turn over the page again from Isaiah 40–55 to Isaiah 56–66, the situation has changed once more. The background to these chapters lies in the time after Yahweh has come back to Jerusalem and some of the exiles have come back with him, though things are by no means as wonderful as we might have expected. Yahweh still has a lot to do, and the people still have a lot to do. To this end the chapters challenge them and challenge God and portray the wonder of what Yahweh intends to do in even more glorious technicolor. At the center of the chapters is that testimony by a "Third Isaiah" to Yahweh's commission (Isa 61), which Jesus takes up in Luke 4. These last chapters of the book leave Judah to respond to Yahweh's challenges and live by his promises. We could say that the church lives in the same circumstances as Judah does. We too live between some fulfillment of God's promises and the day that will see more complete fulfillment. Thus Paul takes up

Third Isaiah's promise of a redeemer and a new covenant and declares that God will fulfill it on that day (Isa 59:20–21; Rom 11:26–27).

Jeremiah

Like Isaiah, the book of Jeremiah can be hard to follow, though it is less dominated by very short units than Isaiah. Like Isaiah, it begins by linking the prophet with a sequence of kings, and a look back at 2 Kings enables us to see that Jeremiah works a century later than Isaiah ben Amoz. Thus the fall of Jerusalem, the end of the monarchy, and the exile of many of its people are about to happen (in other words, we could say that Jeremiah fits in between Isa 1–39 and Isa 40–66). But they have not yet happened, and it's not over until it's over. Jeremiah's thankless job is to keep urging Judah to turn around.

One distinctive feature of the book is that it incorporates a number of stories about Jeremiah. One of these stories tells us about an occasion when Jeremiah had a lot of his prophecies written down, as Isaiah once did (see Jer 36). Taking this action and getting his secretary to read out the scroll in the temple courtyards constituted another, almost final attempt to get people to take some notice. It does bring his prophecies to the renewed attention of the king. On a cold winter Jerusalem day, King Jehoiakim sits in front of an open fire in his palace courtyard, and as the scroll is read out, he cuts it to bits and burns it. Putting things into writing makes them firmer; destroying documents may forestall their contents. But the story ends with Jeremiah dictating the scroll again and making it quite a bit longer.

One reason for incorporating stories about Jeremiah in the book of his prophecies is thus the way they illustrate how people's attitude to Jeremiah and their action toward Jeremiah express their attitude to God and their action in relation to God.

The stories about Jeremiah would have been written by people who did recognize that he was a prophet from Yahweh and did want other people to take notice of him—people like Baruch, the secretary who wrote that scroll. Presumably they would be telling these stories after the disaster that Jeremiah warned about had actually happened. They are longing that maybe *now* people will start taking some notice. A prophet such as Isaiah or Jeremiah does his actual prophesying for his contemporaries, but the reason for turning them into books is so that the next generation, and the generation after that, can read them. The fulfillment of the prophecies proves that they really came from God and that therefore the next generation has the chance to make the response to them that their parents were not sensible enough to offer.

The longest single section of the book (Jer 40–44) tells of what happened after the fall of Jerusalem, a sad story that only partly relates to Jeremiah himself but tells of how people's willful and stupid resistance to God continues. The community has the chance of a new start, but they assassinate the Babylonian-appointed governor of Judah and then realize that they had better run for it. They force Jeremiah to go with them to Egypt, notwithstanding his declaration that this flight will only lead to Yahweh bringing them more trouble. Once again their attitude to Jeremiah is their attitude to God, and Jeremiah's story ends its account of his work as a prophet by portraying vividly his abject failure. Except that somebody ensured that the story got told and the words got preserved, so that we are still reading them and being affected by them.

A parallel significance attaches to another distinctive feature of Jeremiah, a series of protests and prayers that cluster in Jeremiah 11–20. The protests and prayers indicate the frightening pressure people put on Jeremiah. The stories and the prayers give us the outward and the inward version of what people were doing to him. People applied that pressure indirectly by resisting his message, and directly by trying to silence him. The point about the presence of these protests and prayers in the book is once again that in reflecting the response people gave to Jeremiah, they reflect the response people gave to God.

Jeremiah came from a village called Anathoth, which was only five miles north of Jerusalem but was across the important boundary between Judah and Benjamin. Some ambiguity always attached to whether Benjamin belonged to Ephraim or to Judah, and his Benjaminite connections would provide another reason for people in Jerusalem to be a bit suspicious of him. The problem for Jeremiah was that his own village was inclined to be against him too, no doubt in part for the opposite reason (see Jer 12).

Ezekiel

Ezekiel was Jeremiah's younger contemporary, and it would be surprising if he had not heard Jeremiah delivering his messages in the temple courtyard, where Ezekiel would be growing up to begin his ministry as a priest. But before he reached the right age, he was taken off with his family to Babylon with the people who made up the first exile in 597 BC. Then, at the age of thirty when he would have begun his priestly ministry, instead he had a vision in which God commissioned him to be a prophet. For the next decade he and Jeremiah were both fulfilling this ministry, Jeremiah in Jerusalem, Ezekiel in Babylon.

After the confusing arrangement of Isaiah and Jeremiah, it is nice to discover that the book of Ezekiel is quite clearly structured:

chapters 1–3	his commission
chapters 4–24	his messages of warning to Judah
chapters 25–32	his messages about other peoples
chapters 33–48	his messages of promise to Judah

Despite the fact that Ezekiel delivers all his messages in Babylon, his dominant concern is Jerusalem itself: its sins, the trouble coming to it, and its promised future. In all these aspects of his focus on Jerusalem, his vocation as a priest comes out. The nature of the temple worship scandalizes him, the prospect of Yahweh simply leaving the temple appalls him, and the promise of the new temple thrills him.

The reason for his focus on Jerusalem is that the destiny of the city is of central importance for the Judahites who have been moved from there to Babylon. Most of them are Jerusalemites. They have known the disaster of the Babylonian invasion that took them off into exile, but they are inclined to hope that the worst is therefore over. Surely they will soon be able to return home? Ezekiel knows that the situation is more complicated. The disaster the city has gone through has not changed things there. People are still worshiping in ways that mean they have turned their backs on Yahweh. If this pattern continues, a worse disaster is bound to come.

It does continue, and the worse disaster does come: the Babylonians' destruction of Jerusalem in 587. It is the arrival of news concerning this catastrophe that frees Ezekiel to turn from warnings to promises. The irony is that people do not believe him when he gives them promises of restoration any more than they did when he issued warnings of disaster. That phenomenon illustrates why prophets exist. The community does not need prophets to confirm what it thinks. It needs prophets to contradict what it thinks, one way or the other.

There is a series of promises from God that go way back in Israel's story—promises of a land, of increase, of blessing, of God's commitment to David's line and to Jerusalem, and of God's presence in the temple. We could say that all Ezekiel now does is reaffirm those promises in new ways that show how they relate to the people's circumstances as they now are. Ezekiel's promises are visions that involve a radical change in the topography of the Middle East, and they are not literal pictures of what God intends to do or implicit commissions of what God's servants should do. But in imaginative pictures they do portray the wonder of the restoration that God does intend to bring about.

Ezekiel gives most space to a visionary account of a new Jerusalem and a new temple. His vision has a big influence on the book of Revelation, which actually speaks of a "new Jerusalem" (Rev 21:2). We could say that Ezekiel is one of the major inspirations behind Revelation, which also has to be taken metaphorically, yet really seriously.

The Twelve

In the Christian order of the First Testament, Daniel follows Ezekiel; but in the Hebrew Bible, Daniel comes much later (in a group called the Writings). And in his book Daniel is not called a "prophet" but a "man of insight."[9] The First Testament then closes with the twelve "Minor Prophets," which are minor only in the sense that they are shorter than the "Major Prophets." Chapter for chapter, they are just as profound, challenging, and inspiring as the longer books. They appear in three groups, roughly parallel to the times or accents of Isaiah, Jeremiah, and Ezekiel.

Hosea, Joel, Amos, Obadiah, Jonah, and Micah are mostly contemporary with Isaiah ben Amoz, and thus they focus on warning Israel about disaster that is threatened—especially for Ephraim, where Hosea and Amos actually work, and where Jonah comes from. These three are the only prophets who worked in Ephraim who have books named after them (though Elijah, Elisha, and other prophets also worked there). Even their message is adapted in various ways to speak to Judah, with the implication that Judah cannot afford to congratulate itself on dodging the Assyrian bullet.

The point emerges from the way Amos speaks of "the day of the Lord," or "Yahweh's day." In Amos's context, people looked forward to it as the day when Yahweh would fulfill all his promises to his people. Amos warns them that they will experience it as a day when Yahweh implements all his warnings. There is a kind of finality about this day, but the First Testament sees it as a day that can be embodied in events such as the fall of Samaria or the fall of Jerusalem—it is not just a day that brings history to an end. The idea of a final day that also finds interim embodiments provides the New Testament with a way of thinking of the final fulfillment of God's purpose, which also finds embodiment in an event such as the fall of Jerusalem in AD 70. A related motif is the idea of God

---

9. See the discussion of Daniel on pp. 58–59 above.

having a change of mind about whether to bring judgment, which is important to Amos (with regard to trouble coming to Ephraim) and to Jonah (with regard to trouble coming to Nineveh). Hosea's portrait of Yahweh being torn between wrath and mercy makes a parallel point about Yahweh doing justice to both. The talk in 2 Peter 3 about the final coming of Jesus takes up the same issues.

Nahum, Habakkuk, and Zephaniah are contemporary with Jeremiah, and they focus on the threat of Judah's downfall, which is now more imminent. Like Jeremiah, they work in the context of the collapse of Assyria and the rise of Babylon as the Middle Eastern superpower. Like Jonah, they raise questions about Yahweh's relationship with the superpower of the day. Whereas Jonah warns Israel not to be too negative in its stance toward Assyria, Nahum reassures people that Yahweh will not allow its oppression to continue forever; they complement each other as Paul and James complement each other in the New Testament. Habakkuk wrestles more directly with the morality of Yahweh's dealings with Judah and with Babylon (how can God use wicked Babylon to punish wicked Judah?).

Haggai, Zechariah, and Malachi come from the context of Persia's having taken over from Babylon, when the temple needs rebuilding, and from the succeeding period, so they overlap in theme with Ezekiel but overlap in time with Isaiah 56–66. Haggai and Zechariah 1–8 specifically relate to the rebuilding of the temple, and they too complement each other: Haggai emphasizes the human responsibility for this project, while Zechariah emphasizes the divine commitment to it. Malachi belongs to the next century and reflects the problems of that period, problems that also surface in Ezra and Nehemiah. As a prophet, Malachi both confronts the people who need confronting in this context and speaks of the way Yahweh will fulfill his purpose.

Questions for Discussion

1. How do you think the passages from the Prophets quoted in Matthew 1:18–2:23 help us understand Jesus?
2. When you look at those passages in their context in the Prophets, what was their significance as God's message to their original hearers?
3. In what way does Isaiah 61 help us understand Luke's story of Jesus?
4. How do the passages from the Prophets that are quoted in Acts help us understand its story of the beginnings of the church?
5. What do you think are the chief significances of the Prophets for the church as you know it?

CHAPTER 4

Ideas

Matthew's Gospel takes a jump forward in chapter 3: both Jesus and his cousin John are now grown men taking up the work God has called them to. When we compare Matthew with Mark's way of telling the story, though, we discover that Matthew's leap forward only takes us to where the real story begins, with John the Baptizer's ministry. Whereas Mark more or less begins with a quotation from Isaiah 40, by way of transition Matthew 3 incorporates a shorter equivalent to that quotation. It thus continues to show how the First Testament declares the promise of which Jesus is the fulfillment. But it then moves away from talk in terms of promise and fulfillment for a while and takes us in a different direction. Matthew 3 as a whole points us to the way the First Testament provides us with the images, ideas, and words with which to understand Jesus.

4.1 Matthew 3:13–17: The Anointed, the Servant, the Son

We will come back to John the Baptizer, but it will be convenient to skip ahead to the end of Matthew 3 first, to where God directly picks up phrases from the First Testament when he speaks to Jesus.

> Jesus came from Galilee to the Jordan to be baptized by John. But John tried to deter him, saying, "I need to be baptized by you, and do you come to me?"
>
> Jesus replied, "Let it be so now; it is proper for us to do this to fulfill all righteousness." Then John consented.
>
> As soon as Jesus was baptized, he went up out of the water. At that moment heaven was opened, and he saw the Spirit of God descending like

a dove and alighting on him. And a voice from heaven said, "This is my Son, whom I love; with him I am well pleased." (Matt 3:13–17)

The account of John the Baptizer's work thus closes with Jesus coming for baptism. At the moment when God the Holy Spirit comes to alight upon God the Son for his ministry, God the Father speaks from heaven in words that are not made up for the occasion but are taken from the First Testament. They combine phrases from three passages, and thus put us on the track of one aspect of Jesus's significance in relation to the First Testament: he combines a number of roles, and a number of images are required in order to give something like an adequate account of him.

Yahweh's Anointed

God's opening words, "This is my son," recall Psalm 2:7:

> I shall recount Yahweh's decree:
>   he said to me,
> "You are my son;
>   today I myself have fathered you."

Mark and Luke have "You are my son," in conformity with the psalm. Even with that more exact parallel, in isolation the phrase might seem too thin a basis for hypothesizing that God's words allude to the psalm. But given that Psalm 2 is quoted a number of times in the New Testament, we may infer that the Gospels would expect us to make the link.

The psalm is a king's testimony to Yahweh's word to him. The king need not fear being unable to maintain control of subject nations, because Yahweh has made him sovereign over them; the king recalls Yahweh's words of commission and assurance. After the exile, when Israel had no kings, such a psalm could become linked to Israel's hope that one day it would again have a king for whom God would fulfill this commitment. Earlier, the psalm has described the king as Yahweh's "anointed one," using the Hebrew word *mashiah*, which lies behind the English word *messiah*. In Jewish usage in New Testament times, the messiah was the deliverer to whom the Jewish people looked forward, which is what the word thus means in the New Testament itself.

When we go back into the First Testament, an irony emerges. The First

Testament does from time to time promise that God will send such a deliverer who will embody all that the Davidic king was supposed to be. It describes him (for instance) as the shoot from Jesse's stump or as the faithful branch from that tree (Isa 11:1; Jer 23:5). But it does not refer to him as the *mashiah*. Indeed, it does not have a technical term for this person, which is part of the reason why the word *messiah* came to fulfill this function.

When the First Testament uses the word *mashiah*, it is always referring to a king or a priest who already exists, who has been anointed with oil as a sign of his being designated by God. Paradoxically, then, the First Testament talks about the Messiah but it never calls him the *mashiah*; it does use the word *mashiah*, but it is never referring to the Messiah.

So when Psalm 2 speaks of Yahweh's anointed one, Yahweh's *mashiah*, it is referring to the current Davidic king. But Jerusalem had Davidic kings for only four centuries, and by Jesus's day had been without Davidic kings for six centuries. During that period, having an anointed Davidic king became simply a hope based on God's promise to David, not a present reality. The *mashiah* did not start off as a future figure, but he became one, and Psalm 2 comes to describe the anointed one that the Jewish people will have one day.

In taking up words from Psalm 2, then, God the Father declares that Jesus is the anointed one, the *mashiah*, there spoken of. We can imagine that Jesus would pick up the allusion.

Yahweh's Servant

The phrase "my Son, whom I love; with him I am well pleased," also recalls Isaiah 42:1:

> There is my servant whom I support,
>   my chosen in whom I myself delight.

Again, Isaiah 42 is a passage taken up elsewhere in the New Testament, not least in Matthew 12:17–19, which directly quotes Isaiah 42:1–4. Once more, it is no stretch of the imagination that Jesus and the readers of the Gospel would pick up the allusion when God's words take up a phrase from the verse.

Isaiah 42:1–9 describes the role Yahweh's servant is expected to fulfill. In some respects the role is quite similar to the king's calling, but the portrait of the servant in Isaiah 40–55 makes clear that this role is not fulfilled by the regular exercise of power. It involves accepting affliction and paying a price for the restoration of relationships between God and people. It is this calling that God the Father places before Jesus.

The New Testament does not otherwise quote from Isaiah 42, but it does quote from the "twin" passage about Yahweh's servant, Isaiah 52:13–53:12. Perhaps "twin" is the wrong metaphor; they are more like mother and daughter, or a sketch and a filling out. The First Testament often employs the expression "Yahweh's servant," and it uses it of various people—Moses and David are the people it is most often applied to. Like the *mashiah*, then, Yahweh's servant is not essentially a figure who belongs to the future, and the term is not one that belongs to only one person. There are lots of anointed people and lots of servants of Yahweh. One distinctive feature when the image appears in Isaiah 40–55 is that it often describes the relationship between God and Israel as a whole. It is not just important people like Moses or David who have this relationship with God and this vocation.

A prophet such as Isaiah or Jeremiah is also "Yahweh's servant," and the prophet who speaks in Isaiah 49 and 50 speaks of himself in the same terms. The only point where the New Testament quotes either of these passages is when Paul applies Isaiah 49:6 to himself and Barnabas (Acts 13:47),[1] an application that fits nicely.

It has been a myth of First Testament study since the nineteenth century that there are four "Servant Songs" in Isaiah 40–55, in chapters 42, 49, 50, and 52:13–53:12. They are no more songs than other parts of Isaiah 40–55 (less so than some parts), and the chapters become more obscure if we treat the four passages together and in isolation from their context, rather than as part of Isaiah 40–55 with its many other allusions to "Yahweh's servant." But it can be illuminating to treat Isaiah 42:1–9 and 52:13–53:12 together, not least because both focus on describing the role of Yahweh's servant. They are not making a promise about someone who was to appear in five centuries' time. They are describing the role that Yahweh's servant was supposed to fulfill or was fulfilling. That means they are open to being taken up in the New Testament to spell out the role Jesus fulfills.

---

1. See the discussion of Acts 13 on pp. 80–82 above.

Yahweh's Only Son

In Isaiah 42, the Old Greek translation of the Scriptures, the Septuagint, has *pais* for "servant" (so also Matt 12:18). That word can as easily denote a son as a servant, so that these two passages in Psalm 2 and Isaiah 42 could account satisfactorily for all the words that appear in Matthew 3:17. But the middle phrase, "my son, whom I love," also recalls Genesis 22:1–2.

> God tested Abraham. He said to him, "Abraham!" He said, "I am here." He said, "Take your son, will you, your only one, the one you love, Isaac, get yourself out to the Moriah region, and offer him up as a burnt offering there, on one of the mountains that I shall tell you about."

In the end this sacrifice is not exacted, but Abraham shows himself willing to make it.

His action (and Isaac's implicit willingness to be sacrificed) made a deep impression on Israel, and the passage was much pondered among Jews of Jesus's day. It lies behind Paul's talk of God not sparing his only Son in Romans 8:32. Its importance in Jesus's day encourages the idea that it also lies behind God the Father's words in Matthew 3:17: Jesus is the only Son, whom God loves and whom he is willing to sacrifice for the sake of the world, and Jesus is called to imitate Isaac's availability.

Genesis 22 is a hair-raising story. Does God really ask such things of people? What would be the effect on Isaac of such an experience? There is a midrash on the story (an imaginary and imaginative elaboration of it) that looks at it from Sarah's angle. The midrash starts from the fact that the story of Sarah's death immediately follows the story of Abraham's offering of Isaac. Why would Sarah's death thus immediately follow? The midrash imagines Abraham's servants getting back home and telling Sarah what happened; but before they get to the point where the heavenly figure tells Abraham not to go through with the sacrifice, Sarah drops dead.

In an earlier story Abraham has prayed boldly for Sodom (Gen 18), and it might seem odd that he does not also ask God to change his mind about the offering of Isaac. Another Jewish insight on the story is that in Genesis 18 he was praying for someone else, not for himself. Here God is asking something of Abraham in asking him to give up his son, and the trusting thing for Abraham to do is act on what God says. The story is not about Isaac but about Abraham and about his trust in God for the fulfillment of God's promise.

The horror of the story is mitigated by the fact that, in Jesus, God does show himself willing to do what he had asked of Abraham, and to go through with it. God's taking up his own earlier words to Abraham implies this willingness, while also challenging Jesus to be Isaac.

The Man

At Jesus's baptism, then, God the Father gives Jesus and his disciples some idea of who Jesus is and what role he is to fulfill, by taking up images from the First Testament.

It is an extraordinary idea that someone should be Yahweh's anointed son through whom he would enforce authority in the world, and also Yahweh's dear son whom he is prepared to sacrifice, and also Yahweh's servant who is prepared to sacrifice himself. For many Christians, the idea that Jesus is the suffering servant is easy to recognize. So is the idea that he is the son whom God sacrifices.

The idea that he is the one through whom God will enforce authority in the world is harder to accept. Yet at the beginning of his version of Jesus's story, Luke has reported that Jesus's mother associated her son's birth with God's bringing down rulers from their thrones, and that his uncle associated this birth with God's rescuing his people from the hand of their enemies (Luke 1:52, 73). Zechariah also knew that there was another side to this coin: John's coming and Jesus's coming related to the forgiveness of his people's sins (Luke 1:77).

The complexity of the roles Jesus is to fulfill makes it tempting to simplify the implications of God's words at Jesus's baptism. Jesus's disciples were inclined to simplify them in the opposite direction to that of many modern Christians and to focus on the motif that excited Mary, and in this respect they likely had the same instincts as their contemporaries who were not Jesus's disciples. Their inclination was likely a factor behind Jesus's general hesitation about being identified as the promised anointed king.

Jesus prefers the designation that is literalistically translated "the son of man." In Hebrew or Aramaic, such a phrase is simply a roundabout way of saying "man," as "man of faithfulness" is a roundabout way of saying "faithful man." So I shall use the expression "the Man." The expression is Yahweh's default way of addressing Ezekiel, but it also appears once in Daniel 7 to denote a humanlike figure in a vision who receives authority from another, more senior-looking human figure. The image gained a life of its own in the century or two leading up to Jesus's time, and it came to denote a figure of heavenly origin and significance to whom God gave authority in the world. Various works referring to the Man are associated with the figure of Enoch in Genesis. Genesis describes how Enoch went straight to be with God without dying, which makes him an appropriate person to envisage being able to reveal heavenly secrets.

In due course, Jesus asks his disciples what people say about the Man— that is, about himself (see Matt 16:13–28). Peter declares, "You are the Messiah, the Son of the living God." It is a confession that well matches the words from Jesus's baptism, and Jesus congratulates Peter on his insight, but then bids the disciples not to tell people that he is the Messiah, at least in part because that declaration is misleading out of the context of Genesis 22 and Isaiah 42. And he goes on to try unsuccessfully to get the disciples to see that he is going to be attacked and killed, though he will then rise from death.

The portrait of Yahweh's servant in Isaiah 42, and much more explicitly that in Isaiah 52:13–53:12, combines persecution and exaltation. The vision of the Man in Daniel 7 also does so, and it was more prominent in Jewish thinking in Jesus's day. Yet its having only narrow scriptural background made it more like a blank slate that Jesus could adopt as the background for expounding his vocation.

In Many Ways and in His Son

In Jesus's life and ministry, his baptism and the Holy Spirit's coming on him is of key importance, and in the Gospels the account of this event has a key place. In the words he hears from heaven, he receives fundamental guidelines for the way he is to understand himself. He has the authority of the Davidic king, who is given a special relationship of sonship to the God of heaven. He has the calling of the servant with its different form of power, exercised despite or through affliction. And if that point is not explicit enough, he is the beloved Son whom the Father is willing to sacrifice for the world's sake.

When Jesus is given his fundamental theological orientation for his ministry in terms of key motifs embodying central aspects of his calling that come from the First Testament, God works by bringing together three images that were otherwise unrelated.

The description of God's speaking that opens the Letter to the Hebrews resonates with God's way of working when he speaks at Jesus's baptism.

> In the past God spoke to our ancestors through the prophets at many times and in various ways, but in these last days he has spoken to us by his Son, whom he appointed heir of all things, and through whom also he made the universe. (Heb 1:1–2)

Jesus brings a new revelation of God, yet he does not tell people new things about God. He does say scandalous things that deeply offend his disciples. One is the idea that he has to be attacked and killed (e.g., Matt 16:21–27). Another (a couple of chapters later) is the idea that being a disciple risks forgoing the possibility of divorce (Matt 19:10). He also says some scandalous things that deeply offend other people, such as truths about himself by which he claims more significance than they are prepared to give him. But we do not find the disciples responding to Jesus by saying, "Oh, we never knew those things about God that you have told us," nor do we find Pharisees or Sadducees questioning what he says about God.

What is new about Jesus's revelation of God is illustrated by God's words at his baptism and explicated in those opening lines in Hebrews. Before Jesus, no one had thought of putting together the Messiah, the servant in Isaiah, and the offering of Isaac. They are "various ways" in which God spoke in the Scriptures, but it would not be obvious that they fitted into one big picture. They come to do so not because God gives a further or novel revelation but because they converge in Jesus, in whose person God spoke. Hebrews indeed adds that what converges in him is not merely what God was doing in Israel's prehistory and its history, through Abraham and his willingness to offer Isaac, through David and God's promise to him, and through Israel and its vocation to be God's servant. It is also what God had been doing way before ("through whom also he made the universe") and the ultimate goal of God's purpose ("whom he appointed heir of all things").

On one hand, then, we understand Jesus in his complexity through looking at him in light of the "many and various ways" in which God spoke in the First Testament. Beyond Abraham, David, and Israel are (for instance) Abel (as Hebrews also points out), Joseph, Moses, Aaron and the other priests, Joshua, and Samuel and other prophets—and also Hagar, Miriam, Deborah and other judges, Ruth, Hannah, and other mothers. On the other hand, we understand their significance when we look at the way Jesus embodies aspects of what they all exemplify but makes them part of a new whole.

4.2 Matthew 3:1–5: The Baptizer's Theological Dictionary

The end of Matthew 3, then, takes up expressions from the First Testament to make what we might call a theological statement about who Jesus is. But the use of the Scriptures in connection with making theological statements pervades the Gospel's background. Indeed, across a broad front the New Testament as a whole pictures God and humanity and the relationship between them on the basis of the way these realities are described in the First Testament.

A Theological Dictionary

The point can be illustrated from John's exhortation to repent because God's reign is here.

> In those days John the Baptist came, preaching in the wilderness of Judea and saying, "Repent, for the kingdom of heaven has come near." This is he who was spoken of through the prophet Isaiah:
>
>> "A voice of one calling in the wilderness,
>> 'Prepare the way for the Lord,
>>   make straight paths for him.'"
>
> John's clothes were made of camel's hair, and he had a leather belt around his waist. His food was locusts and wild honey. People went out to him from Jerusalem and all Judea and the whole region of the Jordan. Confessing their sins, they were baptized by him in the Jordan River.
>
> (Matt 3:1–6)

John will go on to exhort people to flee from the coming wrath, to warn them that trees that do not produce fruit are to be felled, and to describe one who will come after him harvesting wheat and burning chaff. All these motifs and themes come from the First Testament. It is on the basis of people's knowledge of these Scriptures that John makes his appeal to them.

I do oversimplify the point in making it that way. In our own Christian context, we make much use of terms such as *salvation, heaven, redemption, election, holiness, kingdom of God,* and *justice*. We are hardly aware of the fact that the meaning of these terms comes as much from our Christian tradition as it does from the Scriptures. Yet we are committed to basing our ideas on the Scriptures, and if someone convinces us that at some point we are following Christian tradition rather than the Scriptures, we may well want to change our way of speaking.

This dynamic would have applied to John the Baptizer and his audience. They too were shaped by the Scriptures as interpreted in their community at least as much as by the Scriptures themselves. If they followed a traditional interpretation of the Scriptures, they would have done so in the conviction that the tradition was a proper interpretation of them. The entire community would agree that their way of thinking needed to follow the Scriptures.

Further, there are of course new things that need to be said in light of Jesus's coming. Something of the dynamic of the relationship between the Testaments is illustrated by John's practice of baptism. This practice is innovative, but it overlaps with the Torah's requirement that people bathe as part of purifying themselves from taboos such as contact with a corpse (e.g., Lev 15, 17) and with its requirement that a foreigner who joins Israel should be circumcised (e.g., Exod 12:48). On one hand, baptism is a one-time rite like circumcision; but on the other, it is a rite involving water administered to people of both sexes who already belong to Israel, like that sacramental bathing. And in using the verb *baptizō* to describe it, the New Testament takes a word that had previously referred simply to plunging oneself in water or to being overwhelmed by something in the way one can be overwhelmed by water. This last connotation coheres with John the Baptizer's talk of being baptized with the Holy Spirit and with fire. To understand baptism, then, it is illuminating to understand the rites that already existed among the Jewish people, which they observed on the basis of the First Testament.

So there is continuity and novelty about baptism. One can see a similar dynamic at work within the First Testament. Circumcision itself came in only with Abraham. Bathing ceremonies came in with Leviticus. The building of the temple brought new observances. The celebration of Israel's festivals changed over the centuries. The Festival of Purim came in during the Persian period. Hanukkah came in through the fulfillment of the visionary promises in Daniel. Sabbath worship in the synagogue developed sometime during the exile or the Second Temple period.

When you have seen God embodied in Jesus, you have seen something new. But what you have seen is the embodiment of the God who had been relating to Israel. And what the word *God* means in the New Testament was determined by what it meant in the Jewish Scriptures. The First Testament is the New Testament's theological dictionary or its language world.

Again, if one looks once more at John the Baptizer's ministry as a whole, by no means does every aspect of its teaching derive from the First Testament. Baptism had no precise First Testament antecedents. Jesus's coming brings new religious practices and new religious language as well as new collocations of First Testament texts. It not only supplements but also refocuses and redefines biblical faith. The incarnation does so; we have noted that "God with us" now means something more radical than was the case in First Testament times (though something quite consistent with the view of God and humanity stated in the First Testament). The cross does so, bringing to clearest external expression that unprecedented paradoxical collocation of kingly glory, fatherly sacrifice, and personal suffering stated at Jesus's baptism. The resurrection does so, making the prospect of our resurrection central rather than marginal to biblical faith and promising a resolution of the enigma and incompleteness of human life recognized by the First Testament and instanced by Matthew's story of the death of Bethlehem's children and the prominence even in Israel's history of the likes of Herod and Archelaus. The outpouring of the Holy Spirit does so, bringing home the significance of Jesus and opening up a new possibility of taking the news about him to the nations.

The Reign of God

The expression "kingdom of God" is an example that is illuminating in several ways. First, it is common for Christians to assume that the teaching of Jesus is the starting point for understanding the kingdom of God. Yet we learn from Matthew 3 that it is John the Baptizer who introduces this phrase into the New Testament. When Jesus later says, "Repent, for the kingdom of heaven has come near," he is simply taking up his cousin's proclamation, when John has been put in prison.

Several sidebars may be appropriate here. Mark does not include this aspect of John's proclamation, so in Mark's Gospel Jesus is the first person to speak of God's kingdom. Luke also does not include it, though he does incorporate an angelic message to Mary that refers to Jesus's own kingdom. This expression is rarer in the New Testament, though it fits with Jesus being the Davidic king. In John "kingdom of God" comes only in Jesus's conversation with Nicodemus.

In Matthew's characteristic phrase "kingdom of heaven," "heaven" is more literally "heavens"; the equivalent Hebrew and Aramaic words are plural, as we can refer in English to the "heaven" or to the "heavens," and to "sky" or to "skies." By New Testament times, many Jews were inclined not to refer directly to "God" in order to avoid risking irreverence, and "heavens" was one way of avoiding it. It is plausible to imagine that John and Jesus could have spoken both of "the kingdom of God" and of "the kingdom of the heavens." Matthew usually has the latter but sometimes has the former.

Moreover, "kingdom" is potentially a misleading translation of Greek *basileia* and of equivalent words such as *malkut* in Hebrew and Aramaic. I come from the United Kingdom, which is a place, ruled by a king or queen. The kingdom of God is not a place. The biblical words refer more to the reign of a king.

Second, if Jesus takes up the notion of God's kingdom or reign from John, John and Jesus take it up from the First Testament. There the Davidic king rules in the "kingdom of Yahweh" (1 Chr 28:5; 2 Chr 13:8). Yahweh's victory over Egypt at the Red Sea establishes the fact that Yahweh reigns and that he will do so forever (Exod 15:18). Many psalms affirm that Yahweh reigns (see especially Pss 93–99).

Yet it seems that Yahweh does not enforce his kingly authority in the world or in Israel. In the sixth century, Babylon ruled. Admittedly, the Babylonian king is the real King's servant (e.g., Jer 27:6–7); he does not realize it, but he is acting as Yahweh's agent. But it will not do in the long run for the superpower to focus on doing its own thing and for the people of God to be forcibly subjected to it. In another sense, then, Yahweh is not really reigning among the nations or in Israel. But as the Babylonian empire is about to fall, Isaiah 52 declares:

> How lovely on the mountains are the feet of one who brings news,
>   one who lets people hear, "All is well,"
> one who brings good news, lets people hear of deliverance,
>   who says to Zion, "Your God has begun to reign!"
> A voice!—lookouts are lifting voice,
>   together they resound!
> Because with both eyes
>   they see Yahweh going back to Zion.
> Break out, resound together,
>   wastes of Jerusalem.
> Because Yahweh is comforting his people,
>   he is restoring Jerusalem.
> Yahweh is baring his sacred arm

> before the nations' eyes.
> All the ends of the earth
> > will see our God's deliverance. (Isa 52:7–10)

God's Reign Drawing Near

So Yahweh intends to assert his kingship in the world of the nations and in the life of Israel by inspiring the Persian king Cyrus to put Babylon down and to make it possible for Judahites in exile to go home. Therein lies the encouragement to Judahites to listen to a voice calling:

> In the wilderness clear Yahweh's way,
> > make straight in the steppe a causeway for our God.
> Every ravine is to rise up,
> > every mountain and hill is to fall down.
> The ridge is to become level,
> > the cliffs a valley.
> Yahweh's splendor will appear,
> > and all flesh will see it together,
> > because Yahweh's mouth has spoken. (Isa 40:3–5)

The message is not that the Judahites are to construct this highway; it is that they are to be encouraged by the fact that God is doing so.

The encouragement was both vindicated and disappointed. Cyrus did put Babylon out of business and did commission Judahites to go back home, and the Persian authorities did support the reestablishment of the Judahite community and its rebuilding of the temple in Jerusalem. But Judah stayed under a superpower's authority and had its own well-being compromised by imperial taxes. Has Yahweh's reign arrived? Well, yes and no.

In due course, Persia is replaced by Greece and later by Rome, so that the declarations of Mary and Zechariah[2] then indicate the awareness that things have not changed so much since the time when Babylon was king. It is in this context that John and Jesus come along with the same declaration as Isaiah 52. God is now becoming king in the sense that he is asserting his kingship. He has been leaving the world to its own devices and letting the Jewish people be its victims. The Jewish people acknowledge that in one

2. See the discussion of "The Man" on pp. 109–10 above.

sense they have nothing to complain about. Their continuing subordination to an imperial lordship issues from their resistance to God's lordship. But might enough be enough? The coming of John and of Jesus means that God has determined that indeed enough is enough. But the subordination was deserved, which means that the Jewish people cannot simply rejoice. The message of John and of Jesus is that they need to repent and change as much as Gentiles do.

In the First Testament, God generally encourages Israel to take a negative attitude to the imperial powers that dominated Israel and other little nations. It is the attitude one would expect Israel to take. God encourages Israel by promising to put down these superpowers, and every century or two he does so. But there is another aspect to his attitude, as is also the case with his attitude to the nearer neighbors with whom Israel was often in conflict. He is, after all, the God of the whole world, and ideally he would rather gain acknowledgment by the whole world than devastate it. The story of Jonah is a telling witness to this other side that also has implications for Israel itself. The story testifies to Yahweh's enthusiasm about the Assyrians repenting and thus averting divine judgment for their waywardness.

Does God's Reign Arrive?

The story in Jonah about repentance leading Yahweh to have a change of mind recalls Jeremiah's exposition of that theme, and Jeremiah 18 notes that the principle is one that applies to Israel, not just to foreign peoples. Indeed, that is why Jeremiah discusses the question. So it should not take much for thoughtful Israelites to work out another implication of the Jonah story. As well as warning them about prophets and about hating their enemies, it warned them about the need for them to follow the Assyrians' example and to escape from their judgment by repenting.

In John's and Jesus's day, the Jewish people need to respond to the same insight. That God is asserting his kingship and intends to terminate Roman rule is reason for the Jewish people to repent, not just to gloat.

As usual, there was some slippage between what God had said about his reign starting and the way things turned out; and, as usual, the reasons may be elusive. Jesus does not immediately do the kind of thing that one would have expected of someone who was bringing in God's reign, though he does other things that imply an alternative scriptural yet also revisionist understanding of it. Likewise his submitting to execution does not look like the way to bring in God's reign, though with hindsight the New Testament can see that it was. God's reign did not in the short term dethrone Rome, but it did dethrone some bigger supernatural powers.

Two thousand more years of history do not give the impression that the reign of God has arrived, and this leads many Christians to take on the same attitude as Jews and unbelievers, that it is our responsibility to bring in the kingdom of justice and righteousness. So we speak of furthering God's reign or extending God's kingdom or working for the kingdom or bringing it in, whereas there is no such talk in the New Testament. There we only receive the kingdom or enter it. Bringing it is God's business.

John and Jesus suggest that the business of the people of God in relation to the reign of God is to repent and believe. The expectation is the same as the one in Isaiah 52. Repenting and believing is the way we prepare the way for the Lord. While Matthew's quotation from Isaiah 40 does not correspond with the text's own meaning, the point Matthew makes on the basis of the text is entirely in keeping with what the First Testament says about a response to the announcement that Yahweh's reign is here.

So attempts to understand "the kingdom of God" by starting from the New Testament are unlikely to work. The puzzle of the sense in which the rule of God "is at hand" or "has come" is also less puzzling when considered in light of the way the First Testament speaks. Half a century before the prophecy in Isaiah 52, Ezekiel declares:

> An end! The end is coming upon the four corners of the country. The end is now upon you. I shall send off my anger against you, and I shall exercise authority over you in accordance with your ways. . . . An end is coming! It is coming! The end is rousing itself against you! There, it is coming! The doom is coming upon you, you who inhabit the country. The time is coming. The day is near—tumult, not cheering on the mountains. Now it is near. (Ezek 7:2–7)

A catastrophe is indeed imminent, and it is *an* end, though not *the* end.

Repentance

How would people understand the expectation on the part of John and Jesus that they should repent? Etymologically, Matthew's verb *metanoeō* denotes a change of mind, and this seems to be the nature of Judas's repentance (Matt 27:3; cf. Heb 12:17). John's interest lies in a change of behavior (Matt 3:8; cf. Luke 5:32; 2 Cor 12:21). In his talk of sackcloth and ashes, Jesus adds the note of regret for one's wrongdoing (Matt 11:21; cf. 2 Cor 7:9–10).

Likewise, of the two First Testament words commonly translated "repent," one denotes sorrow and regret, the other a change of life, while changing one's mind or getting a new mind is also a significant image in the First Testament. Ironically, when the First Testament talks about repentance in the sense of regret (the verb *naham*), the person who most often does the repenting is God. God is sorrowful and regretful about making the world and about making Saul king (Gen 6:6–7; 1 Sam 15:11, 35). The good news is that God can also repent about bringing disaster to people, so that one can therefore appeal to him to do so. Anyone who is apprehensive about the idea that God repents can be reassured that he does not do so (Num 23:19; 1 Sam 15:29; Ps 110:4)—in the sense that he is not fickle or unreliable or a pushover. The bad news is that he will not repent if the people themselves do not repent, and that he can repent of the good he intends to do if people do not take the action he looks for them to take (Exod 32:12–14; Jer 4:28; 18:1–10; Amos 7:3, 6).

The other First Testament word for repentance (*shub*) is the ordinary word for "turn," so it means turn around or turn back. It is at least as surprising that God can repent in the sense of changing his behavior, his pattern of action, in response to human turning (Jonah 3:8–10). But this word is much more often used of human beings. In Jeremiah, Yahweh expresses bewilderment that Judah persists in turning away and will not turn back or regret and relent (Jer 8:4–6). But nothing changes, and the people end up in exile. Fortunately, however, Moses's final sermon and Solomon's prayer at the temple dedication already face this possibility and look beyond it. When Yahweh takes Israel into exile, if they turn from their faithlessness and waywardness and rebellion, it is possible to plead with Yahweh for pardon, and for Yahweh to restore them (Deut 30:1–2; 1 Kgs 8:46–50).

It is in this context that the First Testament also talks in terms of getting a new "heart"—that is, a new way of thinking, a new mind (Ezek 11:19; 18:31; 36:26)—something for which they have some responsibility and for which Yahweh needs to have some responsibility.

The prospect of repentance and of a new way of thinking belongs especially in the context of exile and of Israel's need of restoration. It thus fits the context of John's work. Jesus comes to bring the final restoration of the Jewish people, the final implementing of God's reign among them. If God is to bring that about, or when God brings that about, it requires their sorrow, their turning, their seeking a new way of thinking.

John will go on to make a further, related point. In itself, identifying with the First Testament gets us nowhere. John's hearers were children of Abraham; but God could make more children of Abraham if he chose. The dynamics of John's observation again recall the First Testament, here the story of Yahweh's inclination on Sinai to annihilate Israel and start again with Moses.

4.3 Matthew 3:6–12: The Language World

Matthew's account of the wider context of that proclamation, when John warns people not to rely on their position within Abraham's family, further illustrates how the First Testament functions as the New Testament's language world.

> When he saw many of the Pharisees and Sadducees coming to where he was baptizing, he said to them: "You brood of vipers! Who warned you to flee from the coming wrath? Produce fruit in keeping with repentance. And do not think you can say to yourselves, 'We have Abraham as our father.' I tell you that out of these stones God can raise up children for Abraham. The ax is already at the root of the trees, and every tree that does not produce good fruit will be cut down and thrown into the fire.
>
> "I baptize you with water for repentance. But after me comes one who is more powerful than I, whose sandals I am not worthy to carry. He will baptize you with the Holy Spirit and fire. His winnowing fork is in his hand, and he will clear his threshing floor, gathering his wheat into the barn and burning up the chaff with unquenchable fire." (Matt 3:7–12)

As well as urging repentance on the grounds that the rule of heaven is at hand, John exhorts people to flee from the coming wrath, warns them that a tree that does not produce fruit will be felled, and describes one who will come after him and will baptize with the Holy Spirit and with fire, and who will harvest wheat and burn chaff. John thus interweaves a series of further motifs that presuppose a theological dictionary drawn from the First Testament. They are separable images, but their significance overlaps.

First there is the tree that fails to produce good fruit and that therefore gets felled. A tree that produces good fruit is a First Testament image for the individual who walks by God's instruction and also for Israel as the people of God. Psalm 1 declares that individuals who walk by God's instruction produce fruit in season, while people who do not are blown away like chaff— another image that John uses. To put it another way, if you are a deceitful and amoral person,

> God will indeed tear you down permanently,
>> break you and pull you from your tent,
>> uproot you from the land of the living. (Ps 52:5)

The Olive Tree

The same psalm offers a contrast to that image:

> I am like a verdant olive tree
>> in God's house. (Ps 52:8)

But theologically, the image of Israel itself as an olive tree is more significant. In the allegory of Judges 9:7–15, the olive tree, the fig tree, and the vine refuse to be king of the forest because they have something better to do, showing their prominence among the fruit-bearing plants in Israel. All three provide images for thinking about Israel and the Jewish people in the New Testament. To understand the New Testament's use of such images, one needs to appreciate both the way the First Testament employs the image and the everyday reality that lies behind the image. In other words, behind the passages where the three plants serve as meaningful symbols, there are the many more passages where they are simply olive tree, fig tree, and vine. They have an indispensable role in Israel's life before they have an indispensable role in Israel's theology.

The olive is of extraordinary significance because of its importance in two directions. Olives, but even more olive oil, are important as food and in cooking. But olive oil is also a key source of light in oil lamps. Thus the olive does have an indispensable role in the First Testament's theology.

> Verdant olive, beautiful with shapely fruit,
>> Yahweh named you.
> To a big roaring sound he has set fire to it,
>> and its branches have broken.

Yahweh of Armies who planted you—
>he has spoken of bad fortune for you,
On account of the bad action of Israel's household
>and Judah's household. (Jer 11:16–17)

So Yahweh the gardener planted an olive tree. Maybe it was in anticipation that he named it "verdant olive, beautiful with shapely fruit," or maybe Jeremiah implies it was verdant and lovely for a while. In either case, it is not now that way.

That fact is the background to Paul's taking up the image of Israel as an olive tree to great effect and with far-reaching theological implications. The olive tree's failure to produce fruit has led to some drastic pruning in his day: many branches have been cut out. And that pruning has created space to graft in other branches, Gentile branches. But this background would make it unwise for the Gentile branches to behave in a way that meant they do not produce the fruit either.

> If some of the branches have been broken off, and you, though a wild olive shoot, have been grafted in among the others and now share in the nourishing sap from the olive root, do not consider yourself to be superior to those other branches. If you do, consider this: You do not support the root, but the root supports you. (Rom 11:17–18)

The largely Gentile church did not replace the Jewish people as God's people. We are always like children adopted into an existent family.

> You will say then, "Branches were broken off so that I could be grafted in." Granted. But they were broken off because of unbelief, and you stand by faith. Do not be arrogant, but tremble. For if God did not spare the natural branches, he will not spare you either. Consider therefore the kindness and sternness of God: sternness to those who fell, but kindness to you, provided that you continue in his kindness. Otherwise, you also will be cut off. (11:19–22)

So far, so horticultural. The image may seem strained, but that is nothing to where Paul then takes it.

> And if they do not persist in unbelief, they will be grafted in, for God is able to graft them in again. After all, if you were cut out of an olive tree that is

wild by nature, and contrary to nature were grafted into a cultivated olive tree, how much more readily will these, the natural branches, be grafted into their own olive tree! (11:23–24)

No, the Jewish people have not been superseded as God's people. They are destined to enjoy the blessings of salvation, because "God's gifts and his call are irrevocable" (11:29). God's grace is like that.

The Fig Tree

The everyday importance of figs is that they are the main source of sweetness in Israel. "Honey" in the First Testament most often refers to syrup made from figs; this is the honey in the expression "flowing with milk and honey." But figs themselves were also appreciated.

> I found Israel
> > like grapes in the wilderness.
> I saw your fathers
> > like the first fruit on a fig tree in its beginning.
> When those people came to the Master of Peor,
> > they dedicated themselves to Shame,
> > and became abominations like the thing they loved. (Hos 9:10)

While the First Testament does not explicitly speak of Israel as a fig tree, as it does of Israel as an olive tree, this passage hints at that implication. So even more clearly does Jesus's story about a fig tree that has produced no fruit and about his action when he curses such a fig tree (Mark 11:12–14; Matt 21:18–19; cf. Luke 13:6–9).

> Early in the morning, as he was on his way back to the city, he was hungry. Seeing a fig tree by the road, he went up to it but found nothing on it except leaves. Then he said to it, "May you never bear fruit again!" Immediately the tree withered. (Matt 21:18–19)

One of my colleagues who is a professor of preaching was called up by a former student who did not know what to do with Luke 13 when it was the next Sunday's Gospel reading. The preacher did not want to tell his congregation that Jesus said that kind of thing. Maybe the preacher had realized that Jesus was not just talking about a tree. It would not be surprising if Jeremiah, too, sees the fig as more than just a random fruit:

> Yahweh showed me: there, two baskets of figs placed before Yahweh's palace (after Nebuchadnezzar king of Babylon exiled Jeconiah ben Jehoiakim king of Judah, Judah's officials, the craftworkers, and the smiths, from Jerusalem and brought them to Babylon). One basket was very good figs, like early figs; one basket was very bad figs that could not be eaten because of being bad. Yahweh said to me, "What are you looking at, Jeremiah?" I said, "Figs—the good figs very good, the bad very bad, which could not be eaten because of being bad." (Jer 24:1–3)

The parable suggests a distinction between those who really belong to Israel and those who do not, those who are the people to whom the future belongs and those who are not.

> Yahweh's word came to me. . . . "Like these good figs, so I shall mark down for good Judah's exile community that I have sent off from this place to the country of the Chaldeans. I shall set my eye on them for good and bring them back to this country. I shall build them and not overthrow. I shall plant them and not uproot. I shall give them a mind to acknowledge me, that I am Yahweh. They will be a people for me and I shall be God for them, because they will turn back to me with their entire mind.
>
> "But like bad figs that cannot be eaten because of being bad (because Yahweh has said this), so shall I make Zedekiah king of Judah, his officials, and the remainder of Jerusalem who remain in this country and who are living in the country of Egypt—I shall make them a horror, something bad, to all earth's kingdoms, an insult and an example, a taunt and a slighting, in all the places where I drive them. I shall send against them sword, famine, and epidemic until they come to an end from the land that I gave to them and to their ancestors." (Jer 24:4–10)

Jeremiah would not want his hearers to treat his parable as an allegory. The people who have been taken off into exile are not people who actually produced the fruit of faithfulness and acknowledgment of Yahweh when they were in Jerusalem. Jeremiah could find no one like that (Jer 5:1–6). But they are people who represent the future of the Israelite fig tree, unless the Jerusalemites whom Jeremiah is addressing change their ways.

The Vine

Most often, in both Testaments, Israel is a vine, with similar encouraging and threatening implications to the ones that apply to the other trees.

> You moved a vine from Egypt,
>> dispossessed nations and planted it.
> You cleared a way before it,
>> it put its roots down and filled the country.
> Mountains were covered by its shade,
>> supernatural cedars by its branches.
> It put out its boughs as far as the sea,
>> its shoots to the river. (Ps 80:8–11)

The picture parallels one way of understanding Jeremiah's succinct description of Israel as an olive, but it also works with the nature of the vine as a plant that can spread far and near. Then the psalmist makes the same transition to a negative picture as comes in Jeremiah.

> Why have you broken open its walls,
>> so that all the people who pass by the way pluck it?
> The boar from the forest tears at it,
>> the creature of the wild feeds on it.
> God of Armies, please come back,
>> look from the heavens and see,
> attend to this vine,
>> the stock that your right hand planted,
> and over the offspring you took firm hold of for yourself,
>> burned in fire, cut;
>> at the reprimand from your face they perish. (Ps 80:12–16)

Jeremiah presupposed that the ravaging of the olive tree was what it deserved. The psalm is designed for other contexts where Israel has been attacked and invaded when it did not merit it.

Jeremiah himself can use the vine image to issue his judgment.

> I—I planted you as a top-class vine,
>> all of it trustworthy seed.
> So how have you changed for me
>> into the turnings of a foreign vine? (Jer 2:21)

Hosea has a teasing way of making the point:

> Israel is a spreading vine;
>> its fruit resembles it.
> In accordance with the quantity of its fruit,
>> it multiplied its altars.
> In accordance with the goodness of its country,
>> they made good pillars. (Hos 10:1)

"Spreading" sounds like a good thing, but it becomes clear that the vine is spreading itself around in a bad sense.

With typical snide rhetorical skill, Ezekiel points out that even the vine's wood is useless. We cannot make anything from it. It is only fit for use as fuel for a fire. And that will be the destiny of the city and country that the vine symbolizes (Ezek 15:1–8). Ezekiel also uses the vine as an image for the Davidic king, with its possibility of flourishing (Ezek 17; cf. Ezek 19). Jeremiah, too, makes clear what will follow:

> I have abandoned my household,
>> I have deserted my domain. . . .
> Go, gather all the creatures of the wild,
>> bring them to eat.
> Many shepherds have devastated my vineyard,
>> trampled my share.
> They have made my desirable share
>> into a devastated wilderness.
> Someone has made it into a devastation;
>> it mourns before me, devastated. (Jer 12:7, 9–11)

Isaiah's Vineyard Song

Isaiah's song about a vineyard is the classic exposition of this image.

> I want to sing a song for my friend,
>> my love song about his vineyard.
> My friend had a vineyard
>> on a fertile ridge.
> He dug it and de-stoned it,

and planted it with choice vine.
>He built a tower in the middle of it,
>>and also hewed a press in it.
>He hoped it would make grapes,
>>but it made rotten grapes. (Isa 5:1–2)

One is to imagine a crowd of people gathered in the temple courtyards listening to a singer-songwriter and prepared to give him a tip. He advertises a love song he has composed on behalf of his friend. Initially the vineyard image fits his announcement of a love song (e.g., Song 7:8). But the song turns out to tell the story of a courting that went wrong.

>So now, population of Jerusalem,
>>people of Judah,
>>decide, please, between me and my vineyard.
>What more was there to do for my vineyard,
>>and I did not do it in it?
>Why, when I hoped for it to make grapes,
>>did it make rotten grapes?
>So now I want to let you know, please,
>>what I am doing about my vineyard:
>Remove its hedge, so it will be for burning up,
>>break down its wall so it will be for trampling,
>>so that I make an end of it.
>It will not be pruned and it will not be hoed;
>>briar and thorn will grow.
>I shall order the clouds
>>not to send rain on it. (Isa 5:3–6)

One can imagine that the audience is feeling more and more uneasy. Maybe it would like to hear the woman's angle on the story. Maybe it is beginning to think about other things the vineyard could symbolize. Isaiah then reveals all. The audience is hearing about itself. The dynamics are a little like Nathan's onslaught on David (2 Sam 12:1–12).

>Because the vineyard of Yahweh of Armies
>>is the household of Israel.
>The people of Judah
>>are the planting in which he took pleasure.

He hoped for the exercise of authority, but there—blood pouring out;
    for faithfulness, but there—a cry. (Isa 5:7)

Jesus and the Vine

Jesus's taking up the vine image links with its prominence in the First Testament. We may begin from one of his stories, in Matthew 20:1–15. It was
about a landowner who went out at 6:00 one morning to hire workers for his
vineyard, agreeing to pay them the regular day's wage. At 9:00 he saw some
other day laborers who had not found work, so he hired them, too. At 12:00
and at 3:00 and at 5:00 he did the same again. When evening came he got
his foreman to pay them, beginning with the ones who started last, whom
he paid the full day's wage. The people whom he had hired first therefore
expected more, but they got the same, and they did not like it. After all, they
had worked all through the day in the vineyard when it was hot. But they
got what they agreed for, he pointed out. Can he not do what he likes with
his money? Are they resentful because he is generous?

The parable might apply in various ways to Jesus's listeners and to Matthew's audience, but it would be natural to understand it in light of a statement such as Isaiah's, that the divine vineyard is the household of Israel. So
the point about the parable is that people who have worked in the vineyard
get the same reward whether they have worked for a long time or a short time.
It would apply within the Jewish people both to people who have been faithful
to Yahweh all their lives and to people who now come to repent when they
hear John or Jesus. It would apply to the Jewish people who made a covenant
commitment to Yahweh more than a millennium previously and to Gentile
peoples who associate themselves with the Jewish people in light of Jesus's
coming. The same pair of antitheses would be implied by another parable:

> "What do you think? There was a man who had two sons. He went to the
> first and said, 'Son, go and work today in the vineyard.' 'I will not,' he an-
> swered, but later he changed his mind and went. Then the father went to
> the other son and said the same thing. He answered, 'I will, sir,' but he did
> not go. Which of the two did what his father wanted?" "The first," they
> answered. (Matt 21:28–31)

Jesus makes the point more forcefully in the further parable about the vineyard owner who vainly sent a series of agents to collect his fruit from his

tenants. He finally sent his son, whom the tenants killed. The vineyard owner will necessarily "bring those wretches to a wretched end . . . and he will rent the vineyard to other tenants, who will give him his share of the crop at harvest time" (Matt 21:33–41).

Given the First Testament background of the vine image and the way Jesus takes it up in such parables, his further exposition in John 15 make a revolutionary claim.

> I am the true vine, and my Father is the gardener. He cuts off every branch in me that bears no fruit, while every branch that does bear fruit he prunes so that it will be even more fruitful. You are already clean because of the word I have spoken to you. Remain in me, as I also remain in you. No branch can bear fruit by itself; it must remain in the vine. Neither can you bear fruit unless you remain in me.
>
> I am the vine; you are the branches. If you remain in me and I in you, you will bear much fruit; apart from me you can do nothing. If you do not remain in me, you are like a branch that is thrown away and withers; such branches are picked up, thrown into the fire and burned. . . . This is to my Father's glory, that you bear much fruit, showing yourselves to be my disciples.
>
> As the Father has loved me, so have I loved you. Now remain in my love. If you keep my commands, you will remain in my love, just as I have kept my Father's commands and remain in his love. . . . You did not choose me, but I chose you and appointed you so that you might go and bear fruit—fruit that will last. (John 15:1–16)

You want to understand what Jesus means by his being the real vine? He is the actual embodiment of Israel. So people need to stick with him if they want to be part of Israel. And that will be the key to their being able to produce what is essentially the same fruit of which Isaiah spoke, "love" or "faithfulness in the exercise of authority." Otherwise, they will find themselves cut out (compare Paul's parable of the olive tree in Rom 11).

The Harvest

Each year people in Israel would look forward in anticipation and apprehension to the barley harvest, the grain harvest, and the fruit harvest. We could say that being harvested is not much fun for the olives, figs, and grapes; the image of harvest can thus become a worrying one:

Put out the sickle,
    because the harvest has ripened.
Come, tread,
    because the vat is full.
The presses abound,
    because their bad dealing is great.
Hordes, hordes, in Verdict Vale,
    because Yahweh's day is near in Verdict Vale. (Joel 3:13–14)

Who is this coming from Edom,
    marked in clothes from Bozrah,
this person majestic in attire,
    stooping in his mighty energy?
"I am the one speaking in faithfulness,
    mighty to deliver."
Why is your attire red,
    your clothes like someone treading in a wine trough?
"I trod a press alone;
    from the peoples there was no one with me.
I tread them in my anger,
    trample them in my fury.
Their spray spatters on my clothes;
    I have stained all my attire.
Because a day of redress has been in my mind,
    my year of restoration has arrived.
But I look, and there is no helper;
    I stare, and there is no support.
So my arm has effected deliverance for me;
    my fury—it has supported me.
I trample peoples in my anger,
    make them drunk in my fury,
    bring down their eminence to the earth." (Isa 63:1–6)

In Revelation 14, John sees one "like a son of man" wielding a sharp sickle who is bidden to reap the earth with it because harvest time has come; and he sees an angel bidden to cut the grapes from the earth's vine so as to throw them into the great winepress of God's wrath from which blood then flows as high as horses' bridles.

    John the Baptizer reflects how the grain harvest, too, can generate a worrying image, if you are the chaff, the lightweight useless parts of the grain that get blown away. As Psalm 1 applies this image to the wicked (people other than us, we are tempted to think), Isaiah applies it to foreign peoples (Isa 17:13; 29:5), but other prophets apply it to Israel.

> I shall scatter them like chaff
>> passing away before the wilderness wind.
> This will be your fate,
>> your lot measured out from me. (Jer 13:24–25; cf. Hos 13:3; Zeph 2:1–2)

The Coming Wrath

Like Isaiah 63 and Zephaniah, John the Baptizer speaks of harvest and also of the coming wrath. That theme recurs in the prophets, at the end of whose line John and Jesus stand.

> There, Yahweh's day is coming, ruthless,
>> with fury and angry blazing,
> to turn the earth into a desolation,
>> so it can annihilate its wrongdoers from it. . . .
> Therefore I will make the heavens quake,
>> and the earth will shake out of its place,
> at the fury of Yahweh of Armies,
>> on the day of his angry blazing. (Isa 13:9, 13)

> So Yahweh's wrath—I am full of it,
>> I am weary of holding it in.
> "Pour it on the child in the street
>> and on the group of young men, together.
> Because both man and woman will be captured,
>> the elder with the one full of years.
> Their houses will pass to other people,
>> fields and wives together.
> Because I shall stretch out my hand
>> against the inhabitants of the country (Yahweh's declaration).
> Because from their smallest to their biggest,
>> every one of them is greedy for loot.

Prophet and priest alike,
>   every one of them is acting falsely." (Jer 6:11–13)

Lamentations 2 is a particularly dense exposition of the theme of God's wrath as Jerusalem has already experienced it.

Oh!—with his anger the Lord clouds over
>   Miss Zion. . . .
He was not mindful of his footstool
>   on his day of anger. . . .
In his fury he tore down
>   Miss Judah's fortifications. . . .
He cut off every horn of Israel
>   in his angry blazing. . . .
He burned up against Jacob like a flaming fire
>   consuming all round. . . .
In Miss Zion's tent
>   he poured out his wrath like fire. . . .
In his angry condemnation he spurned
>   king and priest. . . .
My girls and my young men
>   fell by the sword.
You killed them on your day of anger,
>   you slaughtered them, you did not spare.
You call (as on the day of a set occasion)—
>   for terrors for me from all round.
On Yahweh's day of anger
>   there was no one escaping or surviving. (Lam 2:1, 2, 3, 4, 21–22)

The Holy Spirit and Fire

Wrath, then, issues in fire, though fire has the distinction of being a purifying as well as a punitive agent.

If the Lord has washed away
>   the filth of Zion's daughters,
and cleanses from within it
>   the shed blood of Jerusalem,

by a spirit of the exercise of authority
and by a spirit of burning away,
Yahweh will create
over the entire establishment of Mount Zion,
and over its meeting place,
a cloud by day, and smoke,
and a brightness of flaming fire by night. (Isa 4:4–5)

The collocation of spirit and fire in John the Baptizer's message is strikingly similar to the collocation of burning and spirit in Isaiah. The two come together again in the prophecy of Joel to which Peter appeals at Pentecost, though the significance of fire there is rather different.

After that, I shall pour my breath on all flesh,
and your sons and your daughters will prophesy.
Your elderly will have dreams,
your young men will see visions.
I shall also pour my breath
on servants and maidservants in those days.

I shall put portents in the heavens and in the earth,
blood, fire, and columns of smoke.
The sun will turn to darkness,
the moon to blood,
before Yahweh's day comes,
great, extraordinary. (Joel 2:28–31)

A similar pairing appears in the story of King Saul's greatest moment. The Ammonites have threatened to gouge out the right eyes of the people in Jabesh-Gilead. "God's spirit thrust itself onto Saul when he heard these words, and his anger raged right up." He leads the Israelites out to take on the Ammonites besieging Jabesh and slaughters them (1 Sam 11:1–11). While anger is commonly a fruit of the flesh, it can be a fruit of the Holy Spirit. It generates the energy to take decisive action against wrongdoing. Such is the implication of John's talk of Jesus baptizing with the Holy Spirit and with fire (e.g., Matt 3:11). It fulfills the messianic promise:

A shoot will go out from Jesse's stump,
a branch will fruit from his roots.

Yahweh's breath will alight on him,
    a breath with smartness and understanding,
a breath with counsel and strength,
    a breath with acknowledgment and awe for Yahweh;
    his scent will be awe for Yahweh. . . .
He will exercise authority with faithfulness for the poor,
    and reprove with uprightness for the humble people in the country.
He will strike the country down with the club in his mouth,
    with the breath from his lips he will put the faithless person to death.
Faithfulness will be the belt round his hips,
    truthfulness the belt round his thighs.
Wolf will reside with lamb,
    leopard will lie down with goat,
calf, lion, and fatling together,
    with a little boy driving them. (Isa 11:1–6; cf. 28:5–6; 30:27–28)

4.4 Romans: The Theological Resource

The principle that the First Testament provides the theological framework for understanding Christian faith emerges clearly in Paul's systematic account of his revolutionary gospel in Romans. After laying out the basics of it in 3:21–26 (itself thought out in fundamentally First Testament terms), he has to face overtly the question whether this gospel is acceptable—that is, whether it is biblical enough. He approaches this question in Romans 4 by considering the key case of Abraham and maintaining that Abraham's relationship with God had a similar basis to the one he speaks of. It too involved a righteousness based on trust. First Testament theology thus supports and illumines the nature of faith in Jesus. Romans 3 alludes also to the question of what effect this understanding of God's ways has on the position of the Jews, and Paul takes up this question systematically in Romans 9–11, where the theological argument is conducted entirely in terms of the exposition of First Testament Scriptures.[3]

3. See pp. 20–28 above.

Faith and Judgment

Paul outlines his gospel with great succinctness immediately after the opening greetings in the letter.

> In the gospel the righteousness of God is revealed—a righteousness that is by faith from first to last, just as it is written: "The righteous will live by faith." (Rom 1:17)

Or as I might prefer to translate it,

> God's doing the right thing is revealed in it [the gospel] through faith for faith, as it stands written: "The one who is right through faith will live."

Paul is quoting Habakkuk 2:4. Habakkuk ministered in Judah about the same time as Jeremiah. Like Jeremiah, he had to confront Judah about its unfaithfulness and also to deal with the depressing experience of living under the domination of a superpower. In relation to both issues, Habakkuk makes this key comment,

> The faithful person will live by his truthfulness. (Hab 2:4)

Habakkuk is talking about the righteous person, the person who does what is right, the person who lives faithfully with God and with other people. And he is talking about the key to being able to carry on living. Further, he is talking about faithfulness or truthfulness or steadfastness as that key.

So what Paul says has little to do with what Habakkuk says. Indeed, Paul risks someone responding that Habakkuk says the opposite to Paul. Habakkuk is not talking about empty-handed trust in God's promise and God's grace but about active faithfulness. Paul does not see our faithfulness as key to our being right with God. Oddly enough, Hebrews quotes the same line from Habakkuk with an understanding that is much closer to Habakkuk's own:

> You need to persevere so that when you have done the will of God, you will receive what he has promised. For,
>
> > "In just a little while,
> > he who is coming will come

and will not delay.
But my righteous one will live by faith,
    and I take no pleasure
    in the one who shrinks back." (Heb 10:36–38)[4]

The celebration of First Testament saints that follows in Hebrews 11 spells out the point.

Now Paul does believe in active faithfulness as a requirement of people who have come to trust in Jesus, as Habakkuk would be committed to trust as fundamental to a relationship with God; that awareness is implicit elsewhere in his prophecy. As usual, the difference between Paul and the First Testament is at a verbal level. Paul is using Habakkuk's words to make a different point from Habakkuk's, but in Romans 4 Paul will go on to show that he can make his point on the basis of the inherent meaning of the First Testament text of Genesis.

Arguably, indeed, Paul presupposes something more like the point in Habakkuk and in Hebrews in his next quotation:

Because of your stubbornness and your unrepentant heart, you are storing up wrath against yourself for the day of God's wrath, when his righteous judgment will be revealed. God "will repay everyone according to what they have done." To those who by persistence in doing good seek glory, honor and immortality, he will give eternal life. But for those who are self-seeking and who reject the truth and follow evil, there will be wrath and anger.
(Rom 2:5–8)

Paul is quoting from Psalm 62:12, which in isolation might seem to teach justification by works:

God spoke of one thing,
    two things that I heard:
That God has vigor and you, Lord, have commitment,
    that you yourself make good for someone in accordance with his
       action. (Ps 62:11–12)

---

4. I have slightly modified TNIV here. In its quotation from Habakkuk 2:3–4, Hebrews partly follows the Septuagint. TNIV also sees the influence of Isa 26:20 in the opening phrase, "In just a little while."

Doing Right and Being Faithful

The explicitly scriptural note in Paul's summary of his gospel in Romans 1:17, when he quotes from Habakkuk, follows up an implicitly scriptural note with which this summary starts. This gospel is a declaration about God's righteousness or God's doing right or God's own faithfulness.

It is the word *dikaiosynē* that is translated "righteousness," but that translation can be misleading. It can suggest personal uprightness and moral integrity. In Romans 3:25 (TNIV), it is translated "justice," which is misleading in another direction. "Justice" suggests acting in accordance with objective moral norms of law in connection with protecting rights and punishing wrongdoers. While both these terms apply to God, they are not what is directly conveyed by *dikaiosynē*, because *dikaiosynē* is Paul's way of referring to the related Hebrew words *tsedeq* and *tsedaqah* in the First Testament.

Key background to Paul's talk about God's *dikaiosynē* is the way Isaiah 40–66 talks about God's *tsedeq/tsedaqah*. The prophecy is speaking of Yahweh's restoring the Judahites, after their rebellion against Yahweh has led to the wrecking of their nation, the destruction of Jerusalem, and the exile of many of their people. The restoring will be an act of *tsedeq/tsedaqah*.

> Listen to me, you who pursue *tsedeq*,
> who seek help from Yahweh. . . .
> In a flash my *tsedeq* is near,
> my deliverance is going out,
> my arm will exercise authority for peoples.
> My deliverance will be permanent,
> my *tsedaqah* will not shatter. . . .
> Listen to me, you who acknowledge my *tsedeq*,
> a people with my instruction in its mind. . . .
> My *tsedaqah* will be permanent,
> my deliverance to all generations. (Isa 51:1, 5–8)

God's restoration of Judah will be an expression of his *tsedeq/tsedaqah*. It will indeed be an expression of his righteousness, his personal integrity, though in a special sense, and it will be an expression of justice, in that they have served their time (Isa 40:2). But the heart of *tsedeq/tsedaqah* lies in doing the right thing by people to whom one has a commitment. It is closer to faithfulness than to righteousness or justice. Yahweh will not restore Judah because Judah deserves restoration, which would make it an act of simple justice. Yahweh will restore Judah because he had made a commitment to his people and has to do the right thing by them in order to be himself.

Yahweh indeed made it possible for exiles to return to Jerusalem, for people to rebuild the city, and for Judah to regain some identity; and by New Testament times the Jewish people more or less occupied the same area as First Testament Israel. Yet the fact that they continued to live under imperial domination meant that they still needed God to fulfill the promises in Isaiah 40–66. Jesus comes to bring that fulfillment. It will take a different form from the one the prophecy will have led them to expect, but it is that faithfulness of God to his purpose for Israel and for the world that the gospel reveals.

Paul's reference to that righteousness or faithfulness of God invites us to read the First Testament as the story of the righteousness or faithfulness of God, of God's doing the right thing by Israel and by the world.

Sin

Paul goes on in Romans 3:9–18 to include a string of quotations about sin.

Jews and Gentiles alike are all under the power of sin. As it is written:

> "There is no one righteous, not even one;
>   there is no one who understands;
>   there is no one who seeks God.
> All have turned away,
>   they have together become worthless;
> there is no one who does good,
>   not even one." [Ps 14:1–3]
>
> "Their throats are open graves;
>   their tongues practice deceit." [Ps 5:9]
>
> "The poison of vipers is on their lips." [Ps 140:3]
>
> "Their mouths are full of cursing and bitterness." [Ps 10:7]

"Their feet are swift to shed blood;
    ruin and misery mark their ways,
and the way of peace they do not know." [Isa 59:7–8]

"There is no fear of God before their eyes." [Ps 36:1]

We make several contrasting and complementary discoveries when we read the Psalms and Isaiah in light of Paul's pointing us in their direction (he is often following the Old Greek translation, but it does not affect the point). On one hand, Paul is talking in general terms about the sinfulness of the world as a whole, whereas the First Testament texts are talking about something more specific. Isaiah 59 began life as a message to the people of Judah in a particular context, sometime in the period covered by Ezra–Nehemiah. It is not a general statement. Likewise these psalms were designed for people to use when they knew themselves surrounded or assailed by people who embodied those negative characteristics that the psalms describe. Paying attention to the text of Isaiah and the psalms means entering into those contexts, identifying with the prophet in his horror at the social and moral state of his people, and identifying with the people for whom the psalms are written, the people who are the victims of the oppressors they describe.

On the other hand, the psalms give no indication of the particular context they come from, and actually the same is true of the prophecy. The location of Isaiah 56–66 following on Isaiah 1–39 (with its specific allusions to Isaiah's own day in the 700s) and Isaiah 40–55 (with its specific allusions to the situation of Judahites in the 540s) encourages us to relate Isaiah 56–66 to the time that follows, which is that period described in Ezra–Nehemiah, a time over the next century; but Isaiah 56–66 makes no specific reference to any people or events of that time. That complementary feature of the chapters encourages us not to limit its reference to one particular time. The chapters relate to how things will continue to be until Yahweh implements the promises that come at the center of this sequence of chapters (that is, Isa 60–62). Likewise the psalms' lack of information about their authorship or date links with the fact that they are not prayers related to one context, like the prayers and praises that appear outside the Psalms in the First Testament. They presuppose that the kind of circumstances they describe, out of which people will need to pray, are recurring ones. (I assume that the introductions to the psalms that describe them as "David's" do not indicate that he wrote them; but even if one assumes he did, they still appear in the

Psalter as prayers for people to use as situations and needs recur.) So Paul's appeal to them alerts us to a complementary aspect of their inherent nature.

Forgiveness

After those quotations from the Psalms about sin, it is interesting that Paul can subsequently appeal to a psalm to back up his declarations about forgiveness. We pick up his argument in Romans 4. Genesis notes that Abraham was right with God on the basis of his trust in him, not on the basis of (for instance) the observance of a rule about circumcision.[5]

> David says the same thing when he speaks of the blessedness of those to whom God credits righteousness apart from works:
>
>> "Blessed are those
>>   whose transgressions are forgiven,
>>   whose sins are covered.
>> Blessed are those
>>   whose sin the Lord will never count against them." [Ps 32:1–2]
>
> Is this blessedness only for the circumcised, or also for the uncircumcised? We have been saying that Abraham's faith was credited to him as righteousness. (Rom 4:6–9)

There is an inbuilt human assumption that when we do something wrong we have to do something to put it right, and it is a good assumption. But a personal relationship has got into trouble if it makes this assumption too basic when things in the relationship need to be put right. The offending party has to say, "Sorry," and mean it and make no excuses; the offended party has to say, "It's okay," and mean it; the offending party has to trust this assurance (and then do something to put things right).

It is how things work between us and God, by us saying, "Sorry," and by God saying, "It's okay"; but Paul knows a lot of believers in Jesus who do not see it that way. They are attached to the idea that we have to do something to put things right between us and God. Abraham's story argues against that assumption. The psalm argues against it more directly. It presupposes that

---

5. See the discussion of "Romans 4" on pp. 17–19 above.

things have gone wrong, and it uses three of the First Testament's images for wrongdoing: rebellion, failure, and waywardness. In the Old Greek and thus in Paul these become transgressions or acts of lawlessness, failures (plural), and failure (singular). (Admittedly, both in Hebrew and in Greek the word for "failure" has become a general-purpose word for wrongdoing, and people may not have been aware of its etymological link with the idea of failure or shortcoming.)

These changes in the images themselves provide another useful illustration of the dynamic involved in the New Testament's references back to the First Testament. Modern readers of the Scriptures commonly read and quote from translations of the Scriptures into their own language even if they know Hebrew or Greek. Similarly a New Testament writer such as Paul who knows Hebrew but is writing in Greek commonly quotes from the Greek translation, and it is this practice that issues in some of the oddities in his references to the First Testament. But as long as we are not too obsessive, the differences and oddities do not really matter, because people can be scriptural even when they quote a questionable translation. Here the Greek translation has *anomia*, which really means lawlessness or transgression, whereas the psalm has *pesha*, the Hebrew word for rebellion (the Greek translation is followed in many English versions). The difference is that one transgresses a law but one rebels against a person. They are different metaphors with different but complementary implications. Now there is a Hebrew word meaning "transgress," *abar*, which Psalm 17:3 (for instance) uses (though many English translations have "sin"!). So once more, Paul makes a point that is not quite the one his text makes, but it is one he could make on the basis of other texts if he were obsessive enough to bother.

Understanding the Mystery

In our study of Romans 9,[6] we did not consider a quotation from Isaiah:

> The Gentiles, who did not pursue righteousness, have obtained it, a righteousness that is by faith; but the people of Israel, who pursued the law as the way of righteousness, have not attained their goal. Why not? Because they pursued it not by faith but as if it were by works. They stumbled over the stumbling stone. As it is written:

6. See pp. 20–28 above.

> "See, I lay in Zion a stone that causes people to stumble
>   and a rock that makes them fall,
>   and the one who believes in him will never be put to shame."
>
> (Rom 9:30–33)

Paul here restates his key point in Romans 1–4 but applies it to the question he has been tackling in Romans 9. His quotation conflates Isaiah 8:14 and 28:16. It again reflects the Greek translation, though not in a way that undermines the significance of the quotation. But the Greek translation's addition "in him" does play into Paul's hands. His appeal to Isaiah in this connection does involve an irony, a sister irony to the one involved in his appeal to Habakkuk 2:4. We do not know what the stone is in Isaiah 28:16: is it the Torah, or the temple, or the Davidic promise, or Jerusalem, or the Messiah, or the remnant, or faith itself, or what?[7]

Beyond Romans 9, Paul continues to use the First Testament as his resource for thinking through the nature of God's dealing with Jews and Gentiles. A key insight is, "Everyone who calls on the name of the Lord will be saved" (Rom 10:13, quoting Joel 2:32)—Jews and Gentiles. For both, it is therefore key that someone should bring the Lord's message to them: thus, "How beautiful are the feet of those who bring good news" (Rom 10:15, quoting Isa 52:7). The trouble is, most of Israel did not listen: "Lord, who has believed our message?" (Rom 10:16, quoting Isa 53:1). This refusal to listen does not alter the fact that they did hear: "Their voice has gone out into all the earth, their words to the end of the world" (Rom 10:18, quoting Ps 19:4). Paul underlines the point with more quotations (Deut 32:21; Isa 65:1–2).

The result has been a situation anticipated by the story of Elijah. When Elijah laments that there are no other faithful people left, God points out the existence of a substantial remnant; such is the case now (Rom 11:1–6, quoting 1 Kgs 19:10, 14, 18). Indeed, God has made it impossible for the majority to see the truth (Rom 11:7–10, quoting Deut 29:4; Isa 29:10; Ps 69:22–23). It is an act of judgment, but it is a means to an act of grace for the Gentiles, and it is not final.

After some expansion on how that can be (Rom 11:13–32),[8] Paul closes his argument with a definitive act of praise:

---

7. Cf. Otto Kaiser, *Isaiah 13–39,* trans. R. A. Wilson, Old Testament Library (Philadelphia: Westminster; London: SCM, 1974), 253.

8. See further the discussion of the olive tree passage on pp. 121–23 above and of the new covenant on pp. 89–92 above.

> Oh, the depth of the riches of the wisdom and knowledge of God!
>> How unsearchable his judgments,
>> and his paths beyond tracing out!
> "Who has known the mind of the Lord?
>> Or who has been his counselor?"
> "Who has ever given to God,
>> that God should repay them?"
> For from him and through him and to him are all things.
>> To him be the glory forever! Amen. (Rom 11:33–36)

The first verse and the last are Paul's own, the second comes from Isaiah 40:13, the third from Job 41:11. It is both a fitting close to the argument of Romans 9–11 and a fitting close to its relationship with the Scriptures, which have constituted Paul's major theological resource for thinking through his question.

Sacrifice

Paul's discussion of forgiveness and his quotation from Psalm 32 suggest a further point. Christians are clear that in the First Testament, forgiveness depends on offering a sacrifice. They are clear, but wrong. Sacrifice is really important, but it is not the way we get forgiveness. Psalm 32 indicates that we get forgiven by our confession, to which God responds in grace, a response in which we trust.

Now Hebrews emphasizes that sacrifices cannot take away sin. Fortunately, they were never designed to do so. They were never the basis on which people were forgiven. Paul has argued on the basis of the Scriptures that forgiveness is not based on something that we do. Indeed, if forgiveness were a response to an offering we made to God, it would not really be forgiveness.

So what is the point of offering sacrifices? Paul mentions several kinds of sacrifice. First, there is the sacrifice God offers, of Jesus himself: "God presented Christ as a sacrifice of atonement, through the shedding of his blood" (Rom 3:25). In Greek, "sacrifice of atonement" is *hilastērion*. New Testament experts disagree about the meaning of that word. I shall start from its meaning in the Greek translation of the First Testament, where it is one way of referring to the lid (Hebrew *kapporet*) on the covenant chest in the wilderness sanctuary, while the related word *hilasmos* is one way of translating the word for "atonement" in the expression "Day of Atonement" (*yom hakkippurim*).

In these contexts, "atonement" signifies expiation or cleansing. Certain things make us taboo in the sense that we cannot go into God's presence in the sanctuary when we are affected by them, because they clash with God's own nature. They include moral wrongdoing but also idolatry as well as contact with death or sex. A sacrifice is one means whereby we may find purification from such taboos. It washes us clean. The Day of Atonement purified the sanctuary from the polluting effect of all the taboos that people may have brought into it over the year. Purification is not all that is required for one to find cleansing (repentance in all its senses would be needed), but the removal of the taboos is one thing that is needed. Such purification is thus different from forgiveness. A wife whose husband had been unfaithful might forgive her husband; but her forgiveness would not in itself remove the stain of his adultery. In John the Baptizer's ministry, people found forgiveness through repentance, but they still needed to plunge into the Jordan. Sacrificing Jesus is God's way of cleansing us from sin.

A second kind of sacrifice is presupposed in Romans 12 when Paul goes on to speak of our offering ourselves to God as a sacrifice. This sacrifice is more like the whole burnt offering in the Torah's system. Noah's sacrifice after the flood, and Abraham's near-sacrifice of Isaac, were burnt offerings. A burnt offering was not designed to be a means of forgiveness or of expiation. It was an act of commitment.

Finally, Paul speaks of himself as a priest making it possible for the Gentiles to be an offering to God (Rom 15:15–16).

Paul thus alerts us to the wide significance of sacrifice in the First Testament, wider than Christians often recognize. On one hand, sacrifice has only an indirect relationship with forgiveness. On the other, sacrifice has as wide a range of significances as worship. It *is* worship. Christian worship costs us nothing; indeed, we may well think that the point of it is what we get out of it. Israel's worship is expressed in a way that costs something.

Prayer

In Romans 15, Paul makes extensive reference to the First Testament in two further connections. The chapter begins,

> We who are strong ought to bear with the failings of the weak and not to please ourselves. We should all please our neighbors for their good, to build them up. For even Christ did not please himself but, as it is written: "The

insults of those who insult you have fallen on me." [Ps 69:9] For everything
that was written in the past was written to teach us, so that through the
endurance taught in the Scriptures and the encouragement they provide we
might have hope. May the God who gives endurance and encouragement
give you the same attitude of mind toward each other that Christ Jesus had,
so that with one mind and one voice you may glorify the God and Father
of our Lord Jesus Christ. (Rom 15:1–6)

Paul once more refers back to Psalm 69, from which he had quoted earlier
in seeking to understand how most of Israel failed to recognize Jesus. God
had given them a spirit of stupor, as the psalm (vv. 22–23) says:

> May their table become a snare and a trap,
>   a stumbling block and a retribution for them.
> May their eyes be darkened so they cannot see,
>   and their backs be bent forever. (Rom 11:9–10)

I have noted that Psalm 69 leaves Western Christians uneasy because of the
bitterness of its prayer, so I find it interesting that it is one of the passages most
often quoted in the New Testament.[9] John 2:17 quotes the previous line in the
psalm and applies it to Jesus. The psalm goes on to pray against the attackers:

> Pour out your condemnation on them;
>   may your angry rage overtake them.
> May their encampment become desolate;
>   may there be no one living in their tents.
> Because you—the person you struck down, they have pursued,
>   and the suffering of the people run through by you, they have
>   heralded.
> Put waywardness on top of their waywardness;
>   may they not come to your faithfulness.
> May they be erased from the document of living people;
>   may they not be written down with the faithful. (Ps 69:24–28)

Maybe Paul and John only noticed the verse they quote and would not have
liked those verses, but it seems unlikely, especially as Acts 1:20 quotes one of
the lines. Paul directs us to the protest psalms and invites us to make them

---

9. See the comments on Acts 1 on pp. 86–87 above.

our prayers. In Romans 8:36, he quotes another of the protest psalms, Psalm 44; and Jesus quotes yet another on the cross when he says, "My God, my God, why have you forsaken me?" (Ps 22:1).

The Gentiles

In Romans 15, Paul goes on,

> Accept one another, then, just as Christ accepted you, in order to bring praise to God. For I tell you that Christ has become a servant of the Jews on behalf of God's truth, so that the promises made to the patriarchs might be confirmed and, moreover, that the Gentiles might glorify God for his mercy. As it is written:

> "Therefore I will praise you among the Gentiles;
>   I will sing the praises of your name." [Ps 18:49]

> Again, it says,

> "Rejoice, you Gentiles, with his people." [Deut 32:43]

> And again,

> "Praise the Lord, all you Gentiles;
>   let all the peoples extol him." [Ps 117:1]

> And again, Isaiah says,

> "The Root of Jesse will spring up,
>   one who will arise to rule over the nations;
>   in him the Gentiles will hope." [Isa 11:10]

> May the God of hope fill you with all joy and peace as you trust in him, so that you may overflow with hope by the power of the Holy Spirit.
>   (Rom 15:7–13)

It is fitting that Paul closes with a reference to Isaiah, because Isaiah has the entire world in its view from more or less the beginning to the very end.

Another "truth" about the First Testament that Christians are quite clear on, but that actually is an untruth, is that the God of the First Testament was interested only in Israel (or that the Israelites thought he was). It is as if we have not noticed that the First Testament begins with God as the God of the whole world and continues with God making a promise to Abraham that is designed to be a means of God blessing all the nations. Now maybe the Israelites often forgot the nature of God's game plan and just thought about themselves (like the church), and in a sense it was no problem if they did so, because God did not give them the job of going out to convert the world. They were designed to be a means of drawing the nations to God simply by being themselves with God in their midst.

But Paul has noted already in Romans 9–11 that the First Testament does keep reminding them of God's intent. It is often said that Deuteronomy is the heart of the First Testament and of its theology, and Deuteronomy is a book that focuses resolutely on Israel itself and ignores the nations except insofar as it talks about God acting in judgment upon them. So Deuteronomy might have accidentally encouraged Israel not to keep in mind God's concern for the nations. But one of Paul's quotations in Romans 15 (v. 10) indicates that even Deuteronomy cannot end without an invitation to the nations to rejoice with God's people. The Greek translation of Deuteronomy 32:43 invites the heavens rather than the Gentiles to rejoice; it is interesting that this time Paul quotes the Hebrew text.

That the Greek version of Deuteronomy refers to the heavens adds importance to the Psalms' many exhortations to the Gentiles to praise the God of Israel. They are to praise God because he is the creator of the whole world and the God of the whole world, because he is sovereign over the whole world, because what he has done for Israel is significant for them, and just because he is God. The invitation to them is largely rhetorical in that few Gentiles actually heard it. But it kept reminding Israel that he was the God of the entire world, and it kept urging Israel to keep the whole world in its perspective.

So Paul's further clue to a faithful reading of the First Testament is: Watch for the expressions of God's concern for the whole world.

4.5 Hebrews: Through the Prophets, through the Son

Hebrews uses the First Testament to illumine who Jesus is and what he did in a denser way than any other part of the New Testament. It begins with one of the New Testament's most illuminating observations about the relationship of Jesus to the First Testament:

> In the past God spoke to our ancestors through the prophets at many times and in various ways, but in these last days he has spoken to us by his Son.
> (Heb 1:1–2)

In other words, what we get in Jesus is unique, something the First Testament does not give us. The new thing is not that the New Testament tells us some new truths about God. It is that it tells us the story of God's embodiment in Jesus, how he embodies the different truths about God that God gave Israel in various ways and various times.[10] He is the Son of God. He realizes our human destiny. He is the priest who opens the gate into eternal life for us.

Jesus the Son of God

After that introduction, Hebrews goes on to describe Jesus as the one whom God

> appointed heir of all things, and through whom also he made the universe. The Son is the radiance of God's glory and the exact representation of his being, sustaining all things by his powerful word. After he had provided purification for sins, he sat down at the right hand of the Majesty in heaven. So he became as much superior to the angels as the name he has inherited is superior to theirs. (1:2–4)

The argument that follows uses the Scriptures in a way parallel to the one in Matthew 1:18–2:23.[11] Jesus came and behaved in a way that made clear to anyone who was prepared to look that he was the embodiment of God. He manifested God's characteristics (love and compassion combined with a willingness to be tough) and God's power (stilling storms, creating food). But there were apparently people who recognized that there was something supernatural about him but who thought of him as a superangel rather than as divine. Hebrews knows that such a characterization will not do and looks back into the Scriptures for ways of talking about him:

10. See the discussion of "In Many Ways and in His Son" on pp. 110–11 above.
11. See pp. 61–74 above.

For to which of the angels did God ever say,

> "You are my Son;
>> today I have become your Father"?

Or again,

> "I will be his Father,
>> and he will be my Son"?

And again, when God brings his firstborn into the world, he says,

> "Let all God's angels worship him."

In speaking of the angels he says,

> "He makes his angels spirits,
>> and his servants flames of fire."

But about the Son he says,

> "Your throne, O God, will last for ever and ever;
>> a scepter of justice will be the scepter of your kingdom.
> You have loved righteousness and hated wickedness;
>> therefore God, your God, has set you above your companions
>> by anointing you with the oil of joy."

He also says,

> "In the beginning, Lord, you laid the foundations of the earth,
>> and the heavens are the work of your hands.
> They will perish, but you remain;
>> they will all wear out like a garment.
> You will roll them up like a robe;
>> like a garment they will be changed.
> But you remain the same,
>> and your years will never end."

To which of the angels did God ever say,

> "Sit at my right hand
>   until I make your enemies a footstool for your feet"? (Heb 1:5–13)

Hebrews 1 incorporates a number of quotations from psalms about the king (Pss 2, 45, and 110) and a phrase from God's promise to David about his successors as king (2 Sam 7:14), all of which talk about the king as God's son and about the king being invited to sit at God's right hand. What they say thus contrasts with the other statements about the angels and creation. The first set of passages refers to the kings of David's line whom God adopted as sons. Hebrews knows that Jesus is God's Son (not just an angel) in his own being. It is not just a metaphor—or it is a metaphor operating at another level.

Jesus Realizing Humanity's Destiny

The First Testament thus helps in the articulation of the real nature of who Jesus is. The application to Jesus comes first and it generates the interpretation of the passages, but they then generate insight. Hebrews is not simply reading things into the texts; it is discovering things from them as a result of approaching them in the way it does.

The same dynamic continues as Hebrews goes on to hint at its own way of expressing the basis for this approach. Jesus makes it possible to be saved from God's wrath.

> This salvation, which was first announced by the Lord, was confirmed to us by those who heard him. God also testified to it by signs, wonders and various miracles, and by gifts of the Holy Spirit distributed according to his will. (Heb 2:3–4)

It then takes further the argument for Jesus's not being a superangel on the basis of his being the one to whom God has subjected the world to come. In this connection it quotes another psalm:

> What are mere mortals that you are mindful of them,
>   human beings that you care for them?
> You made them a little lower than the angels;

you crowned them with glory and honor
and put everything under their feet. (Heb 2:6–8, quoting Ps 8:4–6)

We can see that this does not apply to humanity as a whole, Hebrews comments. But it does apply to Jesus. And he has made us his brothers and sisters. So in the words of some other First Testament passages,

He says,

"I will declare your name to my brothers and sisters;
in the assembly I will sing your praises."

And again,

"I will put my trust in him."

And again he says,

"Here am I, and the children God has given me."
(Heb 2:12–13, quoting Ps 22:22; Isa 8:17–18)

So there are three passages not about the king, but one about all humanity, one a psalm that anyone could pray, and one about Isaiah himself. Again, Hebrews says, look at Jesus in light of these passages.

Jesus the Priest

Most prominent in Hebrews is its looking at Jesus in light of the First Testament priesthood. Hebrews faces a problem in calling Jesus a priest. He belongs to the wrong clan. A man could either be a Levite and be a priest, or he could be a Judahite and be in the kingly line. He could not be both. Hebrews solves the problem by referring to another First Testament priesthood, that of Melchizedek. Melchizedek was the priest-king of Salem (Jerusalem; Gen 14). By virtue of becoming king in Jerusalem, David inherited Melchizedek's priesthood. Early in its exposition of Jesus's priesthood, then, Hebrews repeats its earlier quotation from Psalm 2 and then adds another line from Psalm 110: "You are a priest forever, in the order of Melchizedek" (Heb 5:6).

Hebrews goes on to tell Melchizedek's story from Genesis in such a way as to suggest that his priesthood was more notable than Levi's anyway. Levi's priesthood could not bring people perfection or maturity, Hebrews says, which explains why people needed the new Melchizedek priesthood that Jesus embodied. On the basis of a single "sacrifice" it could give people eternal life. It turns out that the earthly sanctuary was a copy and shadow of the heavenly one into which Jesus has entered on our behalf; after all, Moses was told to build it according to the pattern he was given (Exod 25:40). In the First Testament, people died, and that was it. The sacrifices had only a limited efficacy. The law about sacrifices was "only a shadow of the good things that are coming"; after all, "it is impossible for the blood of bulls and goats to take away sins" (Heb 10:1, 4). As a result of Jesus's sacrifice, people can enter the heavenly sanctuary when they die. He obtains "eternal redemption" for us; we receive an "eternal inheritance" (Heb 9:12, 15).

So Jesus mediates a new covenant.

The days are coming, declares the Lord,
    when I will make a new covenant
with the house of Israel
    and with the house of Judah.
It will not be like the covenant
    I made with their ancestors
when I took them by the hand
    to lead them out of Egypt,
because they did not remain faithful to my covenant,
    and I turned away from them, declares the Lord.
This is the covenant I will establish with the house of Israel
    after that time, declares the Lord.
I will put my laws in their minds
    and write them on their hearts.
I will be their God,
    and they will be my people.
No longer will they teach their neighbors,
    or say to one another, "Know the Lord,"
because they will all know me,
    from the least of them to the greatest.
For I will forgive their wickedness
    and will remember their sins no more.

(Heb 8:8–12, quoting Jer 31:31–34)

Hebrews makes clear enough elsewhere that God has not yet written his laws into people's minds in a way that makes teaching unnecessary; but the subsequent repetition of the last sentence, followed by the comment that therefore no more sacrifice for sin is needed (Heb 10:17–18), suggests that the emphasis in this quotation lies there on God's forgiveness, not on that other aspect of the new covenant.

Approaching the First Testament from the angle of Hebrews generates two insights. First, Hebrews emphasizes the wonder of the fact that Jesus's death and resurrection "opened unto us the gate of everlasting life."[12] It correctly emphasizes that the First Testament holds no hope of eternal life before people. Second, Hebrews correctly notes that the sacrifices prescribed in the First Testament could not deal with sin and thus could not do anything for people with a guilty conscience. It looks as if there were people in its purview who thought they could do so.

Hebrews thereby makes us ask why God wanted people to offer these sacrifices. Its implicit answer is that they foreshadowed the sacrifice of Christ. But like typology, of which it is an aspect, talk in terms of foreshadowing works only retrospectively, from the reality backward. The rules about sacrifice themselves gave no indication that they foreshadowed something else. Indeed, the rules are thin on explicit explanation of their rationale. Perhaps they assumed that everybody knew. The sacrifices are a familiar enough feature of the life of many traditional cultures. The rules are designed to make sure that Israelites offered the sacrifices in the right way. One might compare the rules for worship in a document such as the Episcopal Church's *Book of Common Prayer*.[13]

4.6 Revelation: Hardly a Verse without an Allusion

It has been said that there is hardly a verse in Revelation that directly quotes the First Testament but also that there is a hardly a verse that would survive if the First Testament allusions were taken out of it. I shall proceed by looking at three sample sections of the book that describe, respectively, the beast arising from the sea, the fall of Babylon, and the new Jerusalem.

---

12. From the collect for Easter Day in the Church of England *Book of Common Prayer*.
13. On the significance of the sacrifices in their own right, see pp. 143–44 above.

Revelation 13:1–10: The Beast out of the Sea

The main First Testament background to Revelation 13 lies in Daniel 7–12. The first of these visions in Daniel describes "the four winds of the heavens stirring up the Great Sea, and four huge animals coming up out of the sea, each different from the others." The fourth animal was

> fearsome, terrifying, and extremely powerful. It had huge iron teeth, de-vouring, crushing, and trampling what was left with its feet. It was different from all the animals that were before it. It had ten horns. I looked at the horns, and there—another small horn came up among them, and three of the first horns were uprooted before it. And there—something like human eyes in this horn, and a mouth speaking great things. (Dan 7:2–8)

In Revelation the four animals become one animal, with features like the four, with ten horns but seven heads, and the mouth speaking arrogantly. In Daniel the last king symbolized by the horns is allowed to exercise authority for "a period, periods, and half a period" (Dan 7:25), and in Revelation the animal similarly does so for forty-two months (Rev 13:5).

We have noted that Daniel 7 is the first of a series of revelations about Middle Eastern history during the Babylonian, Median, Persian, and Greek empires.[14] The visions focus on the Greek period, the rule of the Seleucid and Ptolemaic dynasties in Syria and Egypt, Judah being caught between them. In the 160s BC, Judah was under Seleucid domination, and the Seleucid king, Antiochus IV, banned observance of the Torah's rulings about worship in the Jerusalem temple and introduced a form of worship that suited his garrison. This action provoked a rebellion on the part of Jews who were committed to the Torah. The visions in Daniel describe the action of Antiochus, and promise that God will put the despot down and restore God's sovereignty over the Jewish people. Against all odds, the rebels succeed in seeing Antiochus off, and Judah gained a freedom that it then held for a century, until the arrival of the Romans.

Typically, God's promises were thus fulfilled, but not in a final way; hence Jewish people in Jesus's day were still looking for the restoration of Israel. They read back in Daniel's usefully symbolic (not to say cryptic) visions and found they could apply them to their own day. In Daniel 7, four creatures emerge from the sea, of which the fourth stands for Greece. In Jewish think-ing in Jesus's day, the fourth creature comes to stand for Rome. An apocalypse

14. See the discussion of Daniel on pp. 58–59 above.

called 2 Esdras, which somewhat resembles Revelation and has its origin in about the same time, explains that the fourth creature in Daniel stands for Rome, but it acknowledges that this was not the understanding of its author and first readers (for whom it stood for Greece). The New Testament likewise looks at the Roman persecution of its day in light of Daniel's vision that in itself focuses on events in the 160s. Many of the details in John's vision take up features of Daniel's vision: the ten horns, the seven heads, the characterization of the creatures, the way the dragon talks big, the forty-two months.

Daniel implies that the Middle Eastern empires are all variants on the same reality—they are all creatures that arise out of the turbulent sea, an image for tumultuous forces working against God's purpose. Revelation then suggests looking at Daniel on the assumption that this pattern of events continues. It is not that the Turks or the Russians or the English or the Americans simply *are* the fourth creature to which Daniel refers. But they are or can be further embodiments of this dynamic.

Further, while the deliverance from Antiochus did constitute a fulfillment of Daniel's vision, it did not issue in the permanent implementing of God's reign (Dan 7:27). What did happen showed that the vision really came from God and invited the people of God to keep looking for a more complete fulfillment.

Revelation 18: The Fall of Babylon

It might seem surprising that the First Testament includes no account of the actual fall of Babylon to the Persians in 539—or of the earlier fall of Assyria or the later fall of Persia or of Seleucid rule in Jerusalem (the last does come in 1 Maccabees). But its declarations about coming disaster prove strangely useful in a context where Revelation promises the fall of the Babylon of its own day. The First Testament background to Revelation 18 lies in the proclamation of the coming fall of Babylon in Isaiah 13–14, 47, and Jeremiah 50–51, and the coming fall of Tyre in Ezekiel 26–28.

> Ah, you have fallen from the heavens,
> > bright one, son of dawn!
> You have been felled to the earth,
> > enfeebler of nations! (Isa 13:12)

> Get down, sit in the dirt, young Miss Babel,
> > sit on the ground without a throne, Miss Chaldean. . . .

You said, "I shall be here permanently,
    mistress always."
You did not receive these things into your mind;
    you were not mindful of its outcome.
So now listen to this, charming one,
    who sits in confidence,
who says to herself,
    "I and none else am still here,
I shall not sit as a widow,
    I shall not know the loss of children."
The two of these will come to you,
    in a moment, on one day.
The loss of children and widowhood
    in full measure will have come upon you. (Isa 47:1, 7–9)

Adopting the imagery and words used by the prophets to describe the imminent fall of Babylon, Revelation declares in anticipation that the Babylon of its day is fallen, notwithstanding its own conviction that it would never lose its throne. Urging its readers to get out of the city so as not to be implicated in its sins, Revelation takes up words from Jeremiah:

Get out from inside it, my people;
    each of you save his life
    from Yahweh's angry blaze. (Jer 51:45)

The details in John's vision recycle other elements from the prophets (not only visions that relate to Babylon): the land turned into a haunt for wild creatures, the chalice that brings madness to the nation that drinks from it and now passes it to Babylon. The motif of sea trade and wealth from sea trade that appears in the Tyre prophecy in Ezekiel 26–28 especially suits Rome, and Revelation 18 goes on to utilize it.

Who was like Tyre,
    like the one silenced in the middle of the sea?
When your wares went out from the seas,
    you filled many peoples.
With the quantity of your wealth and your merchandise
    you enriched earth's kings. . . .
All the inhabitants of foreign shores

are desolate over you.
Their kings bristled with horror,
    their faces went dark.
The dealers among the peoples whistled at you;
    you became a horror, and you are no more, permanently.

(Ezek 27:32–36)

Revelation 21: The New Jerusalem

I saw a new heaven and a new earth, for the first heaven and the first earth had passed away, and there was no longer any sea. I saw the Holy City, the new Jerusalem, coming down out of heaven from God, prepared as a bride beautifully dressed for her husband. And I heard a loud voice from the throne saying, "Look! God's dwelling place is now among the people, and he will dwell with them. They will be his people, and God himself will be with them and be their God. 'He will wipe every tear from their eyes. There will be no more death' or mourning or crying or pain, for the old order of things has passed away." (Rev 21:1–4)

The new heavens and the new earth, and the new Jerusalem, first appear in Isaiah.

Because here I am, creating
    new heavens and a new earth.
The earlier ones will not be recollected;
    they will not come into mind.
Rather, be glad and celebrate permanently
    what I am creating.
Because here I am, creating Jerusalem as reason for celebration
    and its people as reason for gladness.
I will celebrate Jerusalem
    and be glad in my people.
There will not make itself heard in it any more
    the sound of weeping or the sound of a cry. (Isa 65:17–19)

In Isaiah, the new heavens and the new earth *are* the new Jerusalem, or vice versa. The new world is embodied in the new city. It is quite a physical and sensible city. Its wonder lies in the way people live out their lifespan instead of dying in infancy or in youth, and are able to enjoy the fruits of their work by living in the houses they build and eating the fruit of the trees they plant (and relaxing under their vine and their fig tree, as prophets elsewhere put it). It is hard to know how physical and sensible is Revelation's new Jerusalem, though probably more so than Christians often assume—more so than the average picture of heaven. Revelation adds that there will be no more sea in this new world, thus also recycling an image from Daniel 7.

Those verses from Revelation 21 incorporate a further motif from earlier in Isaiah:

> Yahweh of Armies will make
>> for all peoples on this mountain
> a banquet with rich foods, a banquet with aged wines,
>> juicy rich foods, refined aged wines.
> He will swallow up on this mountain the layer of wrapping,
>> the wrapping over all the peoples,
> the covering that is spread out over all the nations;
>> he will have swallowed up death permanently.
> The Lord Yahweh will wipe the tears
>> from on all faces. (Isa 25:6–8)

Revelation 21 goes on to describe the new Jerusalem in terms derived from the vision of the new city in Isaiah 60–62 and also in Ezekiel 40–48. Ezekiel stands between Isaiah and Revelation on the line between material/sensible and figurative/otherworldly. In contrast to Ezekiel, in Revelation not only is there no sea (from which beasts could arise), there is no temple, because God is there. In Ezekiel the promise is that there will be a temple, because God will be there.

4.7 The Theology of the First Testament in the New Testament

If the New Testament treats the First Testament as its major resource for a theological perspective or context for understanding Jesus, it directs us to a study of First Testament concepts, motifs, and images. In this section we look in outline at the First Testament's understanding of God, the world, humanity, Israel, the nations, and the future.[15]

---

15. See further my *Old Testament Theology,* 3 vols. (Downers Grove, IL: InterVarsity Press; Carlisle, UK: Paternoster, 2003–2009).

God

So who is the God who is incarnate in Jesus? The New Testament gives no indication that Jesus reveals things about God that Israel did not know before. Rather he brings a personal embodiment of the God whom Israel did know or could have known. In Jesus, God speaks in one person who embodies Israel's variegated revelation (Heb 1:1).[16] That fact matches the fundamental First Testament affirmation, "Yahweh our God Yahweh one" (Deut 6:4).[17]

The correlation between the "one" and the "Yahweh" is important. Neither Testament is interested in monotheism as such—in the mere idea that there is only one God. What they are interested in is that Yahweh is the one God. They quite accept that there are lots of gods (with a lower-case *g*; we are fortunate that we can make the distinction that way in English, as neither Hebrew nor New Testament Greek do), and through most of the First Testament period many Israelites had a hard time seeing that Yahweh was so different from other gods. But the First Testament itself acknowledges throughout that Yahweh is God in a unique sense; other supernatural beings are his underlings and agents.

A paradoxical way to make the point is to note that Yahweh is the holy one. It is paradoxical because other Middle Eastern peoples saw all the gods as holy ones, even though they behaved in ways we would think were unholy. The word for "holy" in Hebrew and related languages is in origin a metaphysical term, not a moral one. It originally denoted "supernatural." Yahweh is then the sole truly supernatural one.

It is the one God Yahweh with his variegated revelation who is then embodied in the one Jesus. As a result, and to put it another way, whereas the Torah came through Moses, grace and truth came through Jesus (John 1:17). John's point, too, is hardly that the Israelites did not know that God was the God of grace and truth. God was showing himself to be the God of grace and truth through Israel's story, and these terms are among the ones God uses in his classic self-description on Sinai:

> Yahweh, God compassionate and gracious, long-tempered, big in commitment and truthfulness, preserving commitment toward the thousands,

---

16. See pp. 110–11 and 147–51 above.

17. Hebrew has no word exactly equivalent to English "is," so it is impossible to be sure where to put "is" in that expression. Cf., e.g., New Revised Standard Version: "The Lord is our God, the Lord alone"; TNIV: "the Lord our God, the Lord is one."

carrying waywardness, rebellion, and wrongdoing; he certainly does not treat people as free of guilt, attending to parents' waywardness in connection with children and with grandchildren, with thirds and with fourths.

(Exod 34:6–7)

Yahweh is God of love, and love comes first in his list of characteristics; and what love means is compassion, grace, long-temperedness, and so on. Yet he is not simply God of love. He is capable of taking action against people for their waywardness. Both Testaments see him as acting in wrath. Further, he redefines what holiness means, because he, the sole holy one, is the one who embodies love and toughness. Because he is who he is, holiness comes to have the moral connotations that we attach to it. It is in these qualities, too, that his majesty and glory lie: glory is the visible or external expression of holiness.

The dominant love and the subsidiary wrath express themselves through Israel's story. The story also reveals that he is the living and active God, the God who speaks and does things. It is love that creates the world, makes promises to Abraham, gets the Israelites out of Egypt, gets them into Canaan despite their rebellion, and keeps them going century after century despite their unfaithfulness. From time to time Yahweh says, "That's it!" and acts in wrath. But most centuries go by with Yahweh simply absorbing the effect of their unfaithfulness. He pays the price for the relationship. When Jesus becomes a human being and lets himself be executed for their benefit, he is embodying the way God has behaved in relation to them over the centuries, and giving them an even more vivid and inescapable sense of the way he has let himself be treated.

The World

God made the world and it belongs to him. While the First Testament story starts from its creation by God, this theme is much more prominent in other parts of the First Testament such as Psalms and Job, where as much interest attaches to the world in its ongoing nature as to its origins in God's creative activity.

The creation comprises the heavens and the earth, the one chiefly the abode of God and of the gods, the other the abode of humanity and of the animal world. Humanity thus shares the earth with the animal world. It is evident that the animal world does not exist for humanity's sake, and it was not originally designed to satisfy our appetites. If anything, we were created for the sake of the animal world and the garden that God laid out. But God does provide for us through the world; plants feed us and some animals can help us. Thus we can pray for our material provision as well as work for it.

Throughout, the First Testament marvels at the world's majestic wonder and also at its goodness and graciousness as a gift from God. The world evidences God's commitment to what he has created, including humanity:

> Yahweh, your commitment is in the heavens,
>   your truthfulness reaches as far as the skies.
> Your faithfulness is like supernatural mountains,
>   your authority is like the great deep.
> Human being and animal you deliver, Yahweh;
>   how valuable is your commitment.
> Divine beings and human beings
>   take shelter in the shadow of your wings.
> They feast on the richness of your house,
>   you let them drink from your lovely wadi.
> Because with you there is a living spring;
>   in your light we see light. (Ps 36:5–9)

Implicit in this description is a conviction about the order, regularity, and security of the world as God created it and maintains it. God created the world with the capacity to reproduce apparently on its own. Yet its life is continually dependent on God. Its security comes from God's continuing involvement with it rather than its own inherent robustness.

The world is capable of worshiping God. Worship is something we do with our bodies and voices, not just with our minds, and in these respects the world has what is needed to glorify God with its worship. At the same time, the First Testament recognizes the world's volatility and its forces' capacity to overwhelm humanity. Darkness gave way to light at the beginning, but light gives way to darkness each evening. Nature can be a threat to humanity and a means of God acting against humanity. Indeed, the first temptation came to humanity from one of the creatures that God had made (Gen 3:1), and the result of humanity yielding to temptation is that our life and work in the world are tougher than they were designed to be.

While the First Testament recognizes that the world is not totally submitted to God, it does not suggest that the world is fallen but rather that it has not reached its destiny of submission to God. Though the creation was clearly very good, paradoxically it was not finished. Humanity was designed to be the means of taking it to its destiny, but we yielded to it and joined it in its insubordination rather than pushing it toward that submission.

Humanity

The classic First Testament starting point for understanding humanity is the declaration that humanity is made in God's image, but like much of Genesis 1–3, Genesis 1:26–27 is an allusive and overinterpreted text. The common use of the Latinism *imago Dei* hints that the meaning of that expression in theological discussion emerges from the discussion itself rather than from Genesis.

Genesis gives no hint that the most important things about humanity is that we are made for a relationship with God. Rather the most important thing about us is that we are made to subdue and serve the creation for God's sake, though the pattern of God's activity hints at a point about this activity that will later become explicit: work is not the be-all and end-all of our lives. Perhaps a better way to put it is to say that we are indeed made for a relationship with God, namely the relationship of servants to a committed and caring master. We are created to be God's servants, and God's servants are designed to live by a rhythm of working and stopping, like their master.

A human being as a sole individual hardly exists. In Genesis 1, humanity was created male and female; and in Genesis 2, the man was left as the sole individual for only enough time to discover that he needed someone other than animals to help him fulfill his vocation. The one-to-one relationship of a man and a woman yields to expansion into the nuclear family and the extended family, the local community and the city, the people and the nation. It is not merely that individuals are relational beings. It is that the group is as real as the individual. We are who we are as part of groups. Our obligations and our security work out through our being members of groups. Our natural blessings and our moral constraints issue from our being members of groups. Such relationships are not only horizontal, embracing people living at the same time. They are also vertical; they involve relationships that run through the generations. The blessings and the sins of the parents involve the next generation, and the one after that, and the one after that. We do not lose responsibility because we are one with previous generations. We are responsible for our own decisions. But we come to these decisions as members of vertical as well as horizontal communities.

The individual person comprises an element we can see and feel, and an element we cannot see or feel (the heart or the mind or the soul). There is an outer person and an inner person. Both are equally important to the person, and they are interdependent. In certain circumstances they can operate separately. In a vision or a dream or a daydream, the mind can be in a different place from the body. But in the full sense the heart or soul or mind cannot exist without the body, and the body is a mere corpse without the heart or mind or soul. Life and love and worship involve the whole person.

Death thus involves the whole person. Humanity was created with a view to eating from the tree of life and living a new, resurrection-style life; but we chose another, forbidden tree and thus forfeited access to the life tree. The results of that disobedience abound through the First Testament story and find expression in rebellion against God, failure to fulfill our vocation in the world, and selfishness and faithlessness to one another. These negative qualities manifest themselves in our lives as individuals and in our corporate life in marriages, families, communities, and nations.

And our lives end in death. The First Testament is strangely accepting of this fact. If we have the chance to live a full life, then we can accept its coming to an end. On the other hand, many people do not get the chance to live a full life, and the First Testament does chafe over that fact. It recognizes that suffering can make us face ways in which we have gone wrong, or test what we are really made of, or give us a chance to grow. But suffering may also not clearly have any positive function, and therefore it makes us cry out to God in protest, though possibly only to hear God say, "Tough; the world does not revolve around you; you have to accept the evidence you have that I am trustworthy even when you cannot understand me" (see Job).

Israel

The entire world is the horizon of the First Testament's concern. Yahweh's purpose embraces the whole world. But having failed to tame humanity as a whole, Yahweh devised a new strategy, to start with one person and one family and one people who would form a bridgehead into the world as a whole. The idea would not be that they would actively reach out to the world but that Yahweh would so bless them that the world would be drawn to their God. To this end, Yahweh's people needed to be distinguishable from other peoples and in a sense separate from them, though also open to other people choosing to join them. Such was Israel's position.

As a family, Israel is a place of learning, and specifically a place to learn who Yahweh is and how life with Yahweh works. And as a people chosen as Yahweh's special possession in the world, Israel's responsiveness and submission to Yahweh would be required if they were to become Yahweh's poster child.

The relationship between Yahweh and Israel was thus covenantal, though being covenantal can take different forms. It starts as a covenant commitment on Yahweh's part that simply involves an act of sovereignty and grace whereby Yahweh makes promises to this family. When Yahweh has taken action to deliver the people from serfdom in Egypt, Yahweh renegotiates the arrangement so that it becomes a two-sided covenant that involves Israel accepting a reciprocal commitment to Yahweh in response to his grace. The complicating result is that the covenant can now be imperiled by Israel's failure to maintain its side of the commitment.

This family is chosen by Yahweh for real privilege, but chosen in an inclusive, not an exclusive, way: its choice is designed to be a means of including other people, not of excluding them. It is not chosen on the basis of being worthy of choice; the First Testament emphasizes that there was nothing to commend Israel over other peoples. The notion of choice relates to a people, not to individuals, though Yahweh also chooses individuals, such as Moses and David, with a view to using them in specific ways.

Yahweh's deliverance of Israel from Egypt turns Israel into Yahweh's kingdom and Yahweh's servant. It is a kingdom because Yahweh, not Pharaoh, is the great king, and also Israel's king, as his fight with Pharaoh demonstrated. It means that the idea of Israel having kings compromises the fact that Yahweh is Israel's king. Israel is a servant because this king had taken hold of Israel as an entity to serve him—again in contrast to the idea of Israel serving Pharaoh.

As Yahweh's people, Israel becomes the people of the land promised to Abraham. Paradoxically, Israel's destiny to be the means of blessing the nations is to come about through its displacement of the nation that was then occupying this land, though the displacement (like the victory over the Egyptians) comes about because that nation had earned its fate, not simply because it was in the way. This country becomes Yahweh's home and the context in which Yahweh acts, speaks, and listens. The presence, speaking, and listening come to be focused in a sanctuary in its capital. But Israel's rather consistent failure to give Yahweh its covenantal response leads to Yahweh's abandonment of that home and to his allowing the nations to devastate it.

It is against this background that Yahweh reaffirms the people's status as his servant who is to be the means of announcing his purpose in a world that is looking for some insight on what the world is about and who is at work in it (Isa 42:1–9). That commission is clarified when Israel has made the move from essentially focusing on being the people of a particular land to being a people dispersed through the world, even while aware that that land is its homeland.

The Nations

The development of the world of nations is an outworking of God's creation of humanity. Thus the Psalms frequently invite or challenge the nations to worship Yahweh as king, as deliverer, and as provider, and to acknowledge Israel as Yahweh's people and Israel's king as their real king.

But from the beginning this world of nations was inclined to resist the destiny God had in mind for it. Israel's own history unfolds against the background of the imperial nations that assert themselves as its overlords but sometimes can be its protectors, and of little nations that surround it and can be both threats and allies.

Broadly, the superpowers (Egypt, Assyria, Babylon, Persia, Greece) are entities that pretend to a position in the world that makes them its real rulers. Though they nominally acknowledge the gods, they do not see them as the key players in the world. The Assyrians make the point most explicit (see Isa 36–37). It is explicit in another way when the king of Babylon is portrayed as like a subordinate deity making an assault on the throne of the real top god and being thrown down even from his subordinate position, so that he comes to a shameful end (Isa 14).

The superpowers' interest lies in their own power and in their being able to carve out an empire in order to make themselves wealthier. As far as Yahweh is concerned, they too are his servants—the point is most explicit in Jeremiah with regard to Babylon. The bad news for Israel is that as his servant it can be the means of his bringing trouble to Israel because of its turning to other deities. They invade Israel for their own reasons, but without realizing it they are Yahweh's agents. Because they are acting aggressively and arrogantly for their own aggrandizement rather than seeking to serve Yahweh, Yahweh will act in wrath against them, too, in due course. Yahweh can also use them as his servants to positive ends: he gets Cyrus to commission Judahites to return to Jerusalem to rebuild the temple. Or the story of the empires can simply be one that has no positive meaning, as it is in Daniel's visions.

Yahweh's bringing down the superpower (Egypt, followed by Assyria, Babylon, Persia, and Greece) is good news for little Israel and for the other little peoples that are Israel's neighbors. They are naturally inclined to think that they need to safeguard and protect their own destinies, and Israel is then inclined to look at things the same way and either to fear them or to treat them as potential allies in resistance to the superpower of the day, instead of making Yahweh the object of its fear and its trust.

Yahweh made humanity as a whole, and the development of the nations fitted his purpose for humanity to govern and serve his creation. He still has a positive purpose for them. Even when the First Testament speaks of catastrophe coming on them, it commonly adds a note of hope. Like Israel, they are faced with a choice. They can acknowledge Yahweh now and evade disaster. Or they may experience disaster but may then find restoration. Isaiah says of Israel's great original oppressor:

> On that day, there will be five towns in the country of Egypt speaking the tongue of Canaan and taking oaths to Yahweh of Armies. . . .
>
> On that day there will be an altar for Yahweh in the middle of the country of Egypt and a column for Yahweh at its border. It will be a sign and a testimony for Yahweh of Armies in the country of Egypt; when they cry out to Yahweh before oppressors, he will send them someone to deliver and argue, and he will rescue them.
>
> Yahweh will cause himself to be acknowledged by the Egyptians, and the Egyptians will acknowledge Yahweh on that day. They will serve with sacrifice and offering, and make pledges to Yahweh and make good on them. Yahweh will strike Egypt, striking but healing, and they will turn back to Yahweh, and he will let himself be entreated by them and will heal them.
>
> On that day there will be a causeway from Egypt to Assyria. Assyria will come to Egypt, and Egypt to Assyria. Egypt will serve with Assyria.
>
> On that day Israel will be the third for Egypt and for Assyria, a blessing in the middle of the earth, because Yahweh of Armies has blessed it, saying, "Blessed be my people Egypt, my handiwork Assyria, and my domain Israel." (Isa 19:18–25)

The Future

If the First Testament has an overview term for the destiny that lies ahead of Israel and the nations, it is "Yahweh's day." In the earliest occurrence of the expression (Amos 5), the prophet makes clear that people think of Yahweh's day as a coming day of great blessing. In effect, it will be the fulfillment of God's promise of blessing to Abraham. But Amos knows that the rebellious and wayward state of the people means that the day when Yahweh acts has to be a day of calamity, not a day of blessing. The end is coming (Amos 8:2).

Amos is proved right. The day of disaster comes, and Assyria puts the northern kingdom of Israel out of business. This does not exactly mean that its people cease to exist. While many get exiled, many doubtless return to their homes when the Assyrian army is gone, others move to live in Judah, and Assyria imports people from other countries to form a new community as an Assyrian colony that continues to exist as Samaria into the Second Temple period. So Yahweh's day arrives, but it is not simply "the end." A century or so later, the same dynamic unfolds in Judah. Prophets such as Ezekiel declare that the day of Yahweh, or the end, is coming on Judah (Ezek 7:2–6; 13:5). The Babylonians do put the kingdom of Judah out of business and exile its leaders. Lamentations thus grieves for the end coming on Jerusalem:

> The adversaries saw her,
> > made fun of her coming to an end. (Lam 1:7)
> You brought about the day you called for—
> > they should be like me. (1:21)
> He was not mindful of his footstool
> > on his day of anger. (2:2)
> On Yahweh's day of anger
> > there was no one escaping or surviving. (2:22)
> Our end was near, our days were full,
> > because our end had come. (4:18)

The threat that applies to Israel applies to the nations. Isaiah and Jeremiah proclaim Babylon's downfall:

> Howl, because Yahweh's day is near;
> > like destruction from the Destroyer it comes. (Isa 13:6)

167

You who dwell by much water, abundant in storehouses,
>   your end has come, the time for your cutting off. (Jer 51:13)

So Yahweh's day is the day when Yahweh's purpose is spectacularly put into effect, but in this connection it can be a day of blessing or a day of disaster. Further, while it may sound as if it denotes a final day after which there is simply nothing, life does go on, and after half a century Yahweh enables Judah to start finding its way into new life. For the other nations, too, Yahweh makes clear that the end need not be *the* end. The day of blessing or trouble is a partial embodiment of the End with a capital *E*, yet history continues. On the other hand, Yahweh's purpose had a beginning, and it will have an end in a new heavens and a new earth, embodied in a new Jerusalem, where

>   There will not make itself heard in it any more
>   the sound of weeping or the sound of a cry. . . .
>   They will build houses and dwell [in them],
>   they will plant vineyards and eat their fruit.
>   They will not build and another dwell;
>   they will not plant and another eat.
>   The days of my people will be like a tree's days;
>   my chosen ones will use up the work of their hands.
>   They will not toil with empty result;
>   they will not give birth with fearful outcome.
>   Because they will be offspring blessed by Yahweh,
>   they and their descendants with them.
>   Before they call, I myself will answer;
>   while they are still speaking, I myself will listen. (Isa 65:19–24)[18]

Questions for Discussion

1. How do the passages from Psalm 2, Isaiah 42, and Genesis 22 help us understand Jesus?
2. In light of the way the First Testament and Matthew speak of God's reign or kingdom, what do you think is the significance of the theme of God's reign for the church today?

18. See the discussion of Rev 21 on pp. 157–58 above.

3. In what ways do we need the First Testament in order to understand Romans? In what ways is Romans quite clear without an understanding of the First Testament?
4. How far does a knowledge of the First Testament help to make the Revelation to John easier to understand?
5. What aspects of First Testament theology seem especially important for your church?

CHAPTER 5

Relationship

The First Testament spells out the nature of a relationship with God. Matthew's description of that relationship follows on his account of the story of what God has done (Matt 1:1–17), the promises he has thereby fulfilled (1:18–2:25), and the truth about God and us (3:1–17). Once again his description takes up the dynamics of the First Testament's account, in order to describe the kind of attitudes God expects us to have and the kind of life with God that we can live. It thus invites us to discover more about the nature of a relationship with God by studying the First Testament.

5.1 Matthew 4:1–11: It Is Written

Immediately after his baptism, Jesus is led off into the wilderness to be tempted by the devil—an extraordinary statement. The tempter offers him three suggestions of greater or lesser plausibility: to satisfy his hunger by turning stones into bread, to throw himself down from the pinnacle of the temple trusting the promise from Psalm 91 that God will keep him safe, and to secure the kingdoms of the world and their glory by submitting to the devil. Jesus refuses each of these suggestions. What is relevant to our present concern is his basis for doing so. Each time he responds, "It is written . . . ," and quotes from the First Testament—specifically, from Deuteronomy. We are not dependent merely on bread for life but on God's word, and Jesus must rely on that word rather than unilaterally use the powers available to him as Son of God for his own benefit. He is not to put the Lord his God to the test in order to see whether God will keep his promises of protection but rather to trust God to do so when the moment requires it. He is to worship and serve the Lord alone; it cannot be right to ignore this fundamental principle even to gain the worldwide authority and glory that do ultimately belong to him.

Submission

The story of Jesus's temptations thus begins:

> Then Jesus was led by the Spirit into the wilderness to be tempted by the devil. After fasting forty days and forty nights, he was hungry. The tempter came to him and said, "If you are the Son of God, tell these stones to become bread."
>
> Jesus answered, "It is written: 'People do not live on bread alone, but on every word that comes from the mouth of God.'" (Matt 4:1–4)

When the Scriptures talk about fasting, they do not necessarily imply that one eats nothing. Fasting may mean restraint from meat, or refraining from eating during daylight hours. To clarify the point, Luke adds that Jesus ate nothing. He had the power to act so as to satisfy his hunger. Many of the rocks on top of the Mount of Temptation above Jericho, the traditional site of his tempting, are flat and round, like pita bread. It would be easy to imagine them as little loaves.

The devil's advice has plausibility on its side. Is it not natural to utilize our gifts to meet our personal needs? No compromise need be involved; we have to look after our own needs if we are to be able to minister to others. But Jesus thinks about the tempter's question and remembers a line from the Torah.

> You are to be mindful of the entire way that Yahweh your God had you go these forty years in the wilderness, in order that he might humble you by testing you so as to know what was in your mind, whether you would keep his orders or not. He humbled you and let you be hungry and fed you the *maan* which you had not known and your ancestors had not known, in order that he might get you to acknowledge that human beings do not live on the basis of bread alone but on the basis of everything that comes out of Yahweh's mouth. (Deut 8:2–3)

Forty days, the wilderness, temptation: Jesus is repeating Israel's experience, and doing better than Israel did. Indeed, each of the passages he quotes back at the devil come from Deuteronomy 5–11, the part of the book that describes basic attitudes God expects of his people as they keep their side of the covenant relationship. Jesus presupposes that his life should be shaped by these imperatives expressed in the Torah that God gave Israel. Perhaps there is an implication that here in the wilderness the one true Israelite takes seriously that set of principles given in the wilderness to Israel as a whole but never properly observed by Israel. He is fulfilling his people's calling and beginning to offer an obedience to God on Israel's behalf that might make up for the historical Israel's failure.

More than one significance can attach to the declaration about the word that comes out of God's mouth. Merely having food to put in your mouth does not ensure that you stay alive, as Jesus's story about the rich fool indicates (Luke 12:16–21). Further, there is more to sustenance than physical food. Yet further, God himself can provide when there is no regular, natural food; food comes into being because God says so. And in this story God eventually does provide for Jesus, as he did for Israel.

Trust

The Deuteronomic command will be significant for Israel's ongoing life in the land that they are about to enter. There will be many occasions when Israel experiences poor harvests or a shortage of food for other reasons, and it will be tempting then to turn to other gods if Yahweh has failed them. There are a number of stories of individuals who run out of food and are near death. For all such experiences the command issues a challenge. The devil's second suggestion raises overlapping issues.

> Then the devil took him to the holy city and had him stand on the highest point of the temple. "If you are the Son of God," he said, "throw yourself down. For it is written:
>
> > 'He will command his angels concerning you,
> >   and they will lift you up in their hands,
> >   so that you will not strike your foot against a stone.'"
>
> Jesus answered him, "It is also written: 'Do not put the Lord your God to the test.'" (Matt 4:5–7)

The motif of testing thus reappears more explicitly in connection with this second temptation, where Jesus refers to God's own comment about testing (which precedes that recollection of Yahweh testing Israel, just noted). It is not explicit why Jesus should throw himself down and have God rescue him. Is it to give people a spectacular sign that will lead to their recognizing him? Or is it to prove to himself that he really is the Son of God? The tempter's clever quotation could work for either possibility. He quotes from Psalm 91, which in origin likely applies especially to the king. When there were no longer any kings, the psalm would express the way God would relate to the king when there would be a king again—that is, how God would relate to the Messiah. So Jesus can claim the promise of the psalm either to prove to other people that he is the Messiah or to prove it to himself.

The quotation involves taking the promise out of context. In the context in Psalm 91, the promise is that God will look after his servant when he is under attack; it is not an encouragement to act stupidly. To put it another way (as Jesus does), it involves putting God to the test, something against which Deuteronomy also warns.

> You will not follow other gods from among the gods of the peoples that are round you, because Yahweh your God among you is a passionate God, so that the anger of Yahweh your God does not rage against you and he annihilates you from on the face of the land. You will not test Yahweh your God as you tested him at Massah [Testing]. Keep carefully the orders of Yahweh your God, his affirmations, and his decrees that he has given you.
> (Deut 6:13–17)

The story about Israel testing Yahweh comes in Exodus 17. Not long after Yahweh not only gets them out of Egypt but also rescues them at the Red Sea, they are turning on Moses (not directly on Yahweh, actually) because they have little to eat or drink; and on this occasion "they tested Yahweh, saying: 'Is Yahweh among us or not?'" We might see the test as a challenge to see how far they could push Yahweh, or as tempting him to cast them off.

Obeisance

> Again, the devil took him to a very high mountain and showed him all the kingdoms of the world and their splendor. "All this I will give you," he said, "if you will bow down and worship me."
>
> Jesus said to him, "Away from me, Satan! For it is written:

'Worship the Lord your God, and serve him only.'"

Then the devil left him, and angels came and attended him.

(Matt 4:8–11)

The word for "worship" (*proskyneō*) suggests a body movement of doing obeisance. The word can describe someone's bowing down to another human being such as a king. But the story of Mordecai's refusing to bow down to Haman (Esth 3:2) indicates that Jews were inclined to play safe and not bow down to anyone. And obeisance does suggest submission and a commitment to doing the will of the one to whom one bows down. What the devil is requiring is that Jesus should become his servant and should do as he says. The wording in Deuteronomy is slightly different from that in the Gospels, but the implications are the same.

> When Yahweh your God brings you into the country that he swore to your ancestors, to Abraham, to Isaac, and to Jacob, to give you great and good towns that you have not built, houses full of everything good that you have not filled, cisterns dug that you have not dug, vineyards and olive groves that you have not planted, and you eat and are full, keep watch on yourself so you do not put Yahweh out of mind, the one who got you out of the country of Egypt, out of a household of serfs. You are to live in awe of Yahweh your God, to serve him, and to swear in his name. (Deut 6:10–13)

In other contexts the verb for "live in awe" (*yare'*) means "be afraid," but it commonly denotes a positive fear that issues in obedience. The same idea thus continues in the expectation that people should "serve" Yahweh (*abad*); indeed, this verb is often translated "worship."

At each point in this process of temptation, then, from the stock of knowledge of the Torah that he had acquired as a Jew, Jesus is able to draw a passage that goes to the root of the wrong attitude to God that the devil's suggestions involve. The story implies that people reading the Gospel need also to acquire a knowledge of the Torah good enough to enable them to evaluate suggestions from demonic agencies, whether or not well disguised.

In connection with the Scriptures' application to behavior, the areas of the First Testament that will be especially significant are books in the Torah (e.g., Deuteronomy), stories written to offer examples of how Israel should or should not behave (e.g., in Numbers), the exhortations of the prophets that often crystallize the moral attitudes to be embodied in lifestyle, and the wisdom books (especially Proverbs) that establish the links between areas often kept separate, such as religion and ethics on one side, shrewdness and success on the other.

Reading the First Testament in Light of Matthew 4

The middle of Jesus's three temptations involves an appeal to the First Testament on the part of the devil as well as on the part of Jesus. The devil can quote the Scriptures, too. What is the difference between the use and the abuse of the Scriptures?

One principle is that an insight taken out of the broader context of the Scriptures can be misleading, so that one needs a knowledge of the Torah, the Prophets, and the Writings as a whole in order to set particular insights in a context. That principle applies to an individual book such as Proverbs. It collects a range of material on areas of life such as money and sex, and many individual sayings (commending or downgrading riches, reminding men—and women—of their weaknesses) look odd out of context. The range of the material in the book as a whole implicitly recognizes the complexity of factors that need to be taken into account in coming to decisions about attitudes and behavior.

The devil's application of Psalm 91 was entirely Jesus-centered. That principle did not prevent his abusing the Scriptures. Actually, he needed to be more God-centered, for Jesus responds to the devil by quoting a fundamental principle of our relationship with God. It is, indeed, attitudes to God that are the concern of each of the passages he quotes: submission to God's word, trust in God's promise, and worship of God's name.

Jesus thus sets the clear, direct demand of a fundamental passage in Deuteronomy against the devil's application of another passage to a particular set of circumstances. Personal application of the Scriptures is tested by being set in the context of the direct teaching of the Scriptures elsewhere.

In this particular case, misuse of the Scriptures involved taking verses out of their original context. Psalm 91 promises God's protection to "the one who dwells in the shelter of the Most High, who abides in the shadow of the Almighty." In origin it may have been a psalm of assurance for any believer, though perhaps more likely it promises God's protection to the king. If it was a royal psalm and as such was understood messianically by Jesus's time, we have noted that this would give special point to the devil's quoting it. He is inviting Jesus to prove that the psalm's promise about the (coming) king is true about him. It is here that the devil's hermeneutic goes wrong. The psalm speaks of God protecting someone in whatever danger or attack comes. It says nothing about courting danger or taking risks that one could avoid. The devil is able to abuse the text in applying it because he has abused it in the course of his exegesis, taking particular phrases and promises out of context.

Reading the Scriptures requires the ability to handle passages in a way faithful to their particular witness. Collections of texts in devotional books that work by drawing our attention to verses isolated from their context can express helpful devotional truths, but they risk imitating the devil's hermeneutic. The story of the man seeking God's guidance by opening the Scriptures at random, who found first Matthew 27:5 ("Judas went and hanged himself"), then—seeking something more congenial—Luke 10:37 ("Go and do likewise"), then John 13:27 ("Do quickly what you are going to do"), contains a warning about a devotional use of the Scriptures that risks paralleling the devil's.

There are more serious examples. "Seek the peace and prosperity of the city to which I have carried you" (Jer 29:7). One would never guess from the way this exhortation gets repeated that its logic is simply that the exiles may as well do so because they are going to be stuck there for seventy years. "I know the plans I have for you . . . , plans to give you hope and a future" (Jer 29:11). One would never guess from the way this promise gets repeated that it refers to a future that is seventy years away.

5.2 Matthew 5:1–16: A Disciple's Blessings

After his exchanges with the devil, Jesus began his ministry in Galilee. He took up John the Baptizer's challenge to people to repent in light of the implementing of God's reign, he summoned some disciples, he healed many people, and he attracted crowds of followers. Then, "when Jesus saw the crowds, he went up on a mountainside and sat down. His disciples came to him, and he began to teach them" (Matt 5:1–2). The Beatitudes or Blessings with which the Sermon on the Mount opens analyze fundamental aspects of what it means to live with God. The form and content of these blessings derive substantially from the First Testament. The declaration of blessing on people of a certain style of attitude and life recalls especially the opening psalm in the Psalter (also Ps 128). The Sermon on the Mount thus follows the Psalter in beginning with a blessing on those who are open to walking in God's way.

Lowliness and Mourning

> Blessed are the poor in spirit,
>> for theirs is the kingdom of heaven. (Matt 5:3)

The poor in spirit to whom the kingdom belongs are those to whom Isaiah 61 declared good news of freedom, of vindication, and of restoration. Isaiah 61 is the chapter Jesus quotes in his sermon at Nazareth, in a passage that Luke includes at an equivalent place in his Gospel to the Sermon on the Mount in Matthew (Luke 4:16–21);[1] Jesus also echoes it in describing his ministry to John the Baptizer (Matt 11:2–6). The poor in spirit are people who are neglected, ignored, put down, insignificant, and powerless. They are materially needy but also oppressed and depressed.

Most people who will read this book (like the writer) will not be oppressed, neglected, powerless, materially needy, and so on. We are not poor in spirit, though we should not feel guilty about that. Arguably it is something to thank God for, though it is also something to be wary of. Whereas the poor in spirit are the people to whom the reign of heaven naturally belongs, we are the rich for whom it is hard to enter the reign of heaven (Matt 19:23–24). Fortunately it is not impossible (Matt 19:25–26). But it does not come about through our redefining "poor in spirit" so as to take the description away from the people to whom it belongs. That might well mean we cannot get in.

> Blessed are those who mourn,
>> for they will be comforted. (Matt 5:4)

In Isaiah 61, the prophet goes on to speak of having been anointed

> to comfort all the mourners,
>> to provide for the people who mourn Zion—
> to give them majesty instead of ash,
>> festive oil instead of mourning,
> a praise garment instead of a flickering spirit. (Isa 61:2–3)

The poor in spirit are people who mourn the state of Zion. Jerusalem is still in a state of devastation; the ravages of Babylonian destruction remain. Ev-

---

1. See the comments on Luke 4 on pp. 75–76 above.

idently Nehemiah has not yet arrived to rebuild its walls. There is probably not much of a community that lives in the city, but there are people who live outside the ruined walls, and they continue (metaphorically, at least) to sit in ashes and/or to smear their faces with ashes as if they are mourning the loss of a loved one. Their spirit is flickering; its light is almost gone. They cannot believe that things will ever change. If they gather in the devastated remains of the temple, it is to say prayers like the ones in Lamentations, which keep observing that Zion has no comforter.

"Comfort" in Isaiah has two different meanings. It can denote both consoling words and also action that puts things right. Both meanings could apply in Isaiah 61. God intends to restore the city and thus to restore the community's honor or majesty or beauty. God intends to restore the temple, so that the observances there will be ones of praise rather than lamentation. Their participants will be dressed in splendor rather than ashes, festive rather than mourning, confident rather than flickering.

Although the prophet's promises found some fulfillment in the Second Temple period, in Jesus's day Judea was under Roman control, and it mourned as if it was still in the same state. Jesus promises that Jerusalem is going to be comforted.

Meekness and Hunger

> Blessed are the meek,
> for they will inherit the earth. (Matt 5:5)

Jesus picks up a psalm's promise, "the meek shall possess the land" (Ps 37:11). The word for "meek" in the psalm is the same as the word for "poor" in Isaiah 61, an indicator that there is overlap between the qualities and the promises in these blessings. *Meekness* is another word for lowliness or humbleness, not as an inner attitude but as a position in the community. Psalm 37 is full of exhortations to trust, to accept, and to restrain oneself in the face of the success and hostility of wrongdoers. It promises that the meek will not be put down forever. But whereas Isaiah 61 has in mind the reduced state of the community as a whole, the psalm has in mind a division within the community; hence the promise that the meek will come to gain control of the country.

"Earth" and "land" are the same word in Hebrew (*erets*) and in Greek (*gē*), and it is odd that in the psalm the Hebrew word is usually translated the first way and in Matthew the Greek word is usually translated the second way. The complementariness of Isaiah 61 and Psalm 37 might point to a complementariness within these blessings. Judea as a whole was subject to Rome, but within Judea ordinary people were subject to religious people and theologians. Ordinary people in particular are promised that their subjection will not last forever.

> Blessed are those who hunger and thirst for righteousness,
>> for they will be filled. (Matt 5:6)

When Yahweh was about to make it possible for Judahites in Babylon to return home, he urged, "Everyone who thirsts, come to the waters. . . . Why do you spend . . . your labor for that which does not satisfy?" (Isa 55:1–2). In previous chapters, Yahweh has been promising his righteousness to the Judahites in the sense that he has been promising to do the right thing by them, that is, delivering them from Babylon and restoring their relationship with him.[2] The trouble is that they were not convinced of his plan. To judge from the way he seeks to answer them, they were not convinced that they needed to be put right with him, that he could do what he said, and that his proposal about how to restore Jerusalem (namely, through the up-and-coming Persian king, Cyrus) was viable. Yet we could say that they were hungering and thirsting for someone to do the right thing by them, and in Isaiah 55 God is issuing one last invitation to come to him for that blessing.

In Jesus's day, the people are once again (or are still) in need of his restoring them in their relationship with God and in their position as a people. They are hungering and thirsting for God to do the right thing by them, and Jesus comes to bring it about. The people who hunger for it will be blessed; they are going to be filled.

Mercy, Purity, Peaceableness

The first four blessings relate to people's stance in relation to God. The second four concern their relationships with other people.

> Blessed are the merciful,
>> for they will be shown mercy. (Matt 5:7)

---

2. See the discussion of "Doing Right and Being Faithful" on pp. 136–37 above.

At Psalm 18:25, the Revised Version and the American Standard Version have "with the merciful you will show yourself merciful." Yet the key word is *he-sed*, which suggests the translation, "with the committed you show yourself committed." The psalm is talking about our commitment to God and about God's to us, but that Revised Version/American Standard Version translation suggests a concern with our commitment to other people (of which mercy is a facet) and God's to us (of which mercy is a facet).

> Blessed are the pure in heart,
>> for they will see God. (Matt 5:8)

Is Jesus interested in inner attitude rather than outward life? This would be unlikely. To start with, a Jew would never see it that way. "Who shall ascend Yahweh's hill?" Part of the answer is, "the person who has clean hands and a pure heart" (Ps 24:3–4). Whether we are Jewish or not, how could we have a pure heart and not also have clean hands? In a formal sense it might be possible; we could keep the outward purity rules and still be stained inside, and thus Jesus is not very interested in hands being ritually clean (see Matt 15:1–20). But Jews who were serious about the Torah could not be content with a simple dichotomy between hands and heart. If we have a pure heart, it will issue in hands that are free from the stain of blood. If we have an impure heart, it will issue in bloodstained hands. Only a person who is clean and pure in heart or mind and in action can climb the hill to the sanctuary to come before God. That is the blessed person.

> Blessed are the peacemakers,
>> for they will be called children of God.
> Blessed are those who are persecuted because of righteousness,
>> for theirs is the kingdom of heaven.
> Blessed are you when people insult you, persecute you and falsely say all
>> kinds of evil against you because of me. Rejoice and be glad, because
>> great is your reward in heaven, for in the same way they persecuted
>> the prophets who were before you. (Matt 5:9–12)

Once again Jesus recalls Isaiah 40–55. When her children asked for something as soon as she had sat down, my mother used to say, "There's no peace for the wicked." I did not realize she was quoting from the First Testament (Isa 48:22; 57:21). The prophet who makes that declaration is a great peacemaker. He seeks to restore peace between God and his people. He is also concerned for *shalom* on a broader front than the abolition of hostility and the reestablishment of a relationship. *Shalom* stands for well-being, for things going well in a community's life. That is the prophet's desire. Righteousness is again key to the achievement of that desire—the same righteousness to which the fourth blessing referred.

The prophet who speaks in Isaiah 40–55 is someone who experiences persecution because of righteousness, like other prophets. He proclaims how Yahweh is going to do right by his people, and he gets persecuted for it, possibly both by them and by the superpower authorities who do not care for his declaring that the next superpower is about to take over (49:1–6; 52:13–53:12). But he thus experiences chastisement that will bring his people *shalom* (53:5). He is a great proclaimer of Yahweh's reign (52:7), and he will therefore enjoy it. Persecution for proclaiming God's message happened to him. It happened to Jesus. Jesus's point here is that it will happen to other people who talk about the *shalom* that God intends and about how it comes.

Reading the First Testament in Light of Matthew 5:1–12

The depth of Jesus's insights on what it means to live with God reflects his soaking in the First Testament. Psalms and Isaiah, the books most clearly echoed in these blessings, are the books most often and most widely quoted in the New Testament. The book of Psalms feeds New Testament theology; Psalms is also the First Testament book that most directly concerns itself with our life with God, our spirituality, our life of praise, prayer, and personal commitment. Jesus's own example elsewhere in the Gospels directs us to Psalms as our resource for praise and prayer.

It was the interweaving of petition and praise in a lament such as Psalm 22 that provided Jesus with the means of expression for his anguish at the prospect of betrayal and abandonment (see especially Matt 27:46). From this same psalm Jesus took up the psalmist's characteristic insistence on looking beyond his anguish, as well as on looking that anguish in the face. Claus Westermann exaggerated only slightly (Ps 88 seems to be an exception) when he declared that in the Psalms "there is no petition . . . that did not move at least one step . . . on the road to praise," as "there is also no praise that was fully separated from the experience of God's wonderful intervention in time of need."[3]

---

3. *The Praise of God in the Psalms,* trans. Keith R. Crim (Richmond: John Knox, 1965; London: Epworth, 1966), 154.

Certainly Psalm 22 holds together an openness to God over my feelings and needs with a striving nevertheless to maintain faith and praise toward the God who has cared for me in the past and is still "my God" even though seeming to have abandoned me. The psalm also goes on to an anticipation of renewed praise for God's turning to me at my moment of urgent need, and the psalm's successful battle to look beyond affliction as well as looking it in the face is reflected in the reference to it in Hebrews 2:12. The anticipatory praise of Psalm 22:22–31 can thus be imagined on the lips of Jesus, as was the present lament of the opening part of the psalm.

The resources of the Psalms for our life with God are easily ignored by believers who find it difficult to get beyond the Psalms' culture-related talk of bulls of Bashan and Moabite washpots, but the effort to do so is worthwhile, for in the Psalms we are given the Scriptures' own collection of things that it is okay to say to God. To summarize Athanasius's exposition of this point in his *Letter to Marcellinus*, "Most of Scripture speaks *to* us while the Psalms speak *for* us."[4]

It would be a half-truth to infer from the Sermon on the Mount that the First Testament on its own tells us the kind of life with God that a believer can live. While most of the raw material for Jesus's blessings comes from the First Testament, out of this raw material Jesus creates something fresh and new, and greater than the parts it incorporates. What he does theologically (or what he hears theologically) in bringing together the figures of the anointed king, the beloved son, and the suffering servant, he does devotionally in creating a new and profound whole from elements of largely First Testament origin. The blessings are not merely an anthology of vaguely familiar aphorisms but a new, rounded whole that offers listeners a fresh total portrait of the life with God that was already the First Testament's concern.

Jesus's Crucial Contribution

Yet Jesus's crucial contribution to the shaping of our life with God is not his teaching but his life, and especially his death, resurrection, and giving of the Holy Spirit to his people. Insofar as the New Testament brings insight going beyond that of the First Testament, it is insight that can emerge only on the basis of these events. The reason why fresh things can be said is not

4. See, e.g., B. W. Anderson, *Out of the Depths: The Psalms Speak for Us Today,* 3rd ed. (Louisville: Westminster John Knox, 2000), ix; this summary is actually not from Athanasius.

that the evolution of human thinking or the progress of divine revelation has developed to such a point that new statements can now be added to old, less complete truths, but that new events make new statements possible and necessary. Jesus could not speak of the Holy Spirit before the pouring out of the Holy Spirit (John 7:39); nor could he speak of taking up the cross or enjoying resurrection life until crucifixion and resurrection were taking place. When those events have happened, the dynamics of life with God can be thought through with new depth in light of them (as happens, for instance, in Rom 3–8). It is not that life with God is different at every point; people were put right with God by grace through faith under the old covenant. Rather it is that the way in which life with God works can be freshly conceptualized in light of realities (cross, empty tomb, giving of the Holy Spirit) that can now be pointed to and explicated.

It is particularly instructive to set the "vindicatory" psalms and Jesus's coming alongside each other. There is a big difference between these prayers for redress to be exacted on people who have wronged us (e.g., Ps 137:7–9) or who are opposed to God (e.g., Ps 139:19–24) and any prayers we are told Jesus ever prayed for such people. The psalmists were not insensitive, unspiritual, or immoral people (the rest of Pss 137 and 139 show that), nor was God's love for nations other than Israel unknown in their day, nor did First Testament ethics allow people to do what they liked to their enemies. Theologically, perhaps prayer for one's enemies like that of Jesus on the cross is strictly possible only now, because it is the cross that makes forgiveness available to people; the psalms' prayers for judgment on the wicked are prayers for God's justice to be at work in this world, and it is the cross that is God's yes to their prayer for wickedness to be punished.[5]

So were the psalms' prayers for God's judgment valid before Jesus but inappropriate after Jesus? One should be wary of drawing too sharply the contrast between the attitude of these psalms and that of the New Testament. John the Baptizer did address people as a viper's brood that is about to be overtaken by God's wrath, and as trees that have failed to bear fruit and will be felled and burned (Matt 3:7–10); and the Sermon on the Mount makes clear that Jesus accepts John's understanding of what Jesus's coming will bring for the impenitent (7:19). Those whose righteousness is only up to that of the scribes and Pharisees (!) will be excluded from the kingdom; anger, insults, and contempt will mean fiery judgment; adultery, lust, and divorce

---

5. Cf. Dietrich Bonhoeffer, *Psalms: The Prayer Book of the Bible*, trans. James H. Burtness (Minneapolis: Augsburg, 1974), 56–60.

will mean going to hell (5:20–32). The day of Yahweh will be the occasion of Jesus's repudiation of many who thought they belonged to him (7:21–23). Indeed, a saying from beyond the Sermon on the Mount adds that it will see the "subjects of the kingdom" cast into outer darkness, where people will cry and groan in anguish (8:12). Nor is prayer for judgment like that of the psalms absent from the New Testament, notwithstanding Jesus's own prayer for his killers' forgiveness. He promises that people's prayers for vindication will be heard (Luke 18:1–8).

5.3 Relating to God in the New Testament

When the New Testament more broadly looks at a relationship with God, it assumes that the First Testament is a resource. It directs believers there for an understanding of how to go about worship, praise, and prayer, and how to live in trust and hope. It also illustrates how it has learned from the First Testament how to go about worship, praise, and prayer, and how to live in trust and hope.

Ephesians 5: Praise and Thanksgiving

> Be filled with the Spirit, speaking to one another with psalms, hymns and songs from the Spirit. Sing and make music from your heart to the Lord, always giving thanks to God the Father for everything, in the name of our Lord Jesus Christ. (Eph 5:18–20)

Ephesians assumes that people will use the Psalms in giving praise. It also makes clear that the Psalms will not only be the vehicle whereby people voice their praise, but will also teach people how to express their own praise. The New Testament incorporates one or two examples of such praise composed by believers in Jesus or in the context of his coming. Mary's is properly the first:

> My soul glorifies the Lord
>   and my spirit rejoices in God my Savior,
> for he has been mindful
>   of the humble state of his servant.
> From now on all generations will call me blessed,

for the Mighty One has done great things for me—
   holy is his name.
His mercy extends to those who fear him,
   from generation to generation.
He has performed mighty deeds with his arm;
   he has scattered those who are proud in their inmost thoughts.
He has brought down rulers from their thrones
   but has lifted up the humble.
He has filled the hungry with good things
   but has sent the rich away empty.
He has helped his servant Israel,
   remembering to be merciful
to Abraham and his descendants forever,
   just as he promised our ancestors. (Luke 1:46–55)

Mary's song recalls Hannah's song (1 Sam 2); more generally, it seems to follow the pattern of the Psalms. The same is true of the "prophecy" of John the Baptizer's father. Filled with the Holy Spirit, he proclaimed,

Praise be to the Lord, the God of Israel,
   because he has come to his people and redeemed them.
He has raised up a horn of salvation for us
   in the house of his servant David
(as he said through his holy prophets of long ago),
salvation from our enemies
   and from the hand of all who hate us—
to show mercy to our ancestors
   and to remember his holy covenant,
   the oath he swore to our father Abraham:
to rescue us from the hand of our enemies,
   and to enable us to serve him without fear
   in holiness and righteousness before him all our days. (Luke 1:68–75)

Except perhaps for the phrase in parentheses (and the subsequent verses that refer to John), the act of praise would not look at all out of place in the Psalter. Zechariah's song, too, thus follows the pattern of the Psalms, with that explicit note that it did so as he was filled with the Holy Spirit.

Ephesians 6: Praise and Prayer

Zechariah's praise thus constitutes an anticipatory implementing of the bidding in Ephesians 5. Full of the Holy Spirit, he gives praise in a psalm-like way. But the way Ephesians speaks ("psalms, hymns, and songs from the Spirit . . .") indicates the assumption that believers will also pray the actual Psalms. In Romans 8:35, Paul implies a small example when he speaks of the experience of trouble, hardship, persecution, famine, nakedness, and sword that comes to believers, and refers to Psalm 44:22:

> As it is written:
>
> > "For your sake we face death all day long;
> > we are considered as sheep to be slaughtered." (Rom 8:36)

This takes us to Ephesians 6, for Ephesians 5 is not the letter's last exhortation about praise and prayer.

> Pray in the Spirit on all occasions with all kinds of prayers and requests. With this in mind, be alert and always keep on praying for all the Lord's people. Pray also for me, that whenever I speak, words may be given me so that I will fearlessly make known the mystery of the gospel, for which I am an ambassador in chains. Pray that I may declare it fearlessly, as I should.
> (Eph 6:18–20)

Prayer as much as praise and thanksgiving is uttered in the Holy Spirit. They are all aspects of the way in which both Jews and Gentiles have access to the Father through Jesus "by one Spirit" (Eph 2:18).

The Psalms themselves have three main ways of talking to God: in praise, in prayer, and in thanksgiving. Praise means acknowledging with enthusiasm that Yahweh is God and that he has done great things for his people. Prayer means that things are not working out now in the way one would have expected in light of the truths about God that praise acknowledges. Thanksgiving testifies to the fact that God has now responded to such a prayer.

One would put the songs of Hannah, Mary, and Zechariah in that last category. Like the thanksgiving psalms themselves, they thus illustrate and help us understand what might seem an odd note in the first exhortation in Ephesians when it refers to "speaking to one another." Aren't praise and prayer addressed to God? Shouldn't we pray vertically, not horizontally? Jesus warns about praying in a way that is designed for other people to notice (Matt 6:5–6).

The horizontal aspect to praise and prayer of which Ephesians speaks is one that brings glory to God, not to the person praying. It draws attention away from us to God. It is to that end that it invites other people to listen to our praise, our prayer, and our thanksgiving. Thus the Psalms keep switching between address to God and address to human beings. They are engaged in glorifying God but also in urging other people to glorify God. They are engaged in prayer but also in warning other people of what will happen when God answers the prayer.

Further, the combination of Paul's request that people pray for him and his reference to Psalm 44 reminds us that the prayer psalms need not be for praying only on our own behalf. If we are to respond to a request for prayer like Paul's, we may do so by taking up a prayer psalm as he does and praying it for the people who ask for our intercession.

Revelation 4–6: Worship and Prayer

In his vision, John the prophet looks through a door into heaven and sees a throne with someone seated on it, and some living creatures.

> Day and night they never stop saying:
>
>> "Holy, holy, holy is the Lord God Almighty,
>>   who was, and is, and is to come."
>
> Whenever the living creatures give glory, honor and thanks to him who sits on the throne and who lives for ever and ever, the twenty-four elders fall down before him who sits on the throne and worship him who lives for ever and ever. They lay their crowns before the throne and say:
>
>> "You are worthy, our Lord and God,
>>   to receive glory and honor and power,
>> for you created all things,
>>   and by your will they were created
>>   and have their being." (Rev 4:8–11)

John's vision is inspired by Ezekiel's account of his vision (Ezek 1); the creatures' praise is inspired by the seraphs' praise in Isaiah (Isa 6:3). John goes on to report the praise the creatures give to Jesus:

> And they sang a new song, saying:
>
> > "You are worthy to take the scroll
> > > and to open its seals,
> > because you were slain,
> > > and with your blood you purchased for God
> > > members of every tribe and language and people and nation.
> > You have made them to be a kingdom and priests to serve our God,
> > > and they will reign on the earth."
>
> Then I looked and heard the voice of many angels, numbering thousands upon thousands, and ten thousand times ten thousand. They encircled the throne and the living creatures and the elders. In a loud voice they were saying:
>
> > "Worthy is the Lamb, who was slain,
> > > to receive power and wealth and wisdom and strength
> > > and honor and glory and praise!"
>
> Then I heard every creature in heaven and on earth and under the earth and on the sea, and all that is in them, saying:
>
> > "To him who sits on the throne and to the Lamb
> > > be praise and honor and glory and power,
> > > > for ever and ever!"
>
> The four living creatures said, "Amen," and the elders fell down and worshiped. (Rev 5:9–14)

When the Lamb opens the seals, the fifth is significant for our present concern:

> When he opened the fifth seal, I saw under the altar the souls of those who had been slain because of the word of God and the testimony they had maintained. They called out in a loud voice, "How long, Sovereign Lord,

holy and true, until you judge the inhabitants of the earth and avenge our blood?" Then each of them was given a white robe, and they were told to wait a little longer, until the full number of their fellow servants and brothers and sisters were killed just as they had been. (Rev 6:9–11)

Whereas chapters 4 and 5 recall the praise of the First Testament, chapter 6 recalls its prayer. The prayer expressed in the Psalms is often a protest about how things are and a plea for God to punish attackers and persecutors. If such prayer is legitimate before Jesus, is it legitimate after Jesus? God's response to the martyrs is not that they should not pray this way and should pray for their killers' forgiveness. It is to say that they are going to have to wait, but that their prayer will be answered. No doubt the martyrs' prayer is not motivated simply by personal bitterness. They are praying for the public vindication of God's truth. One can see the same concern in the Psalms. The psalmists pray not merely for God to take action against their enemies but for God to take action against his enemies, against people whom we are prepared to make our enemies because they have made themselves into God's enemies (see, e.g., Ps 139).

Hebrews 11 Again: Trust and Hope

We have looked at Hebrews 11 from one angle (actually from two);[6] we now look at it from another. What are the stances that Hebrews commends? It speaks of faith, and it illustrates faith from the First Testament story. So what is faith? The introduction to the chapter makes one think of faithfulness (Heb 10:35–39). The chapter itself begins by making one think of believing things one did not see happen (Gen 1; Heb 11:1–3). But for the most part, Hebrews 11 identifies faith as hope in God, on the part of Abel, Enoch, Noah, Abraham, Isaac, Jacob, Joseph, Moses's parents, Moses himself, the Israelites, and Rahab.

Although the inferences that Hebrews draws from these stories do not always appear to be part of what the stories themselves say, the theme is a First Testament one, again expressed most systematically in the Psalms. While the Psalms illustrate three main ways of talking to God (praise, prayer, and thanksgiving), half of them are prayers or protests, which makes us

6. See the discussion of Heb 11 on pp. 34–39 above, and that on faith and judgment on pp. 135–36 above.

wonder if we can see distinctions among them. And they do represent points on a spectrum between desperate protest at one end and believing hope at the other.

There is another way in which Hebrews 11 relates to the Psalms. The last part of the chapter refers to some heroes of faith who are even more unlikely candidates for such a list than the people who appear earlier in the chapter.

> What more shall I say? I do not have time to tell about Gideon, Barak, Samson and Jephthah, about David and Samuel and the prophets, who through faith conquered kingdoms, administered justice, and gained what was promised; who shut the mouths of lions, quenched the fury of the flames, and escaped the edge of the sword; whose weakness was turned to strength; and who became powerful in battle and routed foreign armies. Women received back their dead, raised to life again. There were others who were tortured, refusing to be released so that they might gain an even better resurrection. Some faced jeers and flogging, and even chains and imprisonment. They were put to death by stoning; they were sawed in two; they were killed by the sword. They went about in sheepskins and goat-skins, destitute, persecuted and mistreated—the world was not worthy of them. They wandered in deserts and mountains, and in caves and holes in the ground. These were all commended for their faith, yet none of them received what had been promised. (Heb 11:32–39)

The passage refers with enthusiasm in an unself-conscious way to people who "became powerful in battle and routed foreign armies," as it has already referred to the Israelites' taking of Jericho. Many modern Christians speak as if the New Testament has progressed beyond the First Testament's militarism, but hardly any of these contrasts between the Testaments work. Both Testaments have what one might call a peace ideal but also a recognition that God works through war. The attitude to violence in Hebrews compares with Revelation's attitude to praying for God's judgment on people. Ironically, the one real difference between the Testaments is that there is no hope of resurrection in the First Testament, but Hebrews here compromises that difference in the way it speaks of the expectation held by these First Testament figures.

5.4 Relating to God in the First Testament

So the New Testament learned from the First Testament much of what it knows about life with God. What happens when we look in the direction it points? What are the dynamics of life with God in the First Testament itself? They embrace remembering, studying, commitment, celebrating, protesting, interceding, arguing, confessing, trusting, questioning, and thanking.

Remembering

That the First Testament (and then the New Testament) is dominated by narrative would likely in itself imply that life with God involves studying and remembering this story. Both Testaments encourage that assumption by referring back to their story elsewhere, in material that is not narrative. The Prophets and the Psalms do so, as does Paul. In the First Testament, remembering is central to life with God. Life with God is based upon some things that God has done, so we need to know what they are.

When Hans Frei in *The Eclipse of Biblical Narrative* showed how an interest in the history behind the biblical text instead of in the biblical story itself came to dominate scholarly interest,[7] he went on to make another illuminating point about the change in the way people came to approach the biblical story. As they had not thought in terms of a difference between the scriptural story and the events in Israel's history, so they had not thought in terms of a difference between the scriptural story and the story of our own lives. Or they had assumed that if there was a difference, our vocation in reading the scriptural story was to fit our story into its story. It tells the true story, not only historically but theologically.

Frei traces how this assumed link also came apart as people began to look in a different way at the divergence between the dynamics of their own story and the dynamics of the biblical story. It was once the case that they instinctively reframed and rethought and reevaluated their own story by the biblical story. Instead, when people perceived that divergence, they reframed and rethought and reevaluated the biblical story by their story. They could rely on their story and their understanding of their experience; it provided them with a way of reading the biblical story.

The presence of extensive narratives in the Scriptures invites us to re-

7. See the discussion of "Story and History" on pp. 11–13 above.

verse the change Frei perceives. We remember the biblical story in order to set our lives in its context.

As is the case with many (maybe most) significant words, the meaning of the Hebrew word usually translated "remember" (*zakar*) overlaps with its English equivalent but is not quite the same. The English word can denote something we do on purpose, but it more often denotes something we do accidentally. The balance in the use of the Hebrew word (in the Scriptures, anyway) is the reverse. Remembering and forgetting are things we do on purpose. The Hebrew words commonly denote being deliberately mindful or dismissing from our mind. Thus in Hebrew we can remember the future—that is, keep it in mind.

Though the First Testament as a whole implies that remembering is important, Deuteronomy is the work that puts the most explicit emphasis on remembering.

> Do not put out of mind the things that your eyes have seen, and so they do not depart from your mind all the days of your life. And get your children and your grandchildren to acknowledge them. (4:9)
>
> Keep watch on yourselves so you do not put out of mind the pact of Yahweh your God, which he solemnized with you. (4:23)
>
> You are to be mindful that you were a servant in the country of Egypt, but Yahweh your God got you out of there with a strong hand and an extended arm. (5:15)
>
> Keep watch on yourself so you do not put Yahweh out of mind, the one who got you out of the country of Egypt, out of a household of serfs. (6:12)
>
> You are to be mindful of the entire way that Yahweh your God had you go these forty years in the wilderness. (8:2)

And so on.

Studying

If we are going to remember, we have to put things into our memory—we have to study. The book of Psalms begins this way:

> The blessings of someone who has not walked
>   by the counsel of the faithless,
> or stood on the way of wrongdoers,

or lived in the settlement of the arrogant!
Rather, his delight is in Yahweh's instruction,
    and he murmurs about his instruction day and night.
He is like a tree planted by channels of water,
    which gives its fruit in its time,
and its foliage does not fade;
    all that he does succeeds.
Not so the faithless people;
    rather, they are like the chaff that the wind blows away.
Therefore the faithless do not rise up when a ruling is given,
    nor wrongdoers in the assembly of the faithful.
Because Yahweh acknowledges the way of the faithful,
    but the way of the faithless perishes. (Ps 1)

The smart person, we could say, is someone who delights in Yahweh's instruction. "Instruction" here is the Hebrew word *torah*, usually translated into English as "law," but it is an example of translation that is misleading most of the time. *Torah* can be translated "teaching," though that may understate the element of direction implied by the word. The Torah (Genesis through Deuteronomy) tells us the story of what God did with Israel from the beginning to the end of Moses's life. But the story encloses vast amounts of instruction about how Israel should live. So we could say that *torah* embraces both story and expectations.

Its references to integrity and wrongdoing suggest that Psalm 1 has in mind the instruction side to Yahweh's teaching. It is then significant as the opening of the book of Psalms, which comprises five books of teaching on praise and prayer, as indicated in the acts of praise at the end of Psalms 41, 72, 89, and 106. These five books of teaching on praise and prayer correspond to the five books that make up *the* Torah. So maybe the blessing on the person who delights in Yahweh's instruction is a blessing on people who read the five books that follow, and take them as their pattern for praise and prayer. Or maybe the blessing reminds people before they think about praise and prayer that praise and prayer "work" only if the people who engage in them are people who follow the instruction in those other five books, *the* Torah. It might be safe to work from both possibilities.

Psalm 1 implies that people need to shape their lives by what they read. Delight will aid that responsiveness. Murmuring takes the point further. The idea is that when we study the Scriptures, we do not just read them inside our head. We recite them. They occupy our body as well as our mind.

How could Jesus respond to suggestions from a weird character he met in the wilderness by producing the appropriate rejoinder from the Torah? I doubt if this capacity issued simply from the fact that he was God. He could do it because he had studied, perhaps starting on Joseph's knee, as Deuteronomy instructs (see, e.g., Deut 11:19).

Commitment

Israel is commanded to offer several types of sacrifice, but the first and most dominant (Lev 1) is the whole burnt offering. One brings a whole animal and burns up the entirety of it for God. Israel was to do so in the Jerusalem sanctuary at dawn and at dusk each day. One got nothing out of offering such a sacrifice, so that it really was an indication of one's commitment to God. In the First Testament, the word for "sacrifice" (*zebah*) does not in itself draw attention to the costliness (the sacrifice in that sense) involved in making a sacrifice. The word means "killing." But it evidently was a sacrifice in the sense of cost too.

The community as a whole or individuals within it could also offer a burnt offering on special occasions—for instance, when they wanted to ask God for something outrageous. Of course, such an offering could easily become a kind of bribe, so God warns them to keep it simple (Ps 50).

God placed a further constraint on how costly sacrifices should be. While other nations' sacrifices were broadly similar to Israel's, one key difference was that other peoples were prepared to sacrifice their children in special circumstances, when they wanted to ask the deity for something extraordinary. Once during a battle,

> The king of Moab saw that the battle was too hard for him, and he got with him seven hundred men drawing a sword to break through to the king of Edom, but they could not. So he got his eldest son who was to reign in place of him and offered him up as a burnt offering on the wall. A great fury came on Israel, and they moved on from there and went back to the land. (2 Kgs 3:26–27)

We do not know quite what was implied by that last sentence, but it suggests that Israel was overwhelmed in some way by what happened.

Israelites also sometimes offered this kind of sacrifice, but it is forbidden by the Torah and condemned by the prophets and by stories in 2 Kings.

Maybe the story of Abraham and Isaac (Gen 22) is significant in this connection. The birth of Isaac is the long-delayed key miracle that can make possible the fulfillment of God's promise to Abraham and Sarah. Then God tells Abraham to turn Isaac into a burnt offering. Will Abraham make such a burnt offering and imperil that promise? Yes, he will. But when that willingness is established, God can release him from going through with the sacrifice. When this story was told in a context where people were familiar with the idea of sacrificing their child as an expression of commitment to God (and thus to back up their prayer and maybe prevail upon God to grant it), one further significance of the story was that it relates how God did once ask for such a sacrifice but in the end did not want it.

Yet by its nature a burnt offering is indeed costly. When David was to build an altar at that same place where Abraham had been willing to offer Isaac and where people would in due course sacrifice burnt offerings, he needed to acquire the site from its owner. The site was now a threshing floor—an exposed place where a farmer could flail the grain and then throw it into the air so that the wind would carry away the chaff and let the heavier good grain fall to the ground again. When David offered to buy the site, its owner wanted to give it to him for free. David responded, "No, because I will definitely acquire them at the full price, because I will not lift up to Yahweh what belongs to you. I will not offer up a burnt offering that cost nothing" (1 Chr 21:24).

Celebrating

Among the three or four main types of psalm and three or four main ways of speaking to God, logically the psalm of praise comes first. It is the verbal and musical equivalent to the burnt offering. Psalm 95 is an example. It begins:

> Come, let's resound for Yahweh,
>   let's shout for our crag who delivers us.
> Let's draw near to his face with confession;
>   we will shout for him with melodies.
> Because Yahweh is the great God,
>   the great king over all gods,
> the one in whose hand are the far reaches of the earth,
>   and to whom the mountain peaks belong,
> the one to whom the sea belongs (he made it)

and the dry land (his hands shaped it).
Come, let's bow low, let's bend down,
    let's bow the knee before Yahweh our maker.
Because he is our God,
    and we are the people he pastures,
    the sheep in his hand. (Ps 95:1–7)

This celebration involves a loud and enthusiastic self-summons to worship, which is at the same time an expression of worship because the people issuing the summons are already involved in it in the manner of Christian worshipers singing, "O come all ye faithful." In other psalms, such as Psalm 100, the summons is directed at other people like the summons in that carol, but it is really still a self-summons. Psalm 95 goes on to incorporate a proclamation of the reasons for the celebration, which are also the content of the worship. It speaks of the person and the nature of the God we are celebrating. It involves declarations that confront what the rest of the world thinks. It entails body and movement as well as mind and voice, and then also a physical self-lowering that is the outward expression of an inner self-lowering. Perhaps that self-lowering prepares the way for what follows, or perhaps what follows raises a question about all this noise and prostration.

    Today, if you listen to his voice,
        do not toughen your mind as you did at Meribah [Argument].

                                          (Ps 95:7–8)

Perhaps God has had enough of celebration and wants people to be quiet and listen. Certainly he implies that it is possible for celebration to be unaccompanied by trust and by an acknowledgment of Yahweh's ways—that is, by not just a knowing of them but a submitting to them. It is therefore possible for people who engage in enthusiastic, heartfelt celebration to forfeit the possibility of entering the promised land, or to be there physically but not really be there, or to lose their place there.[8]

8. See the discussion of Heb 3 and 4 (where this last part of Ps 95 is expounded) on pp. 30–34 above.

Protesting

So life with God can involve protest on God's side. The Psalms show that it can also involve protest on our side. A key factor in preventing some Israelites from entering into the promised land was their repeated protests about what God was doing with them. But they were always protesting to or at Moses, not to or at God. In the Psalms, people under pressure protest to God as the one who is responsible for their situation and the one who can do something about it. It is the most prominent way of speaking to God in the Psalms, an aspect of the way in which we are invited to relate to God as Father. Children who have a confident relationship with their father can be free in battering on his chest with their protests. The First Testament does not make much explicit use of the actual image of God as Father, but it works with the reality of our being God's children.

It is possible to see this freedom to voice our protests as a freedom to find release by holding nothing back, but that aim is not the chief element when children batter on their father's chest. The point is to get father to do something about the topic of protest, to act differently from the way he is acting at present. So it is with the protest psalms. They are Israel's dominant form of prayer, and they work on the assumption that we can get God to change his mind. They know that such prayer does not always work, but they do not redefine the nature of prayer in light of that fact; they come back and urge God again.

There is no constraint on the Psalms' protests. Psalm 88 begins:

Yahweh, my God who delivers,
    by day I have cried out, by night in front of you.
May my plea come before you;
    bend your ear to my resounding noise.
Because my whole person is full of bad experiences;
    my life has arrived at Sheol. (vv. 1–3)

And it continues in that way for another ten verses, then concludes:

Yahweh, why do you reject me,
    hide your face from me?
I am afflicted, breathing my last since youth;
    I have borne your dreads, I despair.
Your acts of rage have passed over me,

> your acts of terror have destroyed me.
> They are around me like water all day,
>   they have encircled me altogether.
> You have taken friend and neighbor far from me,
>   my acquaintances—darkness. (vv. 14–18)

I said the psalm concludes, but it does not conclude—it just stops. No, there is no constraint on the psalmists' freedom about the way they pour themselves out to God, because he is the person who can do something about situations. There are no feelings (anger, doubt, resentment, despair) that cannot be expressed to the one who can take them. It is no wonder that the martyrs in Revelation 6:9–11 pray the way they do. They will have learned from the Psalms.

Interceding

Outside the Psalter, the First Testament incorporates a number of prayers in which leaders pray for their people; see especially Ezra 9 and Nehemiah 9. Although leaders such as Ezra and Nehemiah are hardly guilty of the faithlessness they acknowledge in these prayers, a feature of the prayers is that the leaders pray for "us" rather than for "them." Ezra, for instance, is appalled to discover that Judahites have been marrying women from the neighboring communities, who would not be followers of Yahweh (they are not like a foreigner such as Ruth who becomes a follower of Yahweh). Ezra prays,

> My God, I am disgraced and ashamed to lift up my face to you, my God, because our wayward acts have grown above our head, and our liability is great, as far as the heavens. From the days of our ancestors until this day we have been in great liability, and through our wayward acts we have been given into the hand of the kings of the countries, we, our kings, our priests, with sword, with captivity, with plunder, and with shame of face, this very day. . . .
>
> After all that is come upon us because of our bad ways and our great liabilities, when you, our God, have held back [in punishing] below our waywardness, and given us an escape group like this, shall we go back to contravening your orders and intermarrying with the peoples who are characterized by these offensive practices? (Ezra 9:6–7, 13–14)

While Ezra is "pleading and making confession, crying and falling down before God's house" (Ezra 10:1), he is neither one of the community whose wayward acts caused the downfall of Judah in the first place, nor is he one of the people who has undertaken one of these marriages. But he prays for them by praying for "us," the people with whom he identifies.

This practice puts us on the track of another significance of the book of Psalms. The Psalms include one or two explicit intercessory prayers. The most striking is the prayer for the king to exercise proper government in his care for the poor and oppressed (Ps 72). This psalm models how to pray for the government.

> God, give the king your rulings,
>   the royal son your faithfulness.
> May he give judgment for your people with faithfulness,
>   your humble ones with authority.
> May the mountains bear well-being for the people,
>   and the hills, in faithfulness.
> May he exercise authority for the humble among the people,
>   deliver the needy, crush the fraud.
> May they live in awe of you while the sun shines,
>   and before the moon, generation after generation.
> May he come down like rain on mowed grass,
>   like downpours, an overflowing on the earth.
> May the faithful person flourish in his days,
>   and abundance of well-being, until the moon is no more. (Ps 72:1–7)

It is also a good example of the usefulness of prayer that works horizontally as well as vertically, if the king is present to hear this prayer that lays out priorities for his reign!

The example of Ezra makes it easy also to imagine that Israel used the protest psalms to pray for other people as well as for themselves.

> Yahweh, do not reprove me in your anger,
>   do not discipline me with your wrath.
> Be gracious to me, Yahweh, because I am faint;
>   heal me, Yahweh, because my bones shake in fearfulness.
> My entire being shakes in great fearfulness,
>   and you, Yahweh—how long?
> Turn back, Yahweh, pull me out,
>   deliver me for the sake of your commitment! (Ps 6:1–4)

One can imagine that someone whose life has collapsed would come to the temple with their family and friends and with an offering, and the company would pray the psalm with this person. Or if the person could not come to the temple because they were ill, or away from the city in battle, or under arrest pending trial, the family and friends might come on their own with a sacrifice and pray this way.

Arguing

The protests in the Psalms presuppose that God does not always respond. People praying these psalms, then, have to live with two sets of facts. Psalm 22 does so:

> My God, my God, why have you abandoned me,
>> far away from delivering me, from the word I yell?
> My God, I call by day but you do not answer,
>> and by night—there is no quietness for me.
> But you sit as the sacred one,
>> the great praise of Israel.
> In you our ancestors trusted;
>> they trusted and you enabled them to survive. (Ps 22:1–4)

The psalm alternates between the fact of how things are and the facts about God that stand in tension with how things are. It will abandon neither set of facts because both are—well, facts.

Psalms 42 and 43 (often considered one psalm) have us arguing with ourselves in an analogous way:

> Why do you bow low, my entire being,
>> and why are you in turmoil within me?
> Wait for God, because I shall yet confess him,
>> as the deliverance of my face and my God. (Ps 42:11)

Such agonizing and arguing are key to the way one lives with personal tragedy. Job agonizes in this way, and the book of Job displays such arguments. It is a gargantuan example of a protest psalm. Job's story opens like the beginning of Psalm 44, which recalls how God had been involved with Israel in the past. Then his life collapses in a series of tragedies. From now on, he has to live with two sets of facts: with the basis on which Yahweh is supposed to deal with us, and with the occurrence of these calamities. His friends urge him to reconcile them by acknowledging the waywardness and rebellion that must lie behind the disasters, but doing so would involve giving up one of the sets of facts. We know from the beginning of the story that Job is a person of unequaled commitment to God, and we can accept his account of his life that he later gives as an exposition of that set of facts (Job 31).

So Job rightly argues both with his "friends" and with God. In due course God appears and takes part in the argument, though not in such a way as to resolve it on the terms it has taken. God offers no critique of Job's life and no direct critique of Job's assumptions about the other set of facts concerning the way God deals with us. Indeed, in due course God acknowledges that Job has spoken the truth about God, as the friends have not. Yet God also sets Job's assumptions about God in a wider framework. The reader of Job's story knows that it takes place on a broader canvas, but Job is never told what that canvas is. God's response to Job's argument is to point out that the world is a much bigger place than he seems to think. Reality does not revolve around him. He is going to have to keep trusting in God and keep submitting to God, even though he cannot see how to reconcile the two sets of facts.

Confessing

Like intercession, explicit confession is more prominent outside the Psalter than within it. This fact draws our attention to a feature of the protests in the Psalter: rather than acknowledging waywardness, they are more inclined to protest relative innocence. The implication is that unless we can realistically claim to have been living a life of commitment to Yahweh, we cannot justifiably protest if things go wrong in our life.

The five prayer-poems that make up the book of Lamentations are examples of confessional prayers. They are also protests, like those in the Psalter, about the extent to which God let Jerusalem suffer when Jerusalem fell in 587 BC and about how long he is letting the city continue in its desolate state. But unlike most protest prayers in the Psalter, they acknowledge systematically that the city's destruction was deserved in light of its waywardness in relation to Yahweh. The prayers in Ezra 9 and Nehemiah 9 are also confessions. And within the Psalter, Psalm 51 is a remarkable confessional psalm.

Be gracious to me, God,
    in accordance with your commitment.
In accordance with the abundance of your compassion,
    wipe away my rebellions.
Wash me thoroughly from my waywardness,
    cleanse me from my wrongdoing.
Because I myself acknowledge my rebellions;
    my wrongdoing is in front of me continually.
In relation to you alone have I acted wrongly,
    and done what is bad in your eyes. . . .
Remove my wrongdoing with hyssop so I am pure,
    wash me so I am whiter than snow. . . .
Hide your face from my wrongdoings,
    wipe away all my wayward acts.
Create for me a pure mind, God;
    renew an established spirit within me.
Do not throw me out of your presence;
    do not take your sacred spirit from me.
Give back to me the joy of being delivered by you;
    may your generous spirit sustain me. (Ps 51:1–4, 7, 9–12)

Whereas Christians often assume that people found forgiveness in Israel by bringing a sacrifice, the psalm recognizes that sacrifices are useless in that connection. When we need forgiveness, all we can do is throw ourselves on God's mercy. The sacrifices that link in some way with expiation are not designed to deal with "proper" sin, only with defilement—which will include the defilement that results from proper sin, but not the sin itself. The psalm uses cleansing language to refer to the supernatural cleansing that God needs to do in response to penitence.

Because you would not delight in a sacrifice, were I to give it;
    you would not accept a burnt offering.
Godly sacrifices are a broken spirit;
    a broken, crushed mind, God, you would not despise. (Ps 51:16–17)

It is when God in grace and mercy has cleansed people that it is then possible to resume the regular life of worship with its sacrifices expressing commitment and faithfulness.

Do good to Zion through your acceptance;
> build up Jerusalem's walls.
Then you will delight in faithful sacrifices . . . ;
> then people will take bulls up onto your altar. (Ps 51:18–19)

Trusting

Whereas Psalm 88 comes at the "extreme protest" end of the spectrum of prayer psalms, other psalms come at the "believing hope" end.

Yahweh is my light, my deliverance:
> of whom should I be afraid?
Yahweh is the stronghold of my life:
> of whom should I be in dread?
When people who deal badly drew near me,
> to devour my flesh,
my adversaries and my enemies:
> those people collapsed, fell.
If an army camps against me,
> my heart will not be afraid.
If battle arises against me,
> during this I trust. (Ps 27:1–3)

The psalm already embraces past, present, and the possible future. In the past, Yahweh has shown himself trustworthy. In the present, I know he is my light and my stronghold. Therefore I can look to future possibilities with confidence. Subsequently in the psalm, it seems that the possibility of another crisis is not just theoretical, but the statements about past and present make it possible to pray in a less agonized way than happens in protest psalms:

So now my head is high,
> above my enemies round me.
In his tent I will offer noisy sacrifices;
> I will sing and make music for Yahweh.
Listen, Yahweh, to my voice when I call;
> be gracious to me, answer me. . . .
Do not leave me, do not abandon me,
> my God who delivers. . . .

In view of the people watching for me,
>   do not give me over to the will of my adversaries.
Because there have arisen against me false witnesses,
>   a person who testifies violence.
Unless I trusted to see good things from Yahweh
>   in the country of the living. . . .
Hope in Yahweh, be strong,
>   may your mind stand firm, hope in Yahweh! (Ps 27:6–14)

Hope is an expression of trust, or another way of describing it.

A further encouraging feature of the Psalms emerges. The difference between psalms of protest and psalms of trust or hope is not that the circumstances of the former are more desperate than the circumstances of the latter. It is that the person who prays the former lacks the trust and hope of the person who prays the latter. But the Psalter does not sit in judgment on the person who lacks hope or trust. It provides a wide variety of prayers that people with different degrees of faith and hope can pray.

Questioning

Thus the First Testament allows that one may find trust hard to maintain, and it does not dismiss us when we find it hard. It permits us to keep mulling over questions when we cannot see the answers. Ecclesiastes is the First Testament's great repository of such mulling.

The way the main body of Ecclesiastes works is by laying out examples of what one is supposed to believe and then saying, "Yes, but. . . ."

I have seen under the sun:

>   In the place for the [proper] exercise of authority, faithlessness was
>   there,
>   in the place for faithfulness, faithlessness was there. (Eccl 3:16)

Those are the facts one can observe. So Ecclesiastes repeats to himself the proper convictions of an Israelite who believes in a just God:

>   Over the faithful person and the faithless,
>   God will exercise authority.

> Because there will be a time for every purpose
> and for every activity there. (3:17)

But he is not satisfied with statements of that kind. So he goes on,

> I myself said inside myself with regard to human beings, it is for God to purify them and for them to see that they are animals. Because the experience of human beings and the experience of animals is a single experience for them. Like the dying of the one, so is the dying of the other. Each has the same spirit. The advantage of humanity over animals—there is none, because each is hollow. Each goes to the same place. Each came into being from dirt and each goes back to dirt. Who knows if the spirit of human beings goes up and the spirit of animals goes down beneath the earth? (3:18–21)

He cannot see any empirical evidence for things people say about what happens after you die—and empirical evidence is very important to Ecclesiastes. Indeed, the empirical can be grievously troubling.

> I again saw all the oppressed people that are appearing under the sun. There, the tears of the oppressed, and there is no comforter for them; yes, from the hand of their oppressors is the energy, and there is no comforter for them. (4:1)

Ecclesiastes thus gives the reader permission to be strong-minded and relentless in facing facts. He faces the facts about death and about chance and about our incapacity to find answers to ultimate questions and about the ultimately unsatisfying nature of the things to which people look for meaning, such as fame and wealth and achievement. Not for a moment does he contemplate giving up on God or giving up on life as a good gift from God, but neither will he give up on asking questions about the realities that lie in front of him. The closing paragraphs of the book comment that we do not need too many books like Ecclesiastes in the Scriptures, but that one such book is a gift of God.

Thanking

Alongside the burnt offering in the description of regular offerings in Leviticus comes the fellowship sacrifice or well-being sacrifice (we are not sure how to translate the Hebrew term *shelamim*). Whereas people give the entirety of a burnt offering to God, a fellowship offering is shared between the offerers and God. Fellowship offerings can be made simply because one wants to, as a "freewill offering," or because one has made a promise, but also because one has particular reason to thank God for something—maybe the safe birth of a baby or a safe return from a battle.

A thank offering thus goes along with a thanksgiving in words, as we ourselves often give practical expression to our gratitude to someone by giving them a gift. The gift without the words might not mean anything; in another sense, the word without the gift might not mean anything.

The words of a thanksgiving are addressed to other people as well as to God, and a psalm of thanksgiving can move easily between the two forms of speech. So Psalm 30 can begin:

> I will exalt you, Yahweh, because you put me down,
>> but did not let my enemies rejoice about me.
> Yahweh my God,
>> I cried for help to you, and you healed me.
> Yahweh, you got my life up from Sheol,
>> you kept me alive from going down into the Pit. (30:1–3)

But then it goes on:

> Make music for Yahweh, you who are committed to him,
>> confess his sacred commemoration,
> because there is a moment in his anger,
>> a life in his acceptance. (30:4–5)

The logic is that thanksgiving and testimony are different ways of describing the significance of the same action. Glorifying God for what he has done for us does not work unless it is expressed outwardly in a way that other people can hear. They need to know about what God has done so that they can glorify God and also so that their faith can be built up. It is the logic implied by Paul's exhortation in Ephesians 5:19.[9] What God has done for someone

---

9. See the discussion of Eph 5 and 6 on pp. 184–87 above.

else establishes what he might do for me, which links with the fact that the occasion when someone makes a fellowship sacrifice as an expression of thanksgiving is another occasion when one's family and friends also gather.

Thanksgiving involves telling a story. The psalm tells the story about how things were when everything was okay, how everything collapsed (possibly through no fault of my own), how I prayed, how God heard, and how God acted. It can be the case that protest psalms already start telling this story, and the distinction between protest psalms and thanksgivings can look unclear. The reason is that God's answering prayer is assumed to have two stages. There is an answer in words and an answer in actions. Sometimes a protest psalm can reach the awareness that God has heard the prayer and has responded in the sense of making a commitment to delivering the person from their predicament; Psalm 22 works that way. But then God needs to take the action, and it is when God has acted as well as spoken that one comes back to the sanctuary with friends and family and offering. Then the story the thanksgiving tells can refer to stage two in the answer to prayer as well as stage one, and it can go on to invite people to join in the thanksgiving and to let their trust in God be built up.

Questions for Discussion

1. Which aspect of the texts from Deuteronomy that Jesus quotes in Matthew 4 seems most important for you personally?
2. Which aspects of the "Disciple's Blessings" in Matthew 5 seem most important for you personally?
3. Which aspects of prayer and worship in the First Testament and the New Testament seem most encouraging or challenging for you personally?
4. Which other aspects of the New Testament's teaching about a relationship with God seem most important to you personally?
5. Which other aspects of the First Testament's teaching about a relationship with God seem most important to you personally?

CHAPTER 6

Life

The First Testament provides the foundation and the raw material for Jesus's moral teaching; his teaching about how human life is to be lived. He is again "fulfilling" or "filling out" the First Testament, speaking like a prophet, helping people to see implications in the Scriptures that they might be avoiding, and inviting us to study what they have to teach us about the way we should live.

His Blessings (Matt 5:1–12) had talked initially about "them" (the people who are lowly, mourning, etc.), but he was teaching his disciples and his "they" concealed a "you." In part he was inviting them to imagine that they are looking at people who are lowly, mourning, and so on, as if they are watching a movie; but he wants them to look so as to recognize, in the characters they are watching, themselves as his disciples as they are supposed to be. In the coda to the Blessings, the point becomes explicit: "Blessed are you. . . ." Jesus keeps that direct form of address when he continues,

> You are the salt of the earth. But if the salt loses its saltiness, how can it be made salty again? It is no longer good for anything, except to be thrown out and trampled underfoot. You are the light of the world. A city on a hill cannot be hidden. Neither do people light a lamp and put it under a bowl. Instead they put it on its stand, and it gives light to everyone in the house. In the same way, let your light shine before others, that they may see your good deeds and glorify your Father in heaven. (Matt 5:13–16)

The form of address is thus similar, but Jesus makes another transition: the plural "you" are now the singular "salt" and "light." When his disciples are lowly, mourning, and so on together, they become salt and light.

The First Testament never tells people that they are salt. It does note that salt makes things tasty (Job 6:6), which seems to be the point here in Matthew. Light is a more prominent image in the First Testament, not least in a connection like the one in Matthew. It appears especially in God's promises in Isaiah 60–62. Yahweh is going to make bright light shine on Jerusalem in a way that will draw the nations to it:

> Get up, be alight, because your light is coming,
> Yahweh's splendor has shone on you!
> Because there—darkness covers the earth,
> gloom, the peoples.
> But on you Yahweh will shine;
> his splendor will appear over you.
> Nations will come to your light,
> kings to your shining brightness. (Isa 60:1–3)

It is another way of promising that the lowly, the mourning, the meek, the hungry, the merciful, the peacemaking, and the persecuted will find comfort, restoration, and blessing.

How will they let their light shine? Part of the answer lies in what now follows.

6.1 Matthew 5:17–20: Not to Annul but to Fulfill

Jesus will soon go on to say, "You have heard that it was said. . . . But I tell you . . ."; and some of the commands that people have heard said, to which he refers, are ones that appear in the Torah. So is he replacing the Torah? Yet he declares that he is fulfilling it. He is doing so in several ways. He is bringing out its implications and challenging people to take seriously its more demanding side and not just to settle for the more basic of its standards. He encourages people to see the Torah and the Prophets as an outworking of love for God and love for one's neighbor.

Fulfillment

Matthew 5:1–16 has taken up many themes from the First Testament and applied them to the question of who we are and how Jesus draws us to relate to God. Now Jesus stands back and offers an inference from what he has been doing.

> Do not think that I have come to abolish the Law or the Prophets; I have not come to abolish them but to fulfill them. (5:17)

What is this "fulfilling"? This word might continue to have the implication it had in Matthew 1–2, where it denoted Jesus filling out promises. One could then think of passages in the Torah that have been interpreted messianically such as the declarations about the woman's offspring crushing the serpent in Genesis 3:15, about the scepter in Genesis 49:9–10, about the star in Numbers 24:17, and about a prophet in Deuteronomy 18:15–19. Yet Matthew refers to none of these passages (though Num 24:17 presumably lies behind Matt 2:2). Peter does see Jesus as the prophet in Deuteronomy (Acts 3:22), but the New Testament does not see Jesus as the fulfillment of the passages in Genesis, even though they had been interpreted messianically by New Testament times. It is Justin Martyr and Irenaeus in the second century who first see Genesis 3:15 as a kind of initial preaching of the gospel.[1] In connection with Genesis, the New Testament focuses more on Jesus being the fulfillment of the promise to Abraham.

Matthew does include many allusions to and quotations from the Torah, not least in the teaching that follows this statement about fulfilling, but these allusions and quotations relate rather to its teaching on behavior. It turns out that this fulfilling of the Torah and the Prophets is different from the fulfilling in Matthew 1–2, though once again fulfilling means filling out. What Jesus does is fill out or spell out the implications of the Torah and the Prophets. His talk of fulfillment, then, resonates with Paul's speaking of the Torah's expectations being "fulfilled" in people who believe in Jesus and in whom the Holy Spirit is at work, through the fact that love is the "fulfilling" of the Torah (Rom 8:4; 9:31; 13:8, 10; Gal 5:14).

Jesus confirms that point in the way he continues:

> Until heaven and earth disappear, not the smallest letter, not the least stroke of a pen, will by any means disappear from the Law until everything is accomplished. Anyone who sets aside one of the least of these commands and teaches others accordingly will be called least in the kingdom of heaven, but whoever practices and teaches these commands will be called great in the

---

1. See Justin Martyr, *Against Trypho*, 100; Irenaeus, *Against Heresies* 3.23.7; 5.21.1.

kingdom of heaven. For I tell you that unless your righteousness surpasses that of the Pharisees and the teachers of the law, you will certainly not enter the kingdom of heaven. (Matt 5:18–20)

More literally, "not an iota" (or *yod*, the smallest letter in the Hebrew alphabet), "not a dot" (the smallest part of a letter; cf. our "dotting the i's and crossing the t's") will disappear. Yet Jesus's subsequent teaching shows that he does not mean he is committed to observing everything that the Torah says.

Admittedly, most of the acts whereby Jesus offends some other Jews, such as his "breaches" of the Sabbath, indicate a different way of understanding the Torah rather than a breaking of it. In another sense, the same is true when he declares that it is what comes out of our mouths, not what goes into them, that makes us impure. Yet Mark infers that he thereby declared all foods pure (Mark 7:19), which does suggest an abrogation of the Torah itself (cf. Acts 10); nevertheless, it is a fulfillment insofar as it means the achieving of the Torah's own aims. It is in this sense that he challenges his disciples to do right and be faithful in a way that goes beyond the doing right and faithfulness of other people who seek to live committed lives and who have a deep understanding of the Scriptures.

Insights and Contexts

"Progressive revelation" is a common model for understanding the relationship between the First Testament and the teaching of Jesus and the New Testament. The idea is that God was gradually training his people through First Testament times until he eventually revealed his ultimate standards. This understanding does not correspond to the way Jesus speaks of the Torah and the Prophets. Progressive revelation looks like a baptized version of the idea of evolutionary development, and it does not work when applied to the Bible (and to most other areas of the humanities, as far as I can tell).

Within the First Testament itself, the most profound understanding of God and of God's ways and of God's expectations does not emerge as the First Testament story unfolds. Indeed, Jesus notes that the most profound understanding is associated with the beginning of the First Testament story. It is there in Genesis 1–2. Paul in Romans 1–3 also assumes that people knew the fundamental truths about God and about right and wrong from the beginning, but they surrendered this awareness, partly because they did not like it. Indeed, one could argue that the development in thinking in the

First Testament as a whole is more degeneration than progress. Paul also notes that the priority of grace over law is clearer at the beginning of the story than it is later.

I do not imply that Genesis was written before the rest of the First Testament, just that the First Testament associates it with the beginning of the world's story. But if we suspend judgment on the date of Genesis and ask what we do know about the dating of the First Testament, then the oldest works are the messages of prophets such as Amos, and they form an ethical high point of the First Testament. Conversely, Western readers are much less happy with the moral stance of Ezra and Nehemiah, the famous breakers-up of marriages (see Ezra 9–10; Nehemiah 13), and they come much later in the First Testament.

There may well be points at which moral insight is more profound later in this story (so there is gain) as well as points at which it is more profound earlier (so there is loss), and there are probably points at which it is more profound in the middle of the story. The insistence in Jeremiah and Ezekiel on the responsibility of individual generations and individual people to make their own decisions rather than blame earlier generations might be an example. It is in the Babylonian period, too, that I would actually date the creation story in Genesis 1, with its affirmation about all humanity, male and female, as being made in God's image. What these examples show is that insight emerges in relation to contexts. It was circumstances in their day that enabled Jeremiah, Ezekiel, and the author of Genesis 1 to see what they saw—in each case over against fallacious views they needed to confront. It is also in relation to the circumstances of a context and the risky action on the part of their contemporaries that Ezra and Nehemiah needed to take the action that they did.

Something similar is true about the New Testament, though again our not knowing the context in which many of the works were written complicates our thinking about the question. But the different stances taken toward the Roman Empire in Romans 13 and Revelation 13 seem likely to reflect different ways in which the empire affects the congregation Paul writes to and the congregations John writes to.

Creation Ideals and Allowances for Human Stubbornness

One consideration behind the different standards expected in different parts of the First Testament reflects the difference between law and ethics. The point about law is to buttress order and restrain disorder in society. It aims to constrain the conflict that imperils the society. Law keeps one eye on ethics, as the society understands it, but its aim is not the enforcement of ethics.

The First Testament embraces both law and ethics. When it is laying down the law, it has the same aim as other law. So the Decalogue proscribes murder, adultery, theft, and perjury, but not hostility, anger, hatred, lust, jealousy, or lying (it does proscribe coveting, which shows that the Decalogue is a hybrid of law and something more like ethics). It is other parts of the First Testament that proscribe those other attitudes and behaviors that show how things go wrong for people characterized by them, and/or that laud love, patience, faithfulness, mercy, grace, contentment, and truthfulness.

The prohibitions mark the boundaries of acceptable behavior, beyond which one is in unequivocally foreign territory. When they are established, one can begin to "possess the land" by filling in the positive content of behavioral style and attitude appropriate to the country in question. But the country always needs the boundary markers. The land needs frontiers as well as policies for internal development. To put it in terms of another image, the building always needs the lower courses of bricks as well as the superstructure. Jesus is not interested in internal attitudes rather than external actions (it is he who tells an adulteress not to sin again; see John 8:11) but in both. The New Testament writers are not interested in the law of Christ rather than the Decalogue. Ephesians supports its teaching by quoting from the latter (Eph 6:1–3), and elsewhere it repeats one of its prohibitions (see Eph 4:28). The New Testament writers are interested in both.

Jesus suggests another model for understanding differences in level among scriptural commands. Some Pharisees ask his opinion on divorce, and he refers them to Genesis 1–2, whose account of the origin of marriage (he infers) indicates that divorce cannot really be recognized. What then of the permission of divorce in Deuteronomy 24:1–4? It was given "for your hardness of heart," he says. In effect, he implies that divorce and remarriage are a form of legalized adultery. Why then does the Torah make a regulation for them? It does so because of human sin. Marriages will break down, so the Torah contains a regulation that applies to that fact (Matt 19:2–9).

Within the Torah, then, one can find both material that expresses the ultimate will of God and material that takes a realistic approach to the fact of human sin and contents itself with the attempt to control the extent to which God's ultimate will is bound to be ignored, and to minimize the ill effects that issue from this. Marriage breakdown is hardly reconcilable with Genesis 1–2, but it is better to acknowledge the fact of marriage breakdown and seek to lessen the further ills to which it can lead (especially for a woman) than to refuse to recognize such realities. The "low standard" of some of the rules in the Torah issues from their being designed for sinners. Such rules contrast not only with the exalted standard of the Sermon on the Mount but with the exalted standard of the creation story and of the challenges of the prophets.

Indeed, Jesus's appeal to Genesis 1–2 reminds us that the First Testament's significance for ethical questions emerges not exclusively from the explicit commands that appear in the Torah, the Prophets, and the wisdom books. This significance also comes from the perspective on human life that appears in the story of creation (humanity as made in God's image) and the story of redemption (humanity as freed from bondage), from the values asserted especially in the Prophets and the wisdom books (values such as justice, faithfulness, and compassion), and from the concerns regarding human life that run through the whole First Testament, concerns with areas such as marriage and sex, politics and land, work and pleasure, family and community.

This element of condescension in the Torah and the background of First Testament ethics in creation as well as in redemption point to the possibility of applying God's standards to our own world. In Israel, God "compromised" in relating to humanity in its stubbornness, rather than either insisting on a standard it would never reach, or abandoning it because it would not reach this standard. The First Testament thus offers us a paradigm for applying God's ultimate standards to the situations of humanity that we encounter.

Indeed, the Torah's application of God's standards to humanity suggests one aspect of the answer to the question whether the expectations attached to Yahweh's covenant with Israel can apply outside the covenant people. They can be generally applicable because they were given to an ordinary people, even though it was a people drawn into a special relationship with God. They can be generally applicable because they are based on creation as well as on redemption; their background lies in the nature of humanity as humanity and in humanity's relationship with its creator. Similar considerations suggest that we can apply the prophets' expectations regarding fairness in society to the ordinary nation today, and apply to it promises about the blessing that can come when a people returns to the ways of God (2 Chr 7:14); indeed, the book of Jonah pictures a prophet doing so.

Prophecy and Torah

So the expectations of the prophets are often higher than those of the rules in the Torah. We could say that the prophets fulfill or fill out the Torah. And when Jesus says, "But I tell you," he is acting as Israel's greatest prophet. Prophets commonly set themselves over against what people think, including what people think on the basis of the Scriptures. The Pharisees and theologians of Jesus's day concerned themselves with the exposition of the Torah in relation to the behavior of people who were sinners. Suppose one adopts a prophetic starting point?

Hosea and Isaiah are models. In their day, the kings of Ephraim and Judah operate on the basis of realpolitik. The nations are under pressure, and the kings seek to make alliances with other nations who may be able to help them to survive. But the prophets expect Ephraim and Judah to conduct their political policies on the basis of trust in Yahweh.

In Ahaz's time, when Ephraim itself, in alliance with Syria, is putting pressure on Judah, Ahaz is out inspecting his defenses. Isaiah confronts him with a promise that Yahweh will sort out the people who are threatening Ahaz. Isaiah declares,

> If you do not stand firm in trust,
>> indeed, you will not stand firm at all. (Isa 7:9)

In Hezekiah's time, the outward international political situation has changed but the inner dynamics are the same, and Hezekiah is seeking support from Egypt. Isaiah declares,

> Hey, defiant sons (Yahweh's declaration),
>> in forming counsel but not from me,
> in pouring a drink offering but not from my spirit,
>> in order to heap wrong on wrong,
> you who go to descend to Egypt,
>> but have not asked my bidding,
> in protecting yourselves by Pharaoh's protection
>> and in taking shelter in Egypt's shade.
> But Pharaoh's protection will become shame for you,
>> and shelter in Egypt's shade, disgrace. (Isa 30:1–3)

The drink offering refers to the religious rites that accompany political exchanges, negotiations, and treaty making.

Hosea's concern with Ephraim's whoring refers at least in part to the same realities. Isaiah's focus lies on the way Judah is treating Egypt as its potential protection, shelter, and shade. Judah is thus involved in blasphemy, because those words describe what Yahweh is supposed to be for his people (see Ps 91).

The prophets expect Israel to live by outrageously impractical standards. They sometimes need to urge people to live by the Torah (see, e.g., Jer 34:8–22). They often focus on a different level of Yahweh's expectations:

> By what means shall I meet Yahweh,
>   bow down to God on High?
> Shall I meet him by means of burnt offerings,
>   bullocks a year old?
> Would Yahweh accept thousands of rams,
>   in myriads of streams of oil?
> Should I give my firstborn for my rebellion,
>   the fruit of my body for my own wrongdoing?
> He has told you, people, what is good,
>   what Yahweh requires from you:
> rather, exercising authority and being loyal to commitment,
>   and being diffident in how you walk with your God. (Mic 6:6–8)

Love for God and Love for Neighbor

When Jesus is asked what is the most important command in the Torah (Matt 22:36–40), he asks if he can have two, and identifies one from Deuteronomy and one from Leviticus. Love for God and love for one's neighbor are the most important rules in the Torah (Deut 6:4–5; Lev 19:18). His additional comment is also important: all the rest of the Torah and the Prophets hangs on these two commands. The entirety of the Torah and the Prophets is an outworking of them. I imagine he would not mind his comment being extended to the Writings (indeed, he may assume that "The Torah and the Prophets" includes the Writings, which did not have that succinct title in his time).

It is therefore possible to ask of any command in the Torah, how is it an expression of love for God or of love for one's neighbor? One can see how the divorce rule is an expression of love. What happens to a woman who is thrown out by her husband, or held onto by him despite the way he abuses her? The requirement that he give her a divorce certificate opens up the possibility of her escaping an abusive relationship and gives her a document that establishes her status. It provides a little safeguard against ending up in the sex trade because it is the only way to get something to eat.

Another rule concerns what happens to a girl whom an Israelite captures in war and takes home as a wife—maybe not his only one (Deut 21:10–14). Why on earth is the Torah issuing a regulation in this connection? Why not simply ban the practice of capturing a girl whom you fancy? The problem is that men may well not simply accept a ban on the practice, and if all the Torah does is ban it, a man who ignores the ban is then subject to no constraint. Offering some protection to the status of such a girl is an expression of love for one's neighbor.

The element of condescension in the Torah is present in New Testament teaching. Although Paul makes observations about slaves and free people that reassert their oneness before God at creation, he nevertheless accepts the institution of slavery (in its Roman form, a much more vicious institution than the debt servitude of which the Torah speaks) and bids slaves obey their masters. Perhaps compromise is present even in Matthew 19, when Jesus's ban on divorce is qualified by his making an exception in the case of *porneia* (the word often means "fornication," but its precise significance here is the subject of debate). No such qualification appears in Mark's account. Does Matthew simply make explicit what the Markan version took for granted? Is Jesus implicitly (in Mark) or explicitly (in Matthew) also condescending to the realities of human sin, failure, and suffering in the lives of his followers?

The principle of condescension may also explain the First Testament's enthusiasm over ritual regulations, from which Jesus turns away in a chapter such as Matthew 15. Both the rites of sacrifice and the place of sacrifice (the temple) first appear in the Scriptures as human ideas. They are accepted by God, with overt misgivings in the latter case, rather than seen as originally divine intentions (Gen 4:3–4; 2 Sam 7). Perhaps regulations concerning cleanness and taboo have a similar status: not *ultimately* good ideas, but helpful to people in certain cultures and capable of being harnessed so as to embody real truth.

In the Bible's teaching on moral questions, then, the Scriptures written before Jesus and the new insights that issue from Jesus's coming complement each other. The Christian church's calling is to let its understanding of history, prophecy, theology, spirituality, and ethics be shaped by the joint witness of the two Testaments. By interpreting Jesus in light of the First Testament, the New Testament invites us to take up the First Testament's own concerns in all their breadth of interest. By interpreting the First Testament in light of Jesus, the New Testament invites us to look at those concerns in light of his coming.

6.2 Matthew 5:21–48: You Have Heard That It Was Said . . .

In the Sermon on the Mount, Jesus goes on to spell out what "fulfillment" looks like. In doing so, he begins from the Torah's commands relating to murder, adultery, false oaths, redress, and love, but then acts more as a prophet than as a Torah teacher, and approaches the Torah as interpreted in his day with a "yes, but." Yet many Torah-loyal Jews would have had no great problem with what he says, as many modern Jews see nothing un-Jewish in his teaching. The relationship of his teaching to the Torah is similar to the relationship of his Blessings to the First Testament. He takes up elements within the Torah and creates something new with them, affirming and developing strands of First Testament attitudes. He challenges people to live by the entirety of the Torah and the Prophets, not just by carefully chosen aspects of them interpreted in a way that suits us.

Hostility: Both Action and Attitude

> You have heard that it was said to the people long ago, "You shall not murder, and anyone who murders will be subject to judgment." But I tell you that anyone who is angry with a brother or sister will be subject to judgment. Again, anyone who says to a brother or sister, "Raca," is answerable to the Sanhedrin. And anyone who says, "You fool!" will be in danger of the fire of hell.
>
> Therefore, if you are offering your gift at the altar and there remember that your brother or sister has something against you, leave your gift there in front of the altar. First go and be reconciled to that person; then come and offer your gift. (Matt 5:21–24)

To say that the prohibition on murder is the sixth of the Ten Commandments sounds uncontroversial, but that simple statement raises several issues.

- Neither of the versions of the Ten Commandments describes them as the Ten Commandments.

- On the three occasions when the number "ten" occurs in relation to them (Exod 34:28; Deut 4:13; 10:13), they are not "Ten Commandments" but "Ten Words" (the phrase "Ten Commandments" goes back only to Luther). And they are phrased as statements, like a parent saying to a child, "You will not do that!" It sounds like a statement, but it is actually a strong command ("Don't even think about it!").
- There are various ways of allocating the numbers from one to ten, and in some traditions murder comes out as number five (because worshiping other gods and not making images are counted as one) or number seven (because in some arrangements adultery comes before murder).
- What does it mean by "murder"? English has several words for taking someone's life, such as *kill, slay,* and *murder.* So does Hebrew, but its words do not necessarily correspond with the English ones. One can say that "murder" in the commandment does not prohibit all killing; the Torah allows for killing in war and for capital punishment. The killing it bans is something like what we call murder, when someone decides for himself or herself to kill someone else.

To the ban on murder, Jesus adds a ban on anger, the attitude that can issue in murder. He thus "fulfills the Torah," which notes how anger can lead to murder, declares a curse on it (Gen 49:6–7), and tells stories about the trouble it can cause (e.g., Gen 27:45; 30:2). Proverbs, too, formulates aphorisms about the wisdom of avoiding anger (e.g., Prov 16:32).

The Psalms offer the best examples of a recognition that we cannot come to worship if our relationships with our neighbors are not right:

Yahweh, who may reside in your tent,
    who may dwell on your sacred mountain?
One who walks with integrity, acts with faithfulness,
    and speaks truth inside.
He has not gone about talking,
    has not done wrong to his neighbor,
    has not taken up reviling against someone near him.
In his eyes a contemptible person is to be rejected,
    but he honors people who live in awe of Yahweh;
    he has sworn to bring about something bad and has not changed it.
He has not given his silver on interest,
    and not taken a bribe against someone free of guilt;
    one who does these things, who does not slip ever. (Ps 15)

Sex: Both Vision and Realism

Adultery accompanies murder in the Ten Words, and so it does in Jesus's teaching.

> You have heard that it was said, "You shall not commit adultery." But I tell you that anyone who looks at a woman lustfully has already committed adultery with her in his heart. If your right eye causes you to stumble, gouge it out and throw it away. It is better for you to lose one part of your body than for your whole body to be thrown into hell. And if your right hand causes you to stumble, cut it off and throw it away. It is better for you to lose one part of your body than for your whole body to go into hell. (Matt 5:27–30)

I take it that the reason the Torah and Jesus are concerned about inner attitude as well as outward action is not that they think that it is really the inner attitude that matters, as if the outward act did not matter; nor that the inner attitude is simply wrong in its own right, though that may be true; but that going astray in inner attitude is what issues in going wrong in deed. Look after the inner attitude, and the outward act is more likely to take care of itself.

The Ten Words implicitly broaden the point about adultery to cover lust when they come to number ten. In the Deuteronomy version:

> You will not desire your neighbor's wife. You will not long for your neighbor's house or his field, his servant or his handmaid, his ox or his donkey, or anything that your neighbor has. (Deut 5:21)

When Paul talks about how we come to recognize that we are sinners, he comments, "I would not have known what coveting really was if the law had not said, 'You shall not covet'" (Rom 7:7). The Ten Words are most demanding at the beginning and the end: no other gods but Yahweh, and no coveting. Jesus fulfills the Torah by noting a demanding area of life where the coveting command is vitally important.

The difference between the two versions of the Decalogue also points toward another insight. The first version (Exod 20:17) has the same verb for desiring wife and desiring neighbor and field and so on, which points to another reason for desiring one's neighbor's wife: she is a more impressive piece of property, perhaps a more impressive embodiment of the ideal in

Proverbs 31. One is to be wary of lust, which may lead to adultery, and of coveting, which may lead to theft.

In the Sermon on the Mount, Jesus adds a brief version of his comment about divorce, whose broader significance we have already noted.

> It has been said, "Anyone who divorces his wife must give her a certificate of divorce." But I tell you that anyone who divorces his wife, except for sexual immorality, causes her to become an adulteress, and anyone who marries the divorced woman commits adultery. (Matt 5:31–32)

In making this declaration, Jesus goes against the Torah, but we have seen that he does so in order to uphold the Torah. He fulfills the Torah by insisting on its visionary standard and not letting people settle too easily for its standard of making allowances.

Oaths: Truthfulness and Trustworthiness

Jesus skips over "You shall not steal," which may be significant; he is not very interested in property. Or perhaps the Decalogue's command about coveting says all that needs to be said by way of getting behind the command about theft.

Something similar is true of the Torah, which talks about property questions less than Middle Eastern documents such as Hammurabi's "law code" (the title is misleading, as it does not seem to be a collection of regulations for implementing in Hammurabi's realm any more than the Torah is a collection of regulations for implementing in Israel). He jumps on to an exhortation that recalls the eighth commandment, the ban on giving false testimony.

> Again, you have heard that it was said to the people long ago, "Do not break your oath, but fulfill to the Lord the vows you have made." But I tell you, do not swear an oath at all: either by heaven, for it is God's throne; or by the earth, for it is his footstool; or by Jerusalem, for it is the city of the Great King. And do not swear by your head, for you cannot make even one hair white or black. All you need to say is simply "Yes," or No"; anything beyond this comes from the evil one. (Matt 5:33–37)

The focus of Jesus's command lies not on perjury but on the taking of oaths, which does not appear in the Ten Words. There is also no warning about breaking oaths in the Torah, though there is warning about not defaulting on vows (Deut 23:21–23; cf. Eccl 5:4–6). James 3:12 repeats Jesus's bidding, and some other New Testament references to oaths imply some critique.

Jesus apparently lives in a context where some people take a casuistic approach to oaths:

> You also say, "If anyone swears by the altar, it means nothing; but whoever swears by the gift on the altar is bound by the oath." You blind men! Which is greater: the gift, or the altar that makes the gift sacred? Therefore, anyone who swears by the altar swears by it and by everything on it. And anyone who swears by the temple swears by it and by the one who dwells in it. And whoever swears by heaven swears by God's throne and by the one who sits on it. (Matt 23:18–22)

It is in his command about oaths that Jesus is most clearly speaking like a prophet and taking up an issue from his context. Metaphorically he is laying down the law about oaths, but not all New Testament references to oaths seem to have taken Jesus to be laying down a new law. Apparently it is okay for God to take oaths (e.g., Luke 1:73; Acts 2:30; Heb 6:17; the First Testament, too, records a number of oaths that God took). It is also okay for an angel to do so (Rev 10:6) or for Paul to do so (Rom 1:9). Jesus is attacking people who are expert at finding ways of avoiding telling the truth. But he is no more laying down a law for literal implementing than he is when he tells people to cut their right hand off.

His concern makes for a comparison and contrast with a related aspect of ethics in the First Testament, where people sometimes lie with impunity; the text offers no critique. The Israelites' midwives lie to Pharaoh to explain their failure to kill the Israelites' babies (Exod 1:15–21). The First Testament may imply two related underlying assumptions. One is that truthfulness is not just a matter of words but of a total relationship. There is no truthfulness in the relationship between Pharaoh and the Israelites, and therefore the question of the midwives giving Pharaoh the real explanation for the babies' survival becomes moot. The other assumption is that masters owe truthfulness to their servants, kings to their subjects, professors to their students, parents to their children; truthfulness is an aspect of the obligation incumbent on people with power. If the people who are not truthful are the people with power, there is even less basis for urging truthfulness toward them. This links with the way it is often parents who want to get their children to tell them the truth.

Redress: The Relationship of Public and Private

> You have heard that it was said, "Eye for eye, and tooth for tooth." But I tell you, do not resist an evil person. If anyone slaps you on the right cheek, turn to them the other cheek also. (Matt 5:38–39)

The formula "eye for eye, and tooth for tooth," occurs several times in the Torah. The fuller version includes life for life, hand for hand, burn for burn, wound for wound, bruise for bruise (Exod 21:23–25). This rule, too, reminds one of Jesus telling people to cut off their right hand: it looks more like a vivid picture statement than a law. In Exodus, its concern lies with the principle that one should make compensation for the problems or the loss one causes to someone. If I hurt a person in such a way that they cannot work their plow, then I must make up for it by plowing for them. If I give false testimony about someone and they are convicted, again I must make compensation for it (cf. Deut 19:16–21).

It is the community's responsibility to exact the punishment, but the punishment must fit the crime. Another aspect of its significance is thus that it prohibits excessive retaliation of the kind that Lamech went in for (Gen 4:23–24). Yet the First Testament does not extend the application of the "eye for eye" principle to everyday personal relationships. There the First Testament principle is that redress is God's business (Prov 25:21–22, which Paul quotes in Rom 12:19–20). As a servant of Yahweh, you are committed to turning the other cheek: actually, you are committed to offering your cheek and your back (Isa 50:6). Sometimes David lived by this principle in circumstances that could have seemed to warrant a tougher stance (see, e.g., 2 Sam 16).

So Jesus is here fulfilling the Torah in two or three ways. He is resisting anyone applying to their personal relationships a principle that belongs in the context of the law and of the discipline it properly exercises. He is positively reminding people of a principle from the Scriptures that they might be inclined to evade. And he is thus pushing people toward taking the Scriptures' visionary stance rather than opting too easily for another allowance for human stubbornness that appears in the Torah.

Jesus goes on,

> And if anyone wants to sue you and take your shirt, hand over your coat as well. If anyone forces you to go one mile, go with them two miles. Give to the one who asks you, and do not turn away from the one who wants to borrow from you. (Matt 5:40–42)

Giving and lending are key principles within the Torah. A local community is structured by families, one of whose vocations is to be generous to people who lack a regular family network—people such as widows and orphans and Levites. The practice of lending complements the practice of giving. You give to people who have no way of giving back. You lend to families that have hit hard times because they have not grown enough to eat—no questions asked about whether it has happened through bad luck or through inefficiency or through laziness. You do not charge interest on such loans; lending is not a way of getting richer but a way of showing love. And you do not think too much about the fact that debts get cancelled every seven years.

> When there is a needy person among you, one of your brothers, inside one of your communities in the country that Yahweh your God is giving you, you will not firm up your mind and you will not close your hand against your needy brother, because you are to open your hand wide to him and generously lend enough for the lack that he has. Keep watch on yourself so a thing does not come into your scoundrel mind, "The seventh year, the release year, is drawing near," so your eye works badly toward your needy brother and you do not give anything to him, and he calls to Yahweh about you and it becomes a wrong done by you. Give generously to him. Your mind must not work badly when you give to him, because the needy person will not leave off from within the country. That is why I am ordering you, "Open your hand wide to your weak and your needy brother in your country." (Deut 15:7–11)

Nothing much needs to be added to the Torah on the subject of giving and lending.

Love: Both Neighbor and Enemy

> You have heard that it was said, "Love your neighbor and hate your enemy." But I tell you, love your enemies and pray for those who persecute you, that you may be children of your Father in heaven. He causes his sun to rise on the evil and the good, and sends rain on the righteous and the unrighteous. If you love those who love you, what reward will you get? Are not even the tax collectors doing that? And if you greet only your own people, what are you doing more than others? Do not even pagans do that? (Matt 5:43–47)

The puzzle about this exhortation is that the Torah does not tell people to hate their enemies, and neither does any Jewish teacher in Jesus's day that we know of. (Jesus himself is the only person in the Bible who ever tells people to hate anyone; see Luke 14:26.)

Maybe "love your neighbor (and hate your enemy)" was a popular saying in which the statement in the Torah was amplified in what might have seemed a logical way. But logic often gets us into trouble—or rather, scriptural logic often works differently from regular human logic. And the context of the Torah's command points in another direction.

> You will not take the stand against your neighbor's life. I am Yahweh. You will not hate your brother in your mind; you will firmly reprove your fellow, so you do not carry liability because of him. You will not take redress and you will not hold onto things in relation to members of your people, but love your neighbor as yourself. I am Yahweh. (Lev 19:16–18)

Anyone who had read the Torah would have been able to see that Jesus's exhortation to love your neighbor and your enemy is an outworking of the Torah's own exhortation, as is not surprising. It is the neighbor you do not get on with, the neighbor who is your enemy, that you need to be told to love. Leviticus urges people to be willing to rebuke their neighbor, which is likely to cause enmity, if it does not presuppose enmity. It urges people not to take redress; in other words, not to operate on the basis of an eye for an eye. It urges people to let go of animus rather than holding onto it. That is the kind of behavior and attitude that are indicated by loving your neighbor who is your enemy.

Now not everyone in the New Testament loves their enemies and prays for them in this way. Here is Paul:

> God is just: He will pay back trouble to those who trouble you and give relief to you who are troubled, and to us as well. This will happen when the Lord Jesus is revealed from heaven in blazing fire with his powerful angels. He will punish those who do not know God and do not obey the gospel of our Lord Jesus. They will be punished with everlasting destruction and shut out from the presence of the Lord and from the glory of his might on the day he comes to be glorified in his holy people and to be marveled at among all those who have believed. (2 Thess 1:6–10)

Paul's attitude to the people who are troubling the Thessalonians looks similar to the attitude the Psalms take to people who are troubling others. There

LIFE

are thus two attitudes to persecutors in the New Testament, as there are two attitudes to enemies in the Psalms and elsewhere in the First Testament.

Godlikeness

Jesus's teaching about fulfillment closes:

> Be perfect, therefore, as your heavenly Father is perfect. (Matt 5:48)

The word *perfect* is pretty worrying, not to say impossible, though it is partly a problem about English translation. The Greek word is *teleios*, which means "mature" or "complete." It is the Septuagint's translation of the Hebrew word *tam* or *tamim*, which also means "complete." It is the word for an animal that one brings as a sacrifice—it is not one leg short, or injured. It is also the Septuagint's word for Noah when he is described as *tam* (Gen 6:9). There and elsewhere English translations have "blameless," but *tam* is not a negative word (a word that indicates the absence of something) and it does not describe Noah as sinless. Positively, people who are *tam* are utterly steadfast in their commitment to what is right. And *teleios* is the Septuagint's word when Deuteronomy challenges every Israelite to be *tam* (Deut 18:13).

So the first part of Jesus's worrying command recalls Deuteronomy. The second part recalls Leviticus.

> You are to be holy, because I, Yahweh your God, am holy. (Lev 19:1)

As Jesus explicitly combines a command from Deuteronomy and a command from Leviticus as the two greatest commands in the Torah, so he is implicitly doing here in urging us to be perfect and to be like God.

What does it mean to be Godlike? What has the Torah suggested by the time we reach Leviticus 19?

- Be creative; be life-giving; bring order (Gen 1–2).
- Be easily hurt; be realistic; but do not give up (Gen 3–11).
- Give people hope; give people land; give people space and scope (Gen 12–50).
- Hear people's pain; be open and self-revealing; fight against oppression; give people freedom (Exod 1–18).

226

- Be categorical; be concrete and practical; be there; be flexible; be more merciful than judgmental (Exod 19–40).
- Be available; be frightening (Lev 1–18).

What has Matthew suggested it means to be Godlike by the time we reach the end of Matthew 5?

- Persist with your purpose; help the people of God get to their destiny (Matt 1:1–17).
- Do what you say you will do, even if it is surprising (1:18–2:23).
- Quote the Scriptures (3:1–17).
- Test people (4:1–11).
- Do good through other people (5:1–16).
- Love your enemies (5:17–47).

The two profiles make for interesting comparison.

6.3 The First Testament's Ethics in Its Own Right

If we look at the First Testament in its own right, what does ethics look like? If we look for something a little more specific than the two commands about love, but a little less detailed than the 613 commands that Jewish tradition enumerates in the Torah, what do we find? There are virtues or traits that the First Testament implicitly or explicitly commends. There are rationales for behavior that emerge from creation, from God's dealings with his people, from experience, from the prospect of what God intends to achieve, and from relationships with God and with people. There are different contexts in life about which the First Testament offers insight, such as family, village, city, people, nation, kingdom, and empire. And there are topics on which it offers insight, such as wealth, sex, speech, violence and death, war in particular, and servanthood.

Virtues

God's Own Traits

What are the character traits or the virtues that the First Testament looks for and wants people to embody? In discussing Godlikeness in the previous section, we could have started from Yahweh's self-description in Exodus 34:6–7:

> Yahweh, God compassionate and gracious, long-tempered, big in commitment and truthfulness, preserving commitment toward the thousands, carrying waywardness, rebellion, and wrongdoing; he certainly does not treat people as free of guilt, attending to parents' waywardness in connection with children and with grandchildren, with thirds and with fourths.[2]

Such are also qualities Yahweh also expects to see embodied in humanity:

1. The Hebrew word for compassion is related to the word for a woman's womb. So compassion is the feelings a mother has for her children (a father, too: Ps 103:13). It is an attitude that even superpowers are expected to show to the people they conquer (Isa 47:6).
2. Grace is a big-hearted attitude to people whether they deserve it or not. A notable embodiment of it is Esau. Jacob had cheated him out of his "blessing" as the senior son who would have responsibility for the family and then decided it was wise to run for his life; but when he eventually returns, still scared of Esau, he finds that his brother simply wants to welcome him back. He thus finds grace with Esau (Gen 33).
3. Long-temperedness is one of the qualities that Proverbs commends. It is better than having a high opinion of oneself, and it encourages harmony rather than strife in the community (Prov 14:29; 15:18; 16:32; see also Eccl 7:8).
4. Commitment is the faithfulness that goes way beyond anything anyone could expect—for instance, when the other person has let you down or been unfaithful to you or has no claim on you. Ruth is a great embodiment of commitment (Ruth 3:10).
5. Truthfulness means reliability or steadfastness in keeping one's word. It is the quality Rahab looks for in the Israelite spies when she takes the

2. That is, to the third and fourth generations.

risk of throwing in her lot with Israel (Josh 2:12, 14). It is expressed in thinking, in speech, and in action (Pss 15:2; 26:3; Prov 12:19). It is thus the opposite of deceptiveness, an important unethical quality in the First Testament.

6. Being like God means carrying people's wrongdoing—that is, instead of making someone else bear the consequences of their doing wrong to me, I bear them myself. It is the Hebrew way of referring to forgiveness. It is the stance Joseph takes to his brothers who had sold him into slavery (Gen 50:15–21).

7. Being like God means not treating people as free of guilt when they are not:

> One who declares a faithless person faithful or declares a faithful
>   person faithless,
>   both of them are an offense to Yahweh. (Prov 17:15)

To put it another way, it attends to waywardness.

When the First Testament simply talks about qualities human beings are expected to show, then the classic expectation is the combination *mishpat* and *tsedaqah*. These words are commonly rendered in English as "justice" and "righteousness," and justice and righteousness are indeed First Testament principles, but they are not what is signified by those two Hebrew words. *Mishpat* denotes the exercise of authority or government. *Tsedaqah* denotes doing the right thing by the people with whom one has a relationship—with the members of one's community. So *mishpat* and *tsedaqah* denote the exercise of authority in a way that does the right thing by the people in one's community.

Integrity

After Noah, the person who is next put forward as an ethical ideal is Job. His story begins by describing him as upright and utterly steadfast (*tam* again). He formulates that claim for himself in his review of his life (Job 31). We might wonder if he is whitewashing himself, but it would not make any difference to the significance of his statement in terms of ethics. It is still an exposition of what utter steadfastness looks like. So Job spells out integrity as meaning:

- not looking lustfully at a girl
- not being covetous and deceiving anyone
- not trying to seduce a neighbor's wife
- not treating servants unjustly
- not neglecting the poor or the widow or the orphan who need food or clothing
- not trusting in one's wealth
- not rejoicing in a neighbor's misfortune
- not neglecting to show hospitality to someone who needs a place to sleep for the night
- not neglecting to pay a fair wage

David also sees himself as *tamim* (2 Sam 22:24, 26), though with some unconscious irony because we are told enough about his life to know that he is far short of that. The claim is part of a psalm that he quotes or that is put on his lips, and maybe we are not expected to press the details of all fifty verses; the emphasis lies on his praise of God for times when God has rescued him. But the wide canvas of the portrait of David does make it possible to infer a profile of integrity in Israel, utilizing the way David fails as well as the way he stands tall. Positively:

- He trusts in God and makes this the basis of his courage.
- He values friendship.
- He will not take action to further his own position.
- He will admit when he has done wrong.
- He is generous to people who fail.
- He is generous to people who critique him.
- He does not forget people who have been generous to him.

Negatively, he needed to learn:

- that lust can lead to adultery and that a husband is committed to being faithful in marriage
- that a commander-in-chief is committed to being faithful to his soldiers
- that a father is committed to being disciplined with his children
- that marriage need not be subordinate to politics or be a means of prestige
- that the feelings of a father may have to be subordinate to the obligations of a commander

For the most part, David's story does not offer evaluations like the ones I have just assumed, but I think it implies most of them. In contrast, his story raises moral questions for us, on which his story seems to imply no comment. For example, he kills hundreds or thousands of people, and he tells lies to protect his own life. His story's moral impact lies in the questions it makes us wrestle with and the way it makes us ask where our moral judgments come from.

Rationales

Creation and Redemption

Why be ethical? The First Testament has a number of answers, all of which also indicate something of what being ethical means.

First, God created the world in a certain way, and being ethical means living in light of the nature of the way God created it. Not surprisingly, this theme features in the opening two chapters of the First Testament. God created humanity male and female to fill the world and thus to subdue it. They do not do so to despoil it in using it for their own benefit. They are not even given permission to eat the animals that they are to tame. Their task is rather to control the world and bring order to it so that it may reach the destiny God intended for it.

God's creating the world by undertaking a week's work and then having a stopping day implicitly sets an example for humanity's rhythm of work and stopping, though the point becomes explicit only much later in the Torah. God's stopping means he looks back at what he has done and rejoices in its goodness. God's thereby making the seventh day special means that humanity should keep off it and consider the goodness of God's creation. Humanity's stopping in this way means people take some rest and find refreshment, and it is the responsibility of the heads of households to see that the entire family and other members of the work force (not to say animals) do so. More generally, the fact that we are created in God's image means that

> One who oppresses a poor person reviles his maker,
> > but one who is gracious to a needy person honors him. (Prov 14:31)
> One who ridicules a destitute person reviles his maker;
> > one who rejoices at disaster will not go free of guilt. (Prov 17:5)

Genesis 2 makes explicit that humanity's task is to serve and take care of the land that God created, the earth. The Hebrew verb that modern translations render "work" in the expression "work the land" is the verb that regularly means "serve." Humanity is creation's servant. People in general are to "serve" for six days, then stop for a day (e.g., Exod 20:9).

While God's creation commission in Genesis 1 also relates to the animal world, some ambiguity emerges in that connection. Yahweh emphasizes to Job that the world as created does not revolve around humanity (Job 38–39). The animal world exists in its own right, and humanity needs to respect that fact.

A second reason for being ethical is that God delivered Israel from Egypt, and being ethical means living in light of that act by God. The Israelites were serfs in Egypt, and the exodus meant God delivered them from serfdom. They were aliens in Egypt, and thus they know what it feels like to be an alien, and they know that God cares for aliens. So it is their responsibility to be like God and to treat aliens well (e.g., Deut 10:19). The same rationale underlies their obligation to be fair, considerate, and generous to people who are less powerful or more vulnerable than them (e.g., Deut 24:17–22).

In bringing the Israelites out of servitude in Egypt, God made them into his servants instead of Egypt's; they must not think they can sell into permanent servitude other members of this body of Yahweh's servants. And if they take people on as temporary servants, they must provide for them generously when they come to the end of their period of service—because Yahweh behaved in this way toward them (e.g., Deut 15:15). God's deliverance from Egypt also provides a second basis for observing the Sabbath—more specifically, for enabling one's servants to observe the Sabbath (Deut 5:12–15). Paradoxically, neither must they despise any Egyptians (Deut 23:7), because they were refugees in their land before they got turned into serfs.

Experience and Expectation

A third reason for being ethical is that, if we look at the way life works out, we will see that being ethical is part of the way God himself makes life work out. The ethical life is thus the smart way of life. This conviction lies behind much of the teaching in Proverbs. Randomly, from the beginning of the section of Proverbs that collects individual aphorisms:

> Treasures that come from faithlessness do not profit,
>   but faithfulness rescues from death.

> Yahweh does not let the faithful person go hungry,
>> but he thwarts the malice of faithless people.
> A lazy fist makes destitute,
>> but the hand of determined people makes wealthy.
> One who gathers in summer is an insightful son;
>> one who sleeps in harvest is a disgraceful son. (Prov 10:2–5)

Proverbs is the First Testament's great collection of insights drawn from experience of the way things work out in life. Some of its aphorisms speak in terms of how things are, some in terms of how God makes them work out, and some in terms of what is right; it assumes no tension among these three.

One aphorism on its own can give an oversimplified impression, or can give the impression that Proverbs' own perspective is oversimplified. But it is commonly the case that another aphorism in the next verse or chapter will express a contrasting insight. A classic collocation is:

> Do not answer a dimwit in accordance to his denseness,
>> so that you do not become like him, you too.
> Answer a dimwit in accordance with his denseness,
>> so he does not become smart in his own eyes. (Prov 26:4–5)

The way life works out is complicated, and smartness involves being discerning in the way one utilizes insights from experience.

Further, the First Testament recognizes that things do not always work out in the way the aphorisms in Proverbs say they do. As Job points out, people do wrong and get away with it. But the First Testament believes that such cases test but do not disprove the rule—and Job's own story does so. Therefore pay close attention to how things are in the world, Proverbs especially says, and live in light of what you see. Awe for God, ethics, and wisdom all point in the same direction.

A fourth reason for being ethical entails living in light of the fact that God is taking the world to its destiny. Being ethical means living in light of where God is taking the world. One could turn to the order of books in the First Testament to illustrate the point.

> Because here I am, creating
>> new heavens and a new earth.

And one of its features will be:

The wolf and the lamb will pasture together,
   the cougar, like cattle, will eat straw,
   but the snake—dirt will be its food.
People will not do badly, they will not devastate,
   in all my sacred mountain (Yahweh has said). (Isa 65:17, 25)

It is because Yahweh intends to take the world to this destiny that he can commission humanity to subdue it. The motivation parallels the motivation in terms of living in light of the way life does work out in the world. That is, God intends to create a new Jerusalem, to which nations will flock so that Yahweh can resolve their conflicts and so that individuals can sit under their vine and fig tree without anyone making them afraid. The implication that the prophets draw is that we should now walk in Yahweh's name, walk in Yahweh's light (Isa 2:5; Mic 4:5).

Relationship with God and with Other People

The First Testament does not obviously support the idea that "Man's chief end is to glorify God, and to enjoy him forever" (so the Westminster Shorter Catechism), but it does presuppose that we are designed to live as servants of God in fellowship with God. Such fellowship requires a kind of moral harmony. The First Testament assumes that close relationships with other human beings require such moral harmony; it is our business to dissociate from people whose ways are devious and deviate from what is proper. How much more would it be the case that God would not wish to associate with us when we are devious or deviant? To put it another way, ethics belongs in the context of a covenant relationship between God and us and a covenant relationship between us and other people.

The First Testament includes considerable teaching on what makes people polluted or unclean or taboo, and unethical behavior is one of those things that make you taboo. It is the person of integrity who can spend time with God, not the person who lends on interest or takes a bribe or reviles other people (Ps 15).[3] If you repent of being that kind of person, the problem disappears; God cleanses you of your taboo. But if you simply come as you are without such repentance, you cannot be in the presence of God. There were security men in the temple who checked people out before allowing

3. See the quotation in the discussion of "Hostility" on pp. 218–19 above.

them to come in, and Psalm 15 lays out a set of moral checks that determine whether you are unclean; you cannot come into God's presence if you fail them.

Unethical behavior also compromises relationships with family and community. The stories of Jacob's cheating his brother and of Joseph's brothers selling him into slavery illustrate the point, and they have an effect not only on the relationships between siblings but on the relationships of parents and children. More generally, as Proverbs points out:

> A smart son rejoices a father,
>> but a dimwit son is a mother's sorrow. (10:1)
> When things are good for the faithful, the township exults;
>> when the faithless perish, there is a roar. (11:10)
> One who withholds grain—the people will curse him,
>> but blessing will be on the head of one who sells. (11:25)
> When Yahweh accepts an individual's ways,
>> he causes even his enemies to be at peace with him. (16:7)
> A crooked person lets loose a dispute,
>> and a gossip separates a friend. (16:28)
> A faithful person walks about with integrity—
>> the blessings of his children after him! (20:7)

Family and community are built on faithfulness and trust, and part of the way in which God has created the world is that ethical behavior builds up community while unethical behavior will be its downfall—which in the end is disaster for the wrongdoers themselves.

Contexts

Family, Village, City

In considering the First Testament's ethics, we started with ethical traits, which can all be exhibited by individuals. Yet these traits are expressed in the contexts of relationships with other people. And while these relationships are sometimes one-on-one, they are also aspects of communal life. I describe the workings of the community as if things actually worked out in this way; of course in practice things were often very different.

The First Testament is interested in the life of the family. It focuses on the family in the sense of what we might call the extended family—for instance, middle-aged or older parents, their adult children and their wives, and these couples' young children. Even when we allow for most people living much shorter lives than people do in the West, the family would likely be too large to live in one house. They might typically occupy three or four houses in settings that were not so different from what we call nuclear families. The extended family is then the structure for work, for teaching, for worship, for hospitality, and for generosity. The family owns its stretch of land, and its members farm it together. There is no regular practice of employment, of people selling their labor, which happens only when things go wrong. When things do go wrong for a family or for individuals, then a family that is doing okay lends them seed and other things they need in the expectation that they will pay them back next year. If they do not, the family takes them on as temporary "servants" (this old translation is less misleading than the modern translation "slaves") to give them time to get their life back together. The family's community commitment extends to adopting widows and orphans who have fallen out of the family-based social structure. It is the family that observes the Sabbath, and it would not be surprising if the Sabbath was the occasion for teaching in the family along the lines expected by Deuteronomy. It is the family that joins together in observing the annual festivals.

Marriage itself is subordinate to family. While the Song of Songs expresses enthusiasm for the romantic and sexual aspects of the man-woman relationship, most First Testament texts on marriage focus on its practical significance: it is the means whereby the earth gets subdued for God and the garden is cared for (Gen 1–2). While lifelong monogamous heterosexual marriage is the ideal implied by Genesis 1–2, the rest of the First Testament recognizes that in practice marriage is not always like that. Men marry more than one wife for reasons of status or because their first wife cannot have children, and perhaps when many men get killed in war.

Most families live in the context of a village. One might think in terms of three or four of these extended families making up a village of 100–150 people. The village can then combine forces for projects such as digging wells or terracing hills, and it may have a local sanctuary where people offer sacrifices, pray, and celebrate what God does. One family and its boys and girls will look to other families in the village for the young people's wives and husbands. Whereas the head of a family will be responsible for resolving conflicts within the family, conflicts will also arise between families over issues such as violence and theft, and it will be the responsibility of the village's elders to resolve them and to see that wrongdoers make restitution to the people they have wronged.

The town becomes more important as centuries pass. In origin it is more an administrative unit than a residential one, though some families living in the town will be people whose land lies nearby. But the town becomes the place to which people drift for economic and other reasons. Further, people of shrewdness and not too much principle are able to evade the implications of the theory that people who are doing okay support people who are not doing okay and help them get back on their feet. Instead they will take over their land and farm it in a way that brings the benefit to them rather than to its proper owners. Thus economic inequality develops and poverty becomes an issue.

People, Nation, Kingdom, Empire

Israel is a people and a nation from the beginning. It is a people in the sense that it sees itself as an ethnic unit. Israel is the family writ large. Deuteronomy is especially fond of the argument that the members of the community should relate to one another and treat one another as brothers and sisters. The implication is not that it is ethnically exclusive. It is open to other people joining it (people such as Rahab the Canaanite, Ruth the Moabite, and Uriah the Hittite) if they commit themselves to it—in particular, to its own commitment to Yahweh. It is open to the foreigner who comes as a refugee or needy immigrant, a "sojourner" or resident alien, and its rule of life urges practical concern for such people.

Israel is also a nation from the beginning in the sense that it has the equivalent of a political structure (the twelve clans) and the leadership of Moses, then of Joshua. But once the Israelites are in the land, they have no central leadership, and the clans function independently or in local groupings from time to time, but not all together. The religious, moral, and social disadvantages of this arrangement emerge, and in due course the Israelites determine to have a central government—namely, a king. They become a state or a kingdom.

This development solves some of their problems. Under the leadership of David, in particular, they are able finally to defeat the Philistines and take over the parts of Canaan that the Philistines held, and the First Testament does not tell horrific stories about the monarchic period such as it tells about the time when Israel had no kings. On the other hand, Samuel warned them about what kingship would cost them (government costs money, and leaders live better than the people who pay them). And it is this reality that issues in the bifurcation of the state after Solomon. Further, it is the development of the state that encourages urbanization and the inequalities and oppression that characterize it.

In the context of a power vacuum in the Levant, Israel's ability under David to deal with rivals such as the Philistines easily becomes the ability to create its own small empire. This empire does not survive the split within Israel itself, and within a couple of centuries the development of big empires further away (successively Assyria, Babylon, Persia, Greece) comes to impinge on the two kingdoms. The First Testament has little good to say about the empires except that Yahweh can use them to fulfill his own purposes without their realizing it, usually to bring trouble but sometimes to bring blessing. But they are critiqued for their concern with gain for themselves, their cruelty, their lack of compassion, and seeing themselves as God.

Topics

Wealth

While Proverbs is one of the First Testament's key ethical resources, like the Scriptures as a whole it does not offer its insight in a systematized way. Many topics recur in different places. The arrangement encourages readers to reflect on one saying at a time. But there is also value in putting together its sayings on different topics, not least to safeguard against treating one saying as the last word when it needs setting in such a context. For instance, is the wealth of the rich their fortress (Prov 10:15)?

Proverbs realistically recognizes the importance of financial resources. They give security, popularity, and enjoyment (10:15; 14:20; 21:20). It is thus realistic about how life works. It does not assume that property is original sin,[4] and it encourages people to seek wealth.

So how may we get hold of some?

Be bold (11:16).
Be generous (11:25): business involves being sharp, but it also profits from getting on with people.

---

4. See Karl Marx, *The Process of Capitalist Production,* vol. 1 of *Capital,* trans. Samuel Moore and Edward Aveling, ed. Friedrich Engels (1887; repr. Chicago: Kerr, 1919), §8.26, p. 784.

Be honest (15:6; cf. 10:2): another surprising comment that assumes we
live in a moral universe.

Be reverent (10:22): prosperity comes from God, so trust is important
(cf. 3:9–10); the prosperity gospel, like most heresies, gets into trouble
by taking a truth out of context.

But be realistic (11:24): prosperity is unpredictable, and Proverbs' "rules"
are broad generalizations, not universals.

On the other hand, Proverbs recognizes the drawbacks or limitations of wealth:

It comes to seem all-important (11:28).

It cannot buy long life (11:4).

It cannot buy wisdom (3:14) or love or forgiveness or God.

It can make people forget its moral connections (11:6).

It can make people forget relationships (15:27): if money becomes all-
important, it affects friends and family.

It can give people inflated ideas (28:11).

In other words, it tends to drive us to the opposite of the attitudes
that will actually lead to our gaining wealth: generosity, honesty,
reverence.

So be moderate (30:8–9). Do not rely on wealth—rely on God; you cannot
serve two masters.

Proverbs further offers advice on how to get rid of wealth:

Honor God with it (3:9).

Serve the community with it (11:26).

Be generous to the needy with it (28:27; cf. 14:31).

The answer to Marx's point about money causing evil is to do good with it.
Usually in the world there are people who have none and people who have
lots that is doing nothing. Proverbs' solution is cash flow.

Sex

Some aspects of behavior do not count as unethical in Western thinking but
do have the same effect as unethical behavior, in that they make it impossible
to be in God's presence. It is not only illicit sex that makes people taboo;

legitimate sex also does so. We cannot have sex and then go straight into worship, not because the sex is wrong, but because Yahweh is not a sexual being (as Canaanite deities were). We would bring into worship something that clashes with who Yahweh is. Sex is not a god. For Western culture, where many think sex is a god, this is an insight of ethical importance.

It may be illuminating to consider the First Testament's perspective on sex and ethics by starting from comments it makes about eunuchs (Isa 56:1–8) to which appeal has been made in connection with thinking about same-sex relationships. "Eunuchs" here likely denotes Judahites who are genitally deformed and emasculated, perhaps with their cooperation or perhaps not, and perhaps so that they can safely supervise (for example) the king's harem in Babylon. God promises such eunuchs an honored place in the community of Israel, even though they cannot contribute to its future by begetting children. Does such acceptance of eunuchs by God mean that God might similarly now accept homosexuals and same-sex marriage?

How might we decide whether that inference is right? One aspect of the answer is that we need to set the question in the context of an understanding of sex and marriage that is developed from the Scriptures as a whole. Such an understanding would see marriage as:

- service-focused, in that the first man and woman were to serve God and serve the world together
- independent; the man and the woman left their parents
- heterosexual
- procreational; the first human beings were to be fruitful
- monogamous
- egalitarian
- covenantal and thus lifelong
- sexually expressed
- amorous
- publicly recognized by the community

The implication is that a marriage falls short of this vision if it involves

- two people with largely separate work lives
- two people failing to separate from their parents
- two people of the same sex
- two people who avoid having children
- polygamy

- husband or wife having authority over the other
- husband or wife having a still-living former spouse
- celibacy
- a platonic relationship
- a clandestine relationship

A same-sex marriage thus falls short of the scriptural vision, but so do lots of other forms of marriage. In Western culture we disapprove of polygamy but not of some of the other shortfalls. Some traditional societies accept polygamy but not same-sex marriage. Traditional conservative Western assumptions about marriage can seem as far away from the vision that emerges in the Scriptures as secular or liberal Christian understandings.

Speech

Speech, especially secret speech, is prominent in the account of qualities required of someone who wishes to come into God's presence (Ps 15). The perniciousness and danger of wrongful speech is a major theme of First Testament ethics.

> The person who conceals repudiation with lying lips
>> and the one who issues charges, he is stupid. (Prov 10:18)
> The words of the faithless are a deadly ambush,
>> but the mouth of the upright rescues them. (12:6)
> A healing tongue is a tree of life,
>> but deviousness in it is brokenness in spirit. (15:4; cf. 4:24; 10:31; 12:22)

Positively, speech can be nurturing, life-giving, healing, and peace-making:

> The lips of a faithful person pasture many,
>> but stupid people die for lack of sense. (10:21)
> The mouth of a faithful person is a fountain of life,
>> but the mouth of faithless people conceals violence. (10:11)
> A town rises up by the blessing of the upright,
>> but by the mouth of the faithless it breaks down. (11:11)
> There is one who rants like sword thrusts,
>> but the tongue of the wise person is a healing. (12:18)
> Anxiety in a person's mind weighs it down,

> but a good word makes it rejoice. (12:25)
> A gentle response turns back wrath,
>> but a hurtful word arouses anger. (15:1)
> Death and life are in the hand of the tongue;
>> those who give themselves to it eat its fruit. (18:21; cf. 15:23; 16:24)

But repeating gossip is a bad idea:

> One who seeks a relationship covers over rebellion,
>> but one who repeats a matter separates a friend. (17:9)
> Someone who reveals a confidence goes about as a slanderer;
>> do not share with someone who has his lips open. (20:19)

And in general, reticence in speech is a good idea, especially if you want either to be smart or to look smart, or to keep out of trouble:

> One who guards his mouth preserves his life,
>> but one who opens his lips wide—ruin is his. (13:3)
> A stupid person expresses all his feelings;
>> a wise person holds them back. (29:11; cf. 10:19; 15:28; 17:27, 28; 18:7, 13;
>> 21:23; 29:20)

But the right word at the right moment can be something wonderful:

> He kisses with the lips,
>> the one who replies with straight words. (24:26)
> Golden apricots in silver settings
>> is a word appropriately spoken. (25:11)

Yet we have already noted that wisdom is required if one is to discern the right moment (26:4–5).[5]

Violence and Death

Violence is a prominent theme in the First Testament. In handling this theme, as in handling others, the First Testament uses various forms of

---

5. See the discussion of "Experience and Expectation" above.

speech—telling stories, laying down laws, sharing nightmares and dreams, reflecting on issues, and formulating praises and prayers.

It tells stories about illicit violence. Very near its beginning are the violent acts of Cain and Lamech, and it goes on to the violence of Jacob's sons at Shechem. It later tells a series of violent stories in the book of Judges. It makes little comment on these stories. They are part of reality. It does imply that they are of a different ethical status from the stories of God's violence and of the violence that God commissions Moses, Joshua, and the Israelites to undertake. In other words, there is licit and illicit violence.

The First Testament lays down rules to constrain illicit violence. One significance of the saying about an eye for an eye and a tooth for a tooth lies here. The punishment must fit the crime. It must not be excessive, as Lamech's was, and as Jacob's sons was.

It is not only illicit violence that raises questions. One of the things the temple security men would check for[6] is any sign of the ailment traditionally known as leprosy, which seems to denotes a skin condition whose problem lies in making it look as if a person is falling apart; it thus suggests death (see the description of Miriam in Num 12:12). Now death clashes with who Yahweh is, as sex does, and not with who Canaanite gods are (they can die). So a commitment such as burying a relative makes you taboo. You cannot rush into Yahweh's presence after such contact with death; you have to become clean before you can go into the sanctuary. Related considerations seem to underlie the taboo attached to menstrual blood, which is a mysterious thing. It is a sign of life, because it indicates that a woman could conceive life; but blood itself is a sign of death: bleed too much, and you die.

For a converse reason to the consideration that applies to sex, these dynamics are ethically suggestive for Western people. On one hand, we have a hard time dealing with death. On the other, we have difficulties with the boundary between life and death, especially at the end of a life, with knowing when the end comes and when life should continue to be honored and when death should be allowed to have its way.

The First Testament incorporates nightmares and dreams about violence (see, e.g., Amos 7–9; Mic 1–4). Such dreams tell Ephraim and Judah that, if they carry on the way they are, they will end up the victims of imperial violence, and behind the imperial agent the prophets may see Yahweh's hand. They also have a vision of nations laying down their weapons because they come to Jerusalem to Yahweh to learn from him and to let him sort out their conflicts.

---

6. See the discussion of "Relationship with God and with Other People" above.

The First Testament thinks about violence. Ecclesiastes notes that there is a time for war and a time for peace (3:8). It does not mean that there is a time when it is proper to pursue the one and a time to pursue the other, as is reflected by the parallel comment that there is a time to be born and a time to die (3:2). It means that both happen, and we may have little control over them or be unable to see why they come when they do.

And the First Testament authors pray about violence, maybe as much as any other subject. The psalmists pray about violence as an alternative to engaging in violence. Instead of acting violently against their attackers, they implore God to do so. On the other hand, they do not urge God to engage in *hamas*, the regular word for "violence," which denotes improper or illicit violence. In distinguishing between proper and improper violence, the Psalms contrast with the current use of the word *violence* in English, which is inclined to see all "violence" as illicit.

War

This study of topics in First Testament ethics focuses on First Testament ethics in its own right—that is, on issues the First Testament sees as issues. I do not here focus on issues that are important to us and on which there is material in the First Testament for us to consider, but which it does not itself see as an issue (say, conservation). Nor do I focus on aspects of the First Testament that raise problems for modern Western readers. But I make an exception for the subject of war. War is not a major issue in First Testament ethics, but it is a major issue for Western readers, so it warrants attention.

The First Testament implies that things were peaceful in Eden at first; it portrays conflict as coming about as a result of humanity's rebellion against God. And it promises a time when the nations will come to Jerusalem to have Yahweh sort out their conflicts. But in the meantime, it takes war for granted and takes for granted that Israel will get involved in war. It does seek to constrain some of the excesses of war.

Amos 1–2 does so in a polemic against Israel's neighbors (Amos is softening up his audience before attacking Israel itself). War should be fought in a way that avoids what we might call war crimes; it should not involve moving a whole people; it should not ignore treaty obligations; it should be tempered by kinship and by compassion; it should respect people who lose their lives.

Deuteronomy does so in laying down a set of conditions for making war that would be the despair of a commander-in-chief. The citizen army has to be given the chance to excuse themselves and go home (I have just built a house, I have just planted a vineyard, I have just gotten married, I am just scared). When the army is about to attack a city, it is first to proclaim peace to that city. If the city surrenders, its people will lose their independence, but they will not lose their lives. If the city resists, there are limits to the way the Israelites can lay siege to it. They can eat the fruit of fruit trees but cannot destroy the trees. When Israel is thinking about trying to defend itself from attack, a prophet such as Isaiah tells it that the key consideration is trust in God. Human alliances and weapons will get it nowhere if God is not protecting it.

The war that especially troubles Western Christians is Joshua's attack on Canaan. We might note two or three things about this action. Its background is the Canaanites' wrongdoing (e.g., sacrificing children); they are not losing their land just because they are in the way (and God treats Israel the same for behaving in a similar way). It is more or less a one-off event; Israel did not take this event as a model for its ongoing life or its ongoing warring. And the New Testament shows only appreciation for Joshua and his achievement, which confirms our suspicion that it is something about Western thinking that makes us troubled about Joshua. It is not just that we are peace-loving like Jesus and the New Testament. There is also the fact that Joshua and Judges make clear that the Israelites did not actually annihilate all the Canaanites.

Servanthood

The First Testament speaks much about leadership, though in the end it does not think leadership is really important. The most telling aspect of its talk about leaders is that it prefers to call them servants—not servants of the people but servants of Yahweh. It is the standard term to describe Moses, but it also applies frequently to Joshua and David.

In Eden Garden everyone was a servant. Adam and Eve were created to serve the ground. Yet somehow by Abraham's day there are servants and masters, though it looks as if the relationship of masters and servants could mean one did not mind being a servant (see Gen 24). But there were no kings in Israel; the only king was Yahweh, and his people were his kingdom of priests and his holy nation (Exod 15:18; 19:6). Deuteronomy does allow for Israel's appointing a human king if it wishes, but it puts stringent constraints around kingship (Deut 17:14–20). The king needs to be a member of the Israelite family and he needs always to remember that he is a member of the family, just a brother among brothers. Further, he needs to keep a copy of the Torah by his side and to keep reading it.

Gideon's best moment is when people want him to be their ruler after his successes in leading them, but he insists that God continue to be their ruler (Judg 8:22–23). The more the book of Judges unfolds, however, the less well this arrangement works; and in the context of telling some horrifying stories, the book closes with the repeated comment that there was no king in Israel, and finally that everyone was doing what was right in their own eyes (Judg 21:25). Later, the people's petition to have a king is met without enthusiasm by Samuel and by Yahweh, both of whom feel rejected (1 Sam 8).

Leaders are both a necessary evil and an evil necessity. Kings do lead people away from Yahweh as much as toward Yahweh, and in due course Yahweh commissions the Assyrians to put Ephraim's monarchy down, then commissions the Babylonians to put Judah's monarchy down. In the meantime, however, Yahweh has made an unequivocal commitment to David's line, and thus Jeremiah promises that the end of the monarchy will not be final. He does so in a naughty way. Understanding the naughtiness requires an awareness of the fact that the king at the time is Zedekiah, whose name means, "Yahweh is my faithfulness." The promise is,

> There, days are coming . . . when I shall set up for David a faithful branch. He will reign as king and show insight and exercise authority and faithfulness in the country. In his days Judah will find deliverance and Israel will dwell with confidence. This is the name by which he will be called: "Yahweh is our faithfulness." (Jer 23:5–6)

The present king does not live up to his name; Jeremiah is promising a future king who will. Isaiah 40–55 moves in several other directions in order to describe what God will do about his promise to David. The prophet declares that the promise is fulfilled in the person of the Persian king Cyrus, who will make it possible for the Judahites to go home to build the temple (44:24–45:7). He declares that it is fulfilled in the experience of the people as a whole (55:3–5). And he declares that it is fulfilled in the work and experience of an anointed servant of Yahweh (52:13–53:12). This servant will end up as exalted as David, but in the meantime:

> He was despised and the most frail of human beings,
> > a man of great suffering and acquainted with weakness. . . .

Yet it was our weaknesses that he carried,
    our great suffering that he bore.
But we ourselves had counted him touched,
    struck down, by God and afflicted.
But he was the one who was wounded through our rebellions,
    crushed through our wayward acts.
Chastisement to bring us well-being was on him,
    and by means of his being hurt there was healing for us.
All of us like sheep had wandered,
    each had turned his face to his own way.
Yahweh—he let fall on him
    the waywardness of all of us. (53:3–6)

That is what it means to be a servant. The First Testament has shown that kingship is theologically inappropriate but practically necessary. It is an act of rebellion that God accommodates himself to, yet an institution that does not work. The gospel sought to reintroduce the kingdom of priests (1 Pet 2:9), and the early church had no place for churches being headed up by one person. But that arrangement ended in chaos, as happened in Israel's story, so the church had to invent the "monarchical episcopate," churches headed up by a senior pastor. This showed the capacity to control error and to encourage abuse, like Israel's monarchy. If only servanthood worked!

Questions for Discussion

1. In light of the reading you have done in connection with this book, what do you think "fulfillment" means?
2. Which aspects of the Scriptures' teaching about God's ultimate vision for human life do you think place the greatest challenge before your church?
3. Which aspects of the Scriptures' allowance for human hardness of heart do you think bring good news to people you know?
4. How do you balance rationales for behavior that come from creation, from experience, and from relationships?
5. Which aspects of the First Testament's teaching on how we should live our lives seem most challenging?

CHAPTER 7

Conclusion

Not long ago, I asked my students to read Romans and to note where and how Paul referred to the First Testament. One of them commented that he had never realized how often Romans refers to the First Testament. Not all the works in the New Testament refer back as much as Romans does, but we have seen that the First Testament is also prominent in Matthew, Luke, Acts, Hebrews, and Revelation—which covers most of the New Testament. These books assume that they need the First Testament if they are to understand Jesus and to understand God and to understand themselves.

Starting from Matthew in particular, we have looked at five facets of the way the New Testament writings relate to the First Testament. First, they note that the First Testament tells a story, and that Jesus is the climax to the story it tells. They implicitly invite us to go and read that story. Its grand narrative is actually composed of a sequence of stories that offer an understanding of what God was doing with Israel that can also help us understand what God is doing with the church.

Second, they understand what God did in Jesus in light of things that the prophets say. Statements the prophets make are filled out in Jesus. And there is much more to be learned from those prophets: Isaiah, Jeremiah, Ezekiel, and the twelve shorter prophets.

Third, they work with a framework of theological ideas and a theological dictionary that comes ultimately from the First Testament. They do not tell us as much about God as we might expect—they assume we learn who God is from the First Testament. And they presuppose countless images and motifs from the First Testament, which we will need to appreciate if we are to understand the New Testament.

Fourth, they talk about the nature of a relationship with God in a way that presupposes how God has been relating to Israel, and they invite people who believe in Jesus to enter into the way the people in the First Testament pray and praise and confess and testify and worship. So they point us toward the First Testament's resources for praise and prayer—and intercession and protest and questioning.

And fifth, they suggest that Jesus brings the filling out and the fulfillment of the First Testament's vision of life lived God's way. They point us to implications in the First Testament that we may have avoided, and they invite us to see the gift of the Holy Spirit as designed to make it possible for us to fulfill what the First Testament itself wants us to be and do.

In light of the importance the New Testament attaches to the First Testament, it is odd that the church does not read it much. And if the church does read it, this reading is more than slightly selective, mainly so as to use it for support in connection with principles we already think are important. As a Brit, I would hardly dare suggest that taking verses in isolation is "the classic American way of deploying biblical verses," but if an American says it, I might dare to quote him.[1]

Karl Barth put my point this way. The words come in an exposition of Psalm 119:67, "Now I Keep Your Word," which he gave when he was about to leave Germany as a result of his opposition to the National Socialist government:

> And now the end has come. . . . So listen to my piece of advice: exegesis, exegesis, and yet more exegesis! . . . Keep to the Word, to the Scripture that has been given us.[2]

Then there is Augustine, who in his testimony in the *Confessions* tells us how he was once sitting outside under a fig tree—a nice motif, given what we have noted about the fig tree.[3] Feeling spiritually tormented, he wept, and he describes how he prayed in the manner if not the actual words of a psalm:

> How long, Yahweh—will you be angry permanently? . . .
> Do not keep in mind the wayward acts of the past for us. (Ps 79:5, 8)

---

1. See Peter J. Thuesen's review of Mark A. Noll, *In the Beginning Was the Word*, in *Books and Culture* 21.6 (2015): 20.

2. As quoted by Eberhard Busch, *Karl Barth: His Life from Letters and Autobiographical Texts*, trans. John Bowden (Philadelphia: Fortress, 1976), 259.

3. See the discussion of "The Fig Tree" on pp. 123–24 above.

Suddenly he heard the voice of a child in a nearby house singing over and over again, "Take up, read; take up, read." He went back to where he had previously been sitting reading the Scriptures, and opened them again.[4]

Yes, take up and read.

4. *Confessions* 8.12.

For Further Reading

Alter, Robert. *The Art of Biblical Narrative.* New York: Basic, 1981.
———, and Frank Kermode, eds. *The Literary Guide to the Bible.* Cambridge, MA: Harvard University Press, 1987.
Bauckham, Richard. *The Bible in Politics.* 2nd ed. Louisville: Westminster John Knox, 2011.
Borowski, Oded. *Daily Life in Biblical Times.* Atlanta: SBL, 2003.
Bright, John. *The Authority of the Old Testament.* Nashville: Abingdon, 1967.
Brueggemann, Walter. *The Prophetic Imagination.* Philadelphia: Fortress, 1978.
Coogan, Michael D., ed. *The Oxford History of the Biblical World.* Oxford: Oxford University Press, 1998.
Dever, William G. *What Did the Biblical Writers Know and When Did They Know It?* Grand Rapids, MI: Eerdmans, 2001.
Dictionary of the Old Testament. 4 volumes. Downers Grove, IL: InterVarsity, 2003–12.
Ebeling, Jennie R. *Women's Lives in Biblical Times.* London: Clark, 2010.
Frei, Hans W. *The Eclipse of Biblical Narrative: A Study in Eighteenth and Nineteenth Century Hermeneutics.* New Haven: Yale University Press, 1974.
Fritz, Volkmar. *The City in Ancient Israel.* Sheffield: Sheffield Academic Press, 1995.
Goldingay, John. *Do We Need the New Testament?* Downers Grove, IL: InterVarsity, 2015.
———. *Introduction to the Old Testament.* Downers Grove, IL: InterVarsity, 2015.
———. *Biblical Theology.* Downers Grove, IL: InterVarsity, 2016.

Hays, Richard B. *Reading Backwards*. Waco, TX: Baylor University Press, 2014.

Josipovici, Gabriel. *The Book of God*. New Haven: Yale University Press, 1988.

MacDonald, Nathan. *What Did the Ancient Israelites Eat?* Grand Rapids, MI: Eerdmans, 2008.

Martens, Elmer. *God's Design*. 2nd ed. Grand Rapids, MI: Baker, 1994.

Miles, J. *God: A Biography*. New York: Simon and Schuster, 1995.

Perdue, Leo, et al. *Families in Ancient Israel*. Louisville: Westminster John Knox, 1997.

Rad, Gerhard von. *Old Testament Theology*. 2 vols. London: Harper, 1962, 1965.

Toorn, Karel van der. "Nine Months among the Peasants." Pages 393–410 in William G. Dever and Seymour Gitin, eds., *Symbiosis, Symbolism, and the Power of the Past*. Winona Lake, IN: Eisenbrauns, 2003.

Trible, Phyllis. *God and the Rhetoric of Sexuality*. Philadelphia: Fortress, 1978.

———. *Texts of Terror*. Philadelphia: Fortress, 1984.

Wolff, Hans Walter. *Anthropology of the Old Testament*. Philadelphia: Fortress, 1974.

Wright, Christopher J. H. *Old Testament Ethics for the People of God*. Downers Grove, IL: InterVarsity, 2004.

Index of Subjects

Abraham, 5–9, 13, 17–22, 24–26, 35–36,
  38, 40, 42–44, 60, 73, 108–9, 111, 113,
  120, 134, 140, 144, 147, 160, 165, 167,
  174, 185, 189, 195, 210, 245
Adam, 13, 15–17, 25, 52–54, 59–60, 245

Babylon, 6, 8, 39, 41–49, 51–53, 55–56,
  58–59, 73, 75, 94, 97, 100–101, 103,
  115–16, 124, 154–56, 165–68, 177, 179,
  212, 238, 240, 246
Barth, Karl, 249n2
Baumgärtel, Friedrich, 63n1
blessing, 12, 38, 40, 42–43, 64, 73, 80, 97,
  101, 123, 147, 163, 165, 167–68, 176–79,
  181–83, 192–93, 207–9, 214, 218, 228,
  235, 238, 241
Bonhoeffer, Dietrich, 183n5
Bright, John, 8

church, 2, 4, 12, 21, 30, 34, 60, 66, 89, 92,
  98, 122, 147, 153, 217, 247–49, 189–90,
  204, 206
circumcision, 18, 19, 20, 37, 44, 113, 140
covenant, 18, 40, 43–44, 46–48, 90, 94,
  128, 143, 164–65, 172, 183, 185, 214, 234,
  240; Abraham and Sarah subjects of,
  43; new, 2, 89, 91–92, 99, 152–53

David, 7–9, 11, 27, 35, 38, 40, 49–51, 53–57,
  59, 70, 79–80, 84–86, 92–93, 95–96,

101, 106–7, 110–11, 127, 139–40, 150–51,
  185, 190, 195, 223, 230–31, 237–38,
  245–46

election, 22, 112
Eve, 15, 25, 60, 245
exile, 7–9, 39–43, 51–53, 55, 58–59, 62, 64,
  72–73, 89, 92, 94, 97–101, 105, 113, 116,
  119, 124, 137–38, 167, 176
exodus, the, 8, 9, 14, 23, 24, 31–32, 35, 46,
  57, 64, 232
Exodus, Book of, 10, 16, 23–24, 31, 39, 47,
  173, 223, 228

faith, 1, 4–6, 9, 17–19, 21, 33–38, 40, 43,
  45–46, 57, 63–65, 85, 114, 122, 134–36,
  140–42, 182–83
faithfulness, 21, 22, 29, 35, 59, 72, 74, 109,
  124, 128–30, 134–38, 145, 161, 189, 199,
  202, 204, 211, 213–14, 219, 228, 232,
  235, 246
Frei, Hans, 11

García Martínez, Florentino, 72n4
Gentiles, 17, 18, 23, 29–30, 62, 70, 80–81,
  83–84, 91, 117, 138, 141–42, 144, 146–47,
  186
God, people of, 2, 18, 27, 33, 36, 46, 54, 56,
  72, 115, 118, 121, 155, 227; purpose, 2,
  22, 40, 42, 63, 80, 89, 91, 102, 111, 155;

Index of Scripture